Dr. Israel brought the earnest intent of serving his patients now to the search for the history of Pernkopf, and as a consequence of this quest became instrumental in providing the world with an important case study of how to deal with the ubiquitous fruits of knowledge gained from medical wrongdoing and even atrocities."

Sabine Hildebrandt, MD
Co-Chair, Lancet Commission on Medicine, Nazism and the Holocaust
Associate Professor of Pediatrics and Member Center for Bioethics,
Harvard Medical School

***

Eduard Pernkopf was one of the key figures in the history of Vienna University during the Nazi period — as dean of the Vienna Medical Faculty, president of the university and author of his famous anatomical atlas, for which he could choose from the bodies of hundreds of victims of the Nazi regime. Howard Israel was instrumental in getting Vienna University to confront this past, more than 50 years after the end of the war. His memoirs provide fascinating insights into this critical chapter in the history of medical science, and the long shadow it casts to this day over institutions and individuals.

Herwig Czech, PhD
Professor of History of Medicine, Medical University of Vienna Co-Chair,
Lancet Commission on Medicine, Nazism and the Holocaust

***

Dr. Howard Israel has written a moving work that is part historical detective story and part memoir. With great humanity and diligence, Dr. Israel uncovers a chilling tale of how physicians and academic institutions blighted their reputations by collaborating—sometimes enthusiastically—with the Nazis. His discoveries should serve as a warning to all about how easily healers can become implicated in horror."

Adam Rovner, PhD
Director of the Center for Judaic Studies, University of Denver
(and/or you can use) author of The Jew Who Would Be King

***

Engaging, intelligent and fiercely original. Dr. Israel takes us on a multi-level journey as he captivates us with his story and illuminates a dark history that resonates brightly today. Clear, fresh prose, vivid and detailed research. Highly recommended.

Linda F. Burghardt, PhD
Scholar-in-Residence Holocaust Memorial & Tolerance Center of Nassau County, N.Y. Journalist and author: The New York Times, USA Today, The Chicago Tribune, Newsday, The New York Daily News, The San Francisco Chronicle

***

In this gripping journey tracing the origins of a medical textbook he relied upon, Dr. Howard Israel confronts the age-old moral dilemma – can good, come from evil?

Lawrence A. Tabak, DDS,
Former Acting Director, National Institutes of Health

NAZI ANATOMY LESSONS

A Dissection of Evil

NAZI ANATOMY LESSONS

A Dissection of Evil

HOWARD ALAN ISRAEL

VALLENTINE MITCHELL
LONDON • CHICAGO

First published in 2026 by Vallentine Mitchell

Catalyst House,
720 Centennial Court,
Centennial Park, Elstree WD6 3SY, UK

814 N. Franklin Street,
Chicago, Illinois,
IL 60610 USA

www.vmbooks.com

British Library Cataloguing in Publication Data:
An entry can be found on request

ISBN 978 1 80371 084 6 HB
ISBN 978 1 80371 085 3 PB
ISBN 978 1 80371 086 0 EB

Library of Congress Cataloging in Publication Data:
An entry can be found on request

There is still time, but, I think, only just time. That is why at whatever cost, I had to write this book – while there is time.

G.E.R. Gedye – Journalist 1938 Vienna, foreword from *Fallen Bastions* 1939

Here is another true picture. Outside a house in Leopoldstadt stands the cart of the Anatomical Institute. Into it are being loaded the bodies of a whole Jewish family. Around the door lounge grinning storm-troopers. Over it hangs a large sign they have just put up – 'Neighbours, please copy.'

G.E.R. Gedye –description of scene in 1938 Vienna, from *Fallen Bastions* 1939

Dental office visit of a long time patient, 1940s Berlin

Patient: *Doctor, what do you think of the situation in Germany right now? What is your impression of the war?*

Doctor: *If you just listen to the daily bulletins from the Fuhrer's headquarters and read the newspapers, and think of the multitude air raids we have, it doesn't look all that good, does it?*

Patient Frowns

Doctor: *But don't worry about it. After all our Fuhrer Hitler is the greatest soldier and field marshall in history. He is going to save us.*

Public trial of doctor following Gestapo arrest

Observer: *For the rest of my life I shall never forget what happened next.*

Chief Justice: *You have been found guilty of crimes of defeatism and sabotage of the war effort, as charged. The penalty is death.*

Observer: *Oh my G-d, I cannot believe what we have just heard. Is that a reason to lose your life?*

William R. Forster - Eyewitness observer to a 1940s Berlin court proceeding from *Farewell Berlin* 2018

To the victims of the Nazis executed at the
Wiener Landesgericht and all victims and their
familes, both those who were murdered and the
survivors of mass genocide.

William E. Seidelman, MD
Emeritus Professor
Department of Family and Community Medicine
Faculty of Medicine, University of Toronto
My friend, colleague and teacher, whose wisdom, expertise,
compassion, bravery and chutzpah
have been a driving force in my life.

Grandpa Max Buchbinder
He emigrated from Poland to the US, hoping to rescue his large
family. Grandpa Max never recovered following their loss as
victims of the Holocaust.

Mindy S. Israel, MS Ed
My wife whose love, support,
and devotion has made this work possible.

Contents

Figures and Illustrations

Figure 1. Anatomical illustrations from the Pernkopf Atlas are superb when preparing for surgery. I was studying the above figure from the 1963 edition[1] when a colleague suggested that Pernkopf was a Nazi. The illustration above is the original painting signed by the artist Eric Lepier, reprinted with permission from the archives of the Josephinum - Ethics, Collections and History of Medicine, MedUni Vienna.

Figure 2. Signature of anatomical artist Eric Lepier with swastika demonstrating allegiance to the Nazi regime appearing in the German language edition of *Eduard Pernkopf Topographische Anatomie des Menschen* published by Urban & Schwarzenberg, Berlin and Wien. The illustration above is the original 1940 painting signed by the artist Eric Lepier, reprinted with permission from the archives of the Josephinum - Ethics, Collections and History of Medicine, MedUni Vienna.

Figure 3. Above left, Franz Batke's 1944 signature followed by what resembles the SS rune, from my copy of the 1963 English language edition of H. Ferner (ed), *Eduard Pernkopf Atlas of Topographical and Applied Human Anatomy, Volume I, Head and Neck*, (Philadelphia Pa and London, W.B. Saunders Company, 1963). Signature on the left, Fig. 263, p. 254, signature on the right, Fig.254, p. 239. Some have interpreted the symbols on the left reflecting an alternative derivation of the number '4' in German. Above right, Batke's signature from the same volume of an illustration from 1943. With permission Elsevier Foreign Rights.

Figure 4a. Pernkopf artist Erich Lepier's signature with swastika erased from my copy of the 1963 English language edition of H. Ferner (ed), *Eduard Pernkopf Atlas of Topographical and Applied Human*

Anatomy, Volume I, Head and Neck, (Philadelphia Pa and London, W.B. Saunders Company, 1963), Fig 289, p 301. Although this was in my copy of the atlas, I never noticed it until 1994. With permission Elsevier Foreign Rights.

Figure 4b. The illustration above first appeared in the 1937 edition of the Pernkopf Atlas, with a swastika connecting 'Lepier' with 'Wien,' in the same format as figure 2. The illustration above is the original painting with the signature modified in 1953 to erase the swastika and was used in the publication of future editions. Reprinted with permission from the archives of the Josephinum - Ethics, Collections and History of Medicine, MedUni Vienna.

Figure 5. The newly appointed Dean of Medicine at the University of Vienna, Eduard Pernkopf, addressing his faculty in 1938 on the role of medicine in the Third Reich to emphasize 'exclusion of the genetically inferior from future generations by sterilization and other means.' Photograph from *Wein 1938* Historical Museum of the City of Vienna, Documentation Archives of the Austrian Resistance. © Austrian National Library, Image rights ÖNB/Wien S 283/30.

Figure 6. Flyer posted throughout the Columbia University Health Sciences Campus in 1994. The program commemorated the victims of the Holocaust and featured Dr. Robert Jay Lifton, the author of *Nazi Doctors: Medical Killing and the Psychology of Genocide,* a book that I had just read prior to the program. Fortuitously, this enabled me to personally meet with Dr. Lifton which ultimately led to my collaboration with Dr. William Seidelman.

Figure 7. Nicholas Wade's article exposes the Pernkopf Atlas controversy to the public. From The New York Times, November 26, 1996, The New York Times. All rights reserved. Used by permission and protected by the Copyright Laws of the United States. The printing, copying, redistribution, or retransmission of this Content without express written permission is prohibited.

Figure 8. During an attack by National Socialist students on the Anatomical Institute at the University of Vienna, Jewish students are

Figure 13. University of Vienna Medical School 2005. Top right, Jewish memorial prayer room. Bottom right, inscription on sidewalk memorializing the victims of the Nazi regime. Top left, the Oral Surgery Clinic building. Photographs taken by H. Israel.

Figure 14. The *Wiener Landesgericht*, Vienna District Court 2005. During the Nazi era many people were sentenced to death by the guillotine in the basement. The human bodies of young, healthy individuals served as a source for dissections and illustrations by Pernkopf's artists for the anatomy atlas. Photograph by H. Israel.

Figure 15. The Anatomy Institute of the University of Vienna 2005. Top left is the street entrance, top right is the statue of Galenus in the lobby. Bottom right is the rear of the Anatomy Institute building. Photographs by H. Israel, with the exception of the bottom left showing a recent picture of a dissection room, photograph courtesy of Dr. Wolfgang Weninger, Anatomy Institute, Medical University of Vienna.

Figure 16. Urban & Schwarzenberg medical bookstore across the street from the entrance of the Anatomy Institute of the University of Vienna 2005. Copies of the 1943 edition of the Pernkopf Atlas were on the shelf in the antique book section of the store. The *Wiener Landesgericht*, Anatomy Institute and Urban and Schwarzenberg were all within a few square blocks, facilitating the creation of the 'masterpiece,' Pernkopf's Atlas of Anatomy. Photographs by H. Israel.

Figure 17. The Seitenstettengasse Temple 2005, the only synagogue in Vienna that survived destruction by the Nazis. Photographs by H. Israel.

Figure 18. The memorial plaque of Chaim and Chana Ben Israel, one of the many memorial plaques surrounding the sanctuary at the Seitenstettengasse Temple, 2005. Photograph by H. Israel.

Figure 19. The Holocaust Memorial in the center of the Judenplatz, Vienna 2005. The memorial was built above the remains of the Viennese synagogue of a flourishing Jewish community, destroyed

2024 dollars) of gold, jewelry and art treasures stolen by the Nazis. This discovery represented less than half of the total amount of plundered valuables (estimated at 11 billion in 2024 dollars). The missing gold was assumed to be in the vaults of Swiss banks. © Everett Collection/Shutterstock with permission.

Figure 25. Memorial plaque honoring the victims of Nazi dentists, from the Holocaust Museum and Tolerance Center, Nassau County, New York, USA. Photograph by H. Israel.

Figure 26. Search terms 'Pernkopf, Nazi, Anatomy, Atlas' in the peer reviewed medical literature reveals a total of 88 publications. Since 1998 following the University of Vienna investigation into the Pernkopf Atlas controversy there have been 70 publications. Of note are the increased numbers of publications following the introduction of the 'Vienna Protocol' providing ethical guidelines for those considering using the atlas for patient care and medical education.

Figure 27. The Josephinum at the Medical University of Vienna, Department of Ethics, Collections and History of Medicine was an appropriate venue for the launch of *The Lancet* Commission on Medicine, Nazism and the Holocaust on November 9, 2023. The original paintings from the Pernkopf Atlas are kept there preserving the historical significance of these meticulous anatomical representations. Photograph courtesy of © Josephinum / Reiner Riedler with permission.

APPENDIX. Ambassador Dafni's historic letter. Yad Vashem Archives AM.2.2/276, P143-146, with permission.

Acknowledgements

There are several individuals who are directly responsible for the story in this book, without which, the events which followed would not have occurred. My wife and soulmate, Mindy, has been instrumental throughout this entire journey. Her active participation, devotion, love and constant support throughout my personal and professional life have made this work possible.

Dr. William Seidelman, who I first met on a lengthy telephone call in 1994, took this desperate, unknowing oral and maxillofacial surgeon under his wing, and provided me with an education, which continues to the present day. The story which follows in this narrative is our story. We collaborated on the important issues to be addressed and Bill and I quickly became very close friends. Bill's wisdom, experience, breadth of knowledge, passion for justice, and bravery were driving forces throughout, and transformed me as a person. Not only did we become partners on this amazing voyage, but our families have become very close as well. Although we have always lived in separate countries, we had the opportunity to meet with both Bill and Racheline, his loving wife on several occasions. Just as Mindy has been my rock and support, Racheline was Bill's brilliant supportive partner throughout the decades. Racheline's recent passing has been a tremendous loss. May her memory be a blessing in our hearts and minds.

Since her emergence as a world-renowned expert on the history of Nazi medicine, Dr. Sabine Hildebrandt has also become a close friend and colleague. The torch from Bill has been passed on to Sabine, who has continued to make enormous contributions to bioethics and medical education. I am grateful for her ceaseless support, review and clarification of important material and answers to the many questions I have had along this road.

The number of individuals for whom I am grateful are so numerous, that I fear listing them, as I would not want to omit those who have been instrumental. Rabbi Josef Polak's responsum, the 'Vienna Protocol, has had a major impact on immortalizing victims of obscene medical experiments and has provided guidelines for doctors confronted with the bioethical dilemmas. Dr. Steven Syrop has been a friend and colleague with expertise in the field of chronic oral and facial pain for decades and he was the individual whose casual remark set me on a path of discovery. Others who have influenced me greatly include Drs. Herwig Czech, Volker Roelcke, Shmuel P. Weiss, Matthew Wynia, William Silvers, Susan MacKinnon, Andrew Yee, Linda Burghardt, Bruce Sanders, Jessica Li and the late Joshua Lilly. I am also grateful to many people in the media profession, who have exposed this important story to the public, including Nicholas Wade, former Science Editor of *The New York Times*, Henry Schuster, producer for CBS News, and the late Art Harris, who was the reporter-moderator of CNN-Time's newsmagazine 'IMPACT –"Nazi Medicine"' which aired in 1997.

I could not have written this book without the love, patience and support of my family, David, Aaron, Heather, Sawako, and my five wonderful grandchildren, who are the future, Arthur, Desi, Kaishu, Hendrick and Mayako.

Foreword

The tale told in these pages is of an encounter between a man and his book,during the course of which an unexpected exposure to radical evil took place such that since then, neither the man nor his book has managed to achieve either refuge or sanctuary from what transpired.

It begins with a young aspiring oral surgeon, lost and frustrated during his study of human anatomy, unable to imagine the streams and valleys, the interior limbs and orifices of the human body in the way doctors must if they are to heal the sick.

Our student eventually comes upon a medical anatomy book of uncommon beauty and accessibility, and it is among its soaring watercolors that he finally achieves the coherence and clarity about the human interior that had so eluded him.

He writes as well of coming upon the provenance of this volume and its illustrations; ***who*** it was who ***posed***, so to speak, for its artists; ***whose*** limbs and blood vessels are these, preserved with such exquisite care and artistic imagination for the benefit of medical science.

He discovers that the body parts so imaginatively copied for this album were from victims of Hitler's civil courts, young and old, guillotined downstairs immediately following trials that had found them guilty of such capital offenses as distributing leaflets. Scholars have suggested that some of the body parts portrayed may also have been from cadavers of Jews murdered for the express purpose of enhancing anatomy collections. None of these victims, regardless of their faith, had been asked to donate his body, none would have conceivably consented to such a request.

The stench of this evil infuses these extraordinary illustrations: the bones, the valves, the sinews, the pipes and the caves. It even penetrates the bodies and souls of those who contemplate these drawings, evoking for some, loathing and revulsion. Such students, surgeons, and anatomists themselves, all redolent from what they have absorbed, become witnesses, become enraged by the injustice, by the con. They emerge chastened by them, and resolve to consult them only for the good and for healing, and only when no other option exists.

The deeper questions about this album, since its origins were exposed over thirty years ago, remain what may be done with it; to what use may it be put, may it be employed by surgeons to aid in their surgery; by anatomy students to help understand this evasive science? May it be used to save lives? To ease pain? Should it be republished? Should it function commercially?

I myself have written about these questions, and there is no need to review this material here. Yet I want to be helpful to our author, indeed, to all who find themselves molested repeatedly by the darkness unfailingly emanating from the album.

To them, as friend and minister, I offer the following less-than-perfect analogy from Jewish law, to provide a way of dealing with these mighty moral questions.

A *Mamzer*, in Jewish law, is an offspring of a forbidden union, such as mother and son, for example, or of one man with another's wife. The *Mamzer*, it turns out, is obligated to observe all the commandments of the Torah, save one: he may not marry and have children, He thus becomes a walking reminder of a sin —a sin, most assuredly, that he did not commit.

Yet the *Mamzer's* status in Jewish society is unambiguous —Whom do we respect more, whom would we give precedence to, who would we honor first, asks the Mishna some 2,000 years ago, the ignoramus High Priest or the scholarly *Mamzer*? The answer is swift and clear: the *Mamzer* goes to the head of the line, he is the one the community must venerate.

There are sins, the *Mamzer's* law tells us, that may not be forgotten, and there are people and institutions whose life-task it is to remind us of these sins. Yet it is crucial not to confuse such people and institutions with the perpetrators, with the sinners themselves.

There is more here; not all has been articulated, Yet surely enough to provoke a larger conversation.

Rabbi Joseph Polak,
Boston University
School of Public Health

Preface

This book is the result of a decades long journey that started with my quest to become an oral and maxillofacial surgeon following graduation from college. My professional education put me on a common course that so many others have traveled, motivated by the desire to become the best doctor possible with the obligation of providing the highest quality of care for all patients. The formula to reach this goal was to study and retain as much knowledge as possible, be diligent to stay on a course of lifelong learning, to always be thoroughly prepared and treat all individuals with compassion, expertise and as a member of one's own family. At the core of attaining these goals was maintenance of the highest degree of ethics. Although the road was not easy, after two decades, I believed that this formula had put me on the correct path. What seemed to be a trivial comment from a colleague, shattered this path forcing me to use a different formula to stay on this course.

The narrative which follows is largely based on my view of the events that unfolded over the span of my career as an academic oral and maxillofacial surgeon. I am neither an historian, anatomist or bioethicist. I have relied on decades of files that I have accumulated over the years, including detailed notes of telephone conversations, e-mails, interviews, articles published in professional journals and in the media, attending meetings and learning from the many experts and colleagues in a field of study about which I had been totally unfamiliar. A significant part of this journey involved my education on the history of the role of the medical profession in the era before, during and after the rise of the Third Reich. I have relied on scholarly references from historians, anatomists, bioethicists, and others, which are included in the bibliography section with more information for those who wish to delve into a more detailed scholarly exploration.

Interestingly, there is no end to this journey. Just as we all aim for perfection, we never quite get there. But we must always strive to reach that plateau.

I alone bear the responsibility for any errors of fact or judgement that are in this book.

Prologue

Grandpa Max - Spring 1961

The Bronx tenement apartment on the third floor was like an oven that day. The windows were open which allowed a scenic view of hanging laundry, clothespins, and lines with pulleys in the alleyway between two dilapidated apartment buildings. There was no breeze and the temperature was soaring, but I did not feel the oppressive heat. Instead, my attention was focused on the confusing scene that I was witnessing.

The ancient black and white Hotpoint television set was turned on and it was just me and Grandpa Max in the living room. I was the nine year old sitting on the couch between Grandpa Max in his easy chair to the right and the TV with the rabbit ears antenna to the left. Grandpa Max rarely watched TV, but he was in a solemn trance on that day, and I am certain that he was totally unaware of my presence. My attention continually shifted between the Hotpoint screen and Grandpa Max. I was not able to comprehend what I was observing, but I knew that something terrible was happening. Grandpa Max, a deeply religious Orthodox Jew was always very quiet and could barely speak English. When he did speak, it was usually the recitation of Hebrew prayers. Suddenly, Grandpa Max erupted, standing up from his chair, cursing in Yiddish and shaking his fist at the TV. I could see the wetting of his pants.

Years later I began to understand. The Nazi Adolph Eichmann was on trial in an Israeli court in Jerusalem. From the perspective of this nine year old, the man in a dark suit and glasses in a protective booth, looked quite ordinary just like anyone's grandpa. Eichmann was eventually sentenced to be executed for crimes against humanity due to his role in the systematic deportation of millions of Jewish people, as well as non-Jews, to extermination camps. Grandpa Max did not demonstrate any elation in the days following the final judgement. Instead, I observed him repeatedly going into lengthy tirades, talking to himself constantly, mumbling angrily, bitterly, followed by spontaneous outbursts repeating the scene I had witnessed.

My knowledge of the Holocaust, which was scant, was limited to what I had seen on television and in the movies. As I grew into an adult I began to realize that besides Grandpa Max, the Holocaust had not touched me or anyone else in my immediate American Jewish family. But I frequently recalled that awful day in the spring of 1961. In the years that followed I reviewed that scene over and over again. Although he continued to put on the Tallis and Tefillin every day, my memory of Grandpa Max the last few years of his life were that of a tormented man with unresolvable pain.

Grandpa Max was not a blood relation of mine. He was my stepgrandfather. But he was the only grandpa I had ever known. I found out that when he was younger, he lived in Poland and had a very big family with a wife, children and many brothers, sisters, aunts and uncles. During the 1930s he saved up enough money to leave Poland and come to the United States, with the hope of earning enough money to rescue his family. Tragically, he was not able to get them out of Poland and he lost his entire family in the Holocaust. He married my grandmother in 1947. I have thought about Grandpa Max frequently over the years. Sometimes tears will come to my eyes when I reminisce about the scene I had witnessed in the Bronx in 1961.

That is what I had learned of the Holocaust as a child.

Thirty-three years later I was confronted directly and personally with the absolute evil of Nazi doctors. This is when my real education of the Holocaust began.

1

Confrontations with Evil

It was an ordinary good life for this baby boomer. Growing up in the post Second World War era, living in the suburbs, graduating from college, marrying the girl next store, becoming a healthcare professional, raising a family, and developing a rising academic career, this life had been shielded from pure evil. The one exception was the scene I had witnessed of my Grandpa Max watching the Eichmann trial as a nine year old in 1961. There were many of the typical challenges life has to offer, but the ups far exceeded the downs. Awareness of the presence of pure evil came from books and movies, but there was no personal confrontation with horror or demons. Therefore, this life was totally unprepared when after four decades it encountered a history of terror, horror and absolute evil. The confrontation with this knowledge was shocking enough but even more terrorizing was the realization that this life's rising star was directly related to this evil. As I advanced in my career, I knew virtually nothing of the history of medicine in Europe before, during and after the Second World War. But that was going to change dramatically.

The healthcare professions include those who have chosen the art and science of healing and obtained vast knowledge to promote life and reduce suffering. However, the potential for human beings to transgress and perform acts of evil, cruelty, and terror with violation of all ethical principles and individual rights are well known. Physicians wield great power in determining the quality of life of each individual patient with significant potential to do great harm and thus, bioethical decision making is an essential component of healthcare. The conditions which ultimately led to the radical departure of physicians as caring healers to killers in Nazi Germany are not unique as history has taught us. Throughout this writing, the terms 'Nazi anatomy,' 'Nazi medicine,' 'Nazi doctors' will be used, and the reader is cautioned that these terms do not imply that the fundamental conditions which led to atrocities during the Nazi era are so unique that it is impossible for this to occur again. Physicians and all human beings have the potential to do great harm as well as perform acts of kindness with great empathy. Healthcare professionals must continually learn from the past and remain acutely aware of the necessity of ethical decision making in the care of each individual patient, as well as their potential to do harm.

In the decades preceding the rise of the Third Reich, German and Austrian academic institutions were the most prestigious in the world. These institutions were known for their leadership in scientific breakthroughs and education producing many Nobel Laureates. The medical academic communities in these institutions set the standards for research and higher education in healthcare. Although it seems incomprehensible that the medical professionals that had been produced by these institutions could change from healers with the highest standards of ethics to killers who committed the heinous crimes against humanity, this is exactly what happened. How did those individuals who pledged an oath to heal and do no harm become perpetrators of pure evil? As these highly educated physicians became convinced that they were 'healing the *Volk*,' by purifying the Aryan race, they viewed that lives that weren't worth living as perfect subjects for research and scientific exploitation. There are those that would argue that any data produced through such unethical means has lost all scientific validity. Most of the experiments conducted by doctors under the Nazi regime produced information that was not scientifically valid and often represented attempts to justify National Socialist racial hygiene theory, and thus, it is easy to discard their results. However, not all of the information produced by unethical and misguided Nazi scientists has been regarded as useless. How should we respond to this data if it could potentially save a life, relieve suffering or benefit humanity? Is it possible that some good can come from evil? If data produced by unethical means that was created in the past, but is scientifically sound and contributes to medical progress, some would argue that it is unethical not to use this information. Others will argue that using this information, regardless of its scientific value, will perpetuate and justify the crime, leading to a repeat of history.

Just ten years prior to Hitler's war machine began its rampage across Europe, German physicians were actively developing the principles of ethics in medicine and in biomedical research. In 1928, the Berlin Medical Association issued a statement on the ethical conduct for research on humans:

> *Any trial on humans must be limited to what is absolutely necessary, must be grounded theoretically and scientifically and must be well defined biologically....for the well-being of the patient is more important than science. Moreover, medical ethics commands that the patient or legal representative be informed of the spirit and purpose of the particular therapeutic test.* [1,2]

The pursuit of ethics involving human experimental subjects continued and in 1931 the German government published 'Guidelines for New Therapy and Human Experimentation' with emphasis on the need for informed consent:

> *Undertaking any test without informed consent is impermissible under any circumstances. Any test on humans that could have been replaced by a test on animals is to be rejected...Experiments performed on children or adolescents under the age of 18 are not allowed if they will endanger the welfare of the child or adolescent in the slightest. Experiments on the dying are incompatible with the principles of medical ethics and thus not permitted.* [1,2]

Although the general principles of ethics in medicine and biomedical research were clearly outlined, the rapid change in attitude of the medical profession mirrored the change in the political environment when the Nazi regime came into power. Now, the medical profession and biomedical research became the scientific rationale for racial hygiene theory. Principles of ethical conduct protecting individual human beings were abandoned, in favor of healing the *Volk*, the body of the Aryan people, with the elimination of those individuals deemed unfit. Physicians were given complete authority over making their own decisions without any significant oversight. Within a period of ten years, the medical professions within the Nazi regime changed from ethical healers to perpetrators of evil. Today, we realize that racial hygiene theory was false, but during the Nazi era, many lay and professional people accepted it as a true and legitimate science.

The data generated by Nazi research was generally regarded as totally without any scientific validity or value in the early years following the Second World War. Brigadier General Telford Taylor was the chief counsel for the prosecution during the Nuremberg trials and he concluded that the experiments conducted by the Nazis had produced nothing of any scientific medical value.[3] However, there are instances in which the data produced by Nazi research may have some potential value and have been cited in the scientific literature. Moe[3] has brought this issue to light and has raised several questions in the evaluation of whether or not it is appropriate to cite this literature:

> 1. *If the experiments were conducted in an unethical manner, can the results be considered reliable?*
> 2. *If the results are useful, can we afford to ignore them?*
> 3. *Does the use of the data imply an endorsement of the methods by which they were gathered, and provide a justification for further unethical research?*[3]

There are examples where data from Nazi research has been cited in the literature, and perhaps the most well-known case is that of Dr. Sigmund Rascher's hypothermia experiments on concentration camp inmates. Rascher's inhumane experiments collected data on immersion of inmates into cold water at freezing temperatures to determine survival limits as well as the best warming options for recovery from the shock of prolonged exposure to cold. Some hypothermia researchers have indicated that there is some benefit in using this data, indicating that they cannot reproduce these experiments in an ethical world.[3]

Others have indicated that there is no scientific validity to the data produced on emaciated concentration camp victims. Berger[4] has concluded:

> *On analysis, the Dachau hypothermia study has all the ingredients of a scientific fraud, and rejection of the data on purely scientific grounds is inevitable. They cannot advance science or save human lives.*[4]

Despite those who have claimed that the hypothermia experiments have no scientific value, these experiments have been cited in numerous publications.

The use of scientific information that had been produced through unethical means did not end when the Nazis were defeated in 1945. These issues have continually been raised with numerous examples in which the data produced through evil means continued to be used. Wernher Von Braun was an eminent rocket scientist who, amongst other German scientists, developed the V2 rocket, based on slave labor, which killed thousands of innocent people before the end of the Second World War. He and his scientists were members of the Nazi party. However, after the war, the US recruited Von Braun and 1600 other German scientists as part of 'Operation Paperclip' and were shielded from prosecution. Von Braun, and his German scientist colleagues were the critical scientific engineering components leading the US space program that ultimately resulted in the first successful lunar mission.[5] The US used the atomic bomb on Hiroshima and Nagasaki with devastating consequences on innocent civilians. For those who initially survived these tragic events, many would eventually succumb to radiation disease giving science the unfortunate opportunity to study the effects of ionizing radiation on the human body.[3] Jewish doctors in the Warsaw ghetto took copious notes of their patients who died of starvation at the hands of their Nazi captors. These notes eventually were smuggled out of the Warsaw ghetto and ultimately provided scientific information on starvation disease, with the tragic loss of so many innocent lives, many of whom were children.[6,7,8]

It is terrifying to realize that there is much scientific data that is available whose source comes from the inhumane suffering of individuals. The narrative which follows represents an unexpected journey taken by this author, involving an anatomy atlas that was deemed a 'masterpiece' of anatomical illustration, providing knowledge of the human body for healthcare professionals throughout the world. How did the creators of such a 'masterpiece' change from healers into killers? Is it possible to salvage anything good from the creation of evil? One surgeon's journey into this world of evil is what follows. The lessons learned changed the person who I was, and this transformation continues to this day.

Notes

1. R. Winau, 'Experimentation on Humans and Informed Consent: How We Arrived Where We Are.' in W. Lafleur, G. Bohme, & S. Shimazono (Eds.), *Dark Medicine: Rationalizing Unethical Medical Research*. Indianapolis, (Indianapolis: Indiana University Press 2007), pp 46-56.

2. Z. Fullerton, 'The Protection of Individual Inviolability: Nazi Doctors and their Mark on Biomedical Research,' *Senior Capstone Projects,* 402, (Vassar College Digital Library, Thesis, Open Access, 2015), pp1-70.
3. K. Moe, 'Should the Nazi research data be cited?' *Hastings Center Report,* 14, 6 (1984), pp.5-7.
4. R.L. Berger, 'Nazi Science - The Dachau Hypothermia Experiments' *N Engl J Med,* 322, 20 (1990), pp.1435-40.
5. M. Neufeld. 'Wernher Von Braun and the Nazis,' *American Experience: Chasing the Moon.* Public Broadcasting Service, 20 May 2019. https://www.youtube.com/watch?v=9e4Hy-Qcs1s
6. M. Winick (ed). *Hunger Disease,* (New York: Wiley,1979).
7. J. Yudkin, 'Hunger Disease: Studies by the Jewish Physicians in the Warsaw Ghetto.' Book review, M. Winick M (ed), *Hunger Disease,* (New York: Wiley, 1979). *J R Soc Med.,* 72, 10 (1979), p790.
8. S.G. Massry, M Smogorzewski, 'The Hunger Disease of the Warsaw Ghetto," *Am J Nephrol,* 22 (2002), pp. 197-201.

2

Basic Anatomy Lessons 1973-77

Introduction to the Anatomy Laboratory and Ms. M

The smell of formaldehyde upon arrival of the anatomy laboratory was sickening to me as well as many first-year students at Columbia University School of Dental and Oral Surgery and the College of Physicians and Surgeons in 1973. The first-year classes of both professional schools were required to complete the anatomy course in eight weeks. This initial exposure to dead people, cadavers, with skin and various tissues in shades of gray has created a striking memory for me, which is emblazoned in my brain. It was truly a shock to this twenty-one-year-old biology major who could not decide whether to pursue a career in medicine or dentistry. Ultimately, I decided on dentistry, thinking 'why should I consider a profession dealing with life or death?' In retrospect, reviewing my career over the decades, that rationale was really a joke, as I ultimately dealt with and struggled with life and death issues for many of my patients over the years.

For the next eight weeks, I was required to learn every blood vessel, nerve, muscle, bone, organ throughout the entire human body. The first time my group gathered around that dissection table, there was a gray body of an elderly woman. I stared, with great difficulty at that body for a long time. Was Ms. M (Mysterious) really a person, who had led a full life, complete with its pleasures, tragedies, triumphs and failures? I looked at this gray mass of tissue and concluded that wasn't possible and I put all of that out of my mind. I had a job to do and tissues to dissect and memorize for posterity.

After one week of anatomy, I thought that I was going to be able to master anatomy of the hand, wrist and upper extremity. I studied the anatomic sketches from *Grant's Atlas of Anatomy*[1] (also referred to as Grant's Atlas) the required atlas for the course and went to the dissection laboratory fully prepared. However, the tissues dissected during the laboratory session did not resemble or correlate with the gray tissues of Ms. M, the cadaver. I left the laboratory sessions feeling frustrated, but not undaunted. I hunkered down with my atlas, studied the movements of my hand and wrist, attempting to identify those muscles that were contracting and correlating them with the pictures I viewed in the atlas. When I returned to the anatomy laboratory, the tissues were still gray and very difficult to correlate with the pictures in the atlas, however, after one week, I felt prepared, thanks to Ms. M, the atlas and my own hand.

It was finally time to rest my weary mind and enjoy the weekend with Mindy, my fiancé. After one week of surviving this grueling pace, it was time for Mindy, and I to celebrate and treat ourselves. A Saturday night reservation for dinner at a very fancy French restaurant, with plenty of wine and good food was set for us. The atmosphere was all set for a perfect evening of fun, relaxation, great food in this expensive restaurant with great ambience. Everything was great until the appetizer was served, and I picked up the fork in my right hand. What muscles did I just use? Was it Flexor Carpi Radius or Ulnaris of the wrist, Flexor Pollicis Brevis or Abductor Pollicis Brevis of the thumb? No matter what I did to try to get anatomy out of my mind for the evening, I just couldn't rid myself of the thought that I had learned nothing after a full week of intense studying. It was obvious to Mindy that I was totally distracted, and an expensive evening had ended in disaster. Not only couldn't I relax, but I couldn't reconcile the thought that I would have seven more weeks of failing to learn anatomy. Something was wrong with my method, and I had to fix this now.

The Professor and IRS Revenue Officer

Having discovered that my strategy for mastering anatomy needed a major change, I reviewed my past study habits which had been successful. I was always willing to put in the time, to study at home and in the library, and through repetition and visual memory, I would eventually comprehend basic key concepts that would remain with me. I figured that it was just a matter of putting in the time to study and prepare prior to the cadaver dissection, so that the anatomy laboratory was just a further reinforcement of knowledge that I had already acquired.

During the second week I studied the required reading from Grant's Atlas in detail for hours prior to each cadaveric laboratory dissection. I attempted to memorize the pictures in the atlas and relate these to the cadaveric dissections which followed. Essentially, I was attempting to use these anatomic pictures as a simulation for identification of the structures that I was going to be dissecting in the cadaver laboratory. My comprehension and memorization improved, but only slightly over the course of weeks two and three. Something was missing. No matter how much I studied and prepared for the laboratory using the atlas, I found it very difficult to correlate the pictures that I was viewing and the structures that I was dissecting in the cadaver laboratory.

I contacted a world-famous anatomist, 'The Professor', about my issues with learning anatomy. He indicated that the problem with my studying technique was that I was trying to simulate the cadaveric laboratory by studying anatomical pictures that were not realistic enough. The Professor, recognizing that I was a serious student, indicated that Pernkopf 's *Atlas of Topographical and Applied Human Anatomy*[2] (also referred to as Pernkopf's Atlas or Pernkopf's Anatomy) was unique in the superb detail and depiction of anatomical details which would come closest to bringing the cadaver laboratory experience as a study guide in preparation for the dissections that were to follow. The Professor did warn me that the cost of purchasing such an atlas was usually prohibitive for those on a student budget.

I was extremely thankful for this renowned professor's advice and my first reaction was to discuss with Mindy, who was going to be the sole source of our income when we were to be married in the months to come. Mindy was going to graduate from Queens College, New York one semester earlier so that she could secure a position and support us through the difficult years while I was a student. When we discussed the purchase of the Pernkopf 's Atlas we both decided that the cost was prohibitive at this time, especially with our unknown source of income for the future following our upcoming wedding. Therefore, I struggled through the eight-week anatomy course with my Grant's Atlas and laboratory dissections. I performed well on my examinations and received an excellent final grade. However, I recognized that I really did not master anatomy or retain the necessary information. The thought of having to treat a patient with my knowledge of anatomy was frightening.

As I proceeded through the early years of my education at Columbia University School of Dental & Oral Surgery, I realized that specialization in the field of oral and maxillofacial surgery was going to be my goal. But how can I become a surgeon, or be accepted into a highly competitive position in an accredited Oral & Maxillofacial Surgery Residency Training Program if I had not mastered anatomy?

Following our wedding, in 1974, Mindy was accepted for a position with the IRS (Internal Revenue Service) as a revenue officer for the Lower East Side of Manhattan. Essentially, any business that was deemed to be consistently delinquent in their Federal Tax, required a visit by the revenue officer to either collect the tax, negotiate a deal to collect the tax in installments, or 'lock the place up' until the taxes were collected. I find it amazing that my 21-year-old bride with her sweet disposition and pretty face, was walking into bars, and other seedy businesses, on what was then, the slums of lower Manhattan, to support our new family. For all of this her salary was $7,000 per year, our sole source of income. Therefore, I was shocked when one day Mindy came home with a surprise gift for me, *Pernkopf's Atlas of Topographical and Applied Human Anatomy, Volume One, Head & Neck.* [2] After thanking her profusely for this wonderful gift, I asked her how much did this cost? Mindy informed me that she found a medical bookstore in lower Manhattan and was able to purchase the book for $50, which was an extremely expensive investment. At that time, we struggled to meet our 1974 budget which included the exorbitant rent of our apartment for $175 per month, a very high inflation rate of 12.3% and long lines at gas stations with the escalating costs of fuel due to the embargo of oil by OAPEC (Organization of Arab Petroleum Exporting Countries) against countries that supported Israel. Needless to say, I accepted this very precious gift, which to this day has had a profound influence on my life.

Notes

1. J.C. Boileau Grant (ed.), *Grant's Atlas of Anatomy*, Sixth Edition, (Baltimore: The Williams & Wilkins Company 1972). 665 illustrations.
2. H. Ferner (ed), *Eduard Pernkopf Atlas of Topographical and Applied Human Anatomy, Volume I, Head and Neck*, (Philadelphia Pa and London, W.B. Saunders Company, 1963), pp.1-345.

3

Monstrous Deeds from the Past – An Education 1994 to Present

Throughout this book the term innocent 'Nazi victims' will be referred to extensively. It is easy to write the words 'Nazi victims' but what does this really mean? Academic scholars commonly use this term to include victims of euthanasia, mass extermination, suicide, forced sterilization, and forced labor. Loss of justice, severe punishment out of proportion to the alleged crime, sadistic cruelty, torture, loss of dignity and public display and humiliation are just some of the characteristics that were commonplace for victims of the court system under the Third Reich. Although there were so many ways for an individual to be victimized during the Nazi era, one specific example crystallized the definition of 'Nazi victim' for me.

Just recently I was scanning through the channels on YouTube, when I found a short segment that affected me greatly. There was an interview of the 92 year old Dr. Wolfram R. Forster. He was born in Germany, served in Hitler's army toward the end of the Second World War, was captured by the allies and eventually emigrated to the US. He and members of his family despised what Hitler stood for but had to remain silent. Forster revealed that his liberation came when he was captured by the Allied Forces. After he completed his medical studies in Germany, he emigrated to the US, practiced as a radiologist and also served in the US Army eventually reaching the rank of Colonel. At the end of the YouTube segment, it was noted that further details of his story were available in the book he had authored, *Farewell, Berlin*.[1] There is one section of this book which clearly describes what it meant to be an innocent Nazi victim. Forster recalls an experience early in his medical school career, when he and a friend skipped a boring lecture and went to sit in the People's Court, to observe the trials that were taking place in Berlin, that were open to the public. Forster recounts the story of the trial of a Berlin dentist who was having a casual conversation with a woman who was a long-time patient of his during a routine visit.

> *Doctor, what do you think of the situation in Germany right now? What is your impression of the war?*

The dentist replied:

> *If you just listen to the daily bulletins from the Fuhrer's headquarters and read the newspapers, and think of the multitude air raids we have, it doesn't look all that good, does it? We have lost Africa, our troops are retreating in Russia, we've lost Stalingrad, our cities are being bombed to ashes – every night a different city. So the situation looks a little disconcerting, don't you agree?*

After the dentist noticed a piercing look in the woman's eyes he added:

> *But don't worry about it. After all our Fuhrer Hitler is the greatest soldier and field marshall in history. He is going to save us.*

Forster recalls that the patient reported this conversation to the Gestapo, and the dentist was arrested and charged with defeatism and sabotage of the war effort.

> *For the rest of my life I shall never forget what happened next.*

After several minutes of deliberation, the Chief Justice issued the verdict:

> *You have been found guilty of crimes of defeatism and sabotage of the war effort, as charged. The penalty is death.*

Forster and his friend were in disbelief that the dentist was going to be executed for expressing his opinion. He turned to his friend and very quietly said:

> *Oh my G-d, I cannot believe what we have just heard. Is that a reason to lose your life?*

Forster goes on to describe what happened next:

> *Forty-eight hours later, the dentist's poster size photograph appeared in a bulletin with a red background and black frame, along with a description of the accusations against him, the verdict, and his already performed execution. This was posted in all public places in Berlin for every citizen to read.*

When Forster retold this story while being filmed for the YouTube segment, you could see through the tears in his eyes that this 92-year-old man had been deeply affected and outraged by this experience throughout his life. How could human beings do this to one another? How is it possible for experiences like this to be repeated, leading to the murder of millions of innocent lives? And yet, this did occur and has occurred so many times throughout history. Therefore, it is our responsibility to never forget this history and repeat the stories that can hopefully teach humankind not to fall into the depths of that slippery slope that leads to the unthinkable.

When I graduated from Columbia University School of Dental and Oral Surgery in 1977, I did not know anything about the history of monsters in medicine, except for the case of the infamous 'Angel of Death,' Josef Mengele. My concept of the role of a doctor was simple: be committed to lifelong learning and do the best you can for the benefit of your patients. You could never know everything about the art and science of being a practicing doctor, but one had to be committed to learn as much as possible and stay up to date with the advances in healthcare. Therefore, one is 'in practice' as there is always room for improvement and learning something new. My education proceeded to postgraduate training in the specialty of oral and maxillofacial surgery with my focus and obsession for perfection. In 1994 I was forced to acknowledge that in my drive to become the best surgeon possible, much of my education was coming from the lessons of a Nazi anatomist. The realization that I had benefited greatly from this teacher represented my initial confrontation with pure evil. Over the past three decades I have learned about the many examples of doctors actively participating in obscene medical experiments, torture and executions that they rationalized as science for the greater good of the people. The knowledge of this history has transformed me as a healer, educator and person. The past thirty years have become a continual education on the history of monstrous acts by the health professions that really existed and had directly influenced me.

An understanding of the history of the medical profession and academic institutions during the Nazi regime is necessary for future healthcare professionals. Physicians, dentists, academic administrators during the Nazi regime played a major role in the implementation of the National Socialist ideology to create a master race. The role of medicine was the healing of the body of the people through 'exclusion of the genetically inferior from future generations by sterilization and other means,' as the Dean of the Medical School at the University of Vienna had addressed his faculty in 1938.[2]

Dr. Julius Hallervorden, Neuropathologist

An investigation by the Senate of the University of Tübingen in Germany and subsequent report in 1989 documented the presence of hundreds of cadavers from persons executed by the Gestapo, which had been delivered to the university's Anatomy Department, and still had been in use for the education of medical students. Although an investigation was initially met with resistance, only through the continued forceful efforts of the students and Professor Jurgen Peiffer, a neuropathologist, did the investigation come to fruition, leading to the removal of specimens. A memorial ceremony with burial of the victims' mortal remains was conducted in July, 1990 and Dr. Peiffer's transcribed speech was published in *Brain Pathology.*[20] Peiffer's heartfelt speech indicated that the years of denial of their Nazi past and delayed memorialization of victims reflected a time when the quest for scientific knowledge as well as loyalty to National Socialist ideology, outweighed any instinct to maintain the ethical principles that had been pledged. The time was long overdue to reveal the deviations from morality in the name of science, and thus Peiffer revealed the truth about a former colleague, Professor Julius Hallervorden, a world-renowned neuropathologist/psychiatrist who became Chair of the Department of Neuropathology of the Kaiser Wilhelm Institute for Brain Research (later renamed the Max Planck Institute). Hallervorden's main research interests included the neuropathological findings in the brains of children with epilepsy and disturbed mental development. On his own initiative, Hallervorden amassed a huge neuropathological collection which included the brain specimens of children with brain disorders and adult psychiatric patients who had been murdered as part of the T-4 euthanasia program at the

Brandenburg-Gorden Psychiatric hospital. Many executions took place in a designated section of this Psychiatric hospital and the methods used included starvation, poison medications, and gas chambers. Following the end of the Second World War, the Kaiser Wilhelm Institute was renamed the Max Planck Society Institute, which moved to Frankfurt, where the brain specimen collections were maintained. Despite the revelations that had been exposed, the Max Planck Institute did not conduct a thorough detailed investigation into the role played by Hallervorden and other professors in the euthanasia programs of the Nazis, nor was Hallervorden brought up on any official charges. He remained at the institute until his death in 1965. The Max Planck organization buried a collection of brain specimens derived from victims of euthanasia in 1990. Physicians and victim's groups called for a further detailed review which revealed more victim specimens.[3,4] It is anticipated that the Max Planck Society's historical project will result in the complete burial of its remaining specimens and memorialization of victims in the near future.

Dr. Hermann Voss, Professor and Head of Anatomy Reich Universität of Posen, German-occupied Poland

Voss directed the preparation of skeletal specimens from Polish resistance fighters who had been executed by the Nazis and used these specimens for teaching. His skull collection also included the remains of Jewish Holocaust victims. Professor Voss took impressions of the faces of Jewish Holocaust victims and prepared plaster stone death masks and sold these, as well as portions of the skull collection to the Vienna Museum of Natural History. The plaster death masks and other artifacts from Jews who were to be transported to Vienna from the Buchenwald concentration camp, were destined to appear in the Vienna Museum's Race Gallery, showcasing evidence of what was expected to soon be an extinct race of humans. Following the war, the death masks, skulls of Nazi victims and other artifacts remained in the archives of the museum. In 1991 the skulls of the Jewish victims were buried in a Jewish Cemetery in Vienna. The plaster stone death masks of the Jews were donated to the Jewish Community in Vienna. Eventually, the skulls of the Polish resistance victims from the Voss collection were given to the Polish government. After the Second World War, Voss continued his academic career as an acclaimed anatomist at the Universities of Jena, followed by Greifswald Medical School and became the editor of *Anatomischer Anzeiger.* In 1959 Voss was honored as 'Outstanding People's Scientist' by East Germany for 'contributions to the development of science in the service of peace.'[4,5]

Dr. August Hirt Anatomist

The case of the notorious anatomist, Dr. August Hirt, had been well documented by Kasten, in 1991.[6] Hirt was a Professor at the University of Strasbourg Medical School and served as the Director of the Anatomical Institute in Nazi occupied France. His early academic career was at Heidelberg University where he taught anatomy and performed research on microscopes. Between 1925 and 1932 Hirt developed a close collaboration with Dr. Philipp Ellinger, a well-respected influential Professor of Pharmacology at Heidelberg. Professor Ellinger was also Jewish. Under Ellinger's leadership, their collaborative research led to the development of an intravital fluorescent microscope, obtaining an international patent and commercialization with Zeiss/Jena, a leading manufacturing company of microscopes and other fine optical equipment founded in Jena, Germany. After 1932 the collaboration ended with Ellinger's promotion to another institution. Within a few years Hirt was promoted to full professor, became a devout member of the Nazi party, and claimed full and exclusive credit for the development of the intravital fluorescent microscope.

Influenced by his active participation in the Nazi party, as well as being an active member of the Waffen SS, in 1941 Hirt was selected to be the Director of Anatomy at Strasbourg University in France. His racial hygiene research was well supported by the powerful head of the SS, Heinrich Himmler. Strasbourg University's location within forty miles of the Natzweiler Concentration Camp, also in Nazi occupied France, facilitated Hirt's notorious research projects. One of Hirt's horrific racial hygiene research projects focused on obtaining a collection of Jewish skulls, which was enthusiastically supported by the Nazi hierarchy and *Ahnenerbe*, the Ancestral Hereditary Society. *Ahnenerbe* was a powerful component of the SS designed to make racial hygiene research in the Third Reich, scientifically legitimate, and thus provide the scientific rationale for the racial superiority of the Aryan peoples and reinforcing racial hygiene policies. Hirt's plan was to select prisoners from the Auschwitz concentration camp, obtain measurements of the head while alive, followed by murder, decapitation, and preparation of the soft tissues for dissolution to create the skull collection. Apparently, there were several logistical issues encountered, resulting in delays, requiring assistance and approval by Lieutenant Colonel Adolf Eichmann, who had the overall responsibility for managing logistics in Nazi extermination camps. In 1943 approximately 100-150 Jewish prisoners from Auschwitz were selected and data for head measurements recorded. The prisoners were then transported to Natzweiler camp from Poland, where further measurements and X-rays were obtained and recorded. Hirt then had them murdered with cyanide poison gas. The bodies were then injected with a preservative and placed in storage where they remained until Hirt was ordered to destroy all evidence of the corpses by the Nazi authorities, as the allied invasion of France advanced. Hirt attempted to obliterate the mortal remains with caustic chemicals, cremation and other techniques; however, he was not able to complete this task on all of the corpses in time.

At the time of liberation of Strasbourg in 1944, Hirt had already fled to the safety of the Reichsuniversität in Tübingen. Press reports arising from the French military judiciary revealed that a total of 86 dead bodies of previously healthy men and women were discovered. The Berlin foreign office requested an official response from Hirt, who hid the truth in his written report:[9]

> *The corpses present were the usual cadavers for dissection training which can be found in every anatomical institute in the world, the majority of which have expired from some form of disease, with the exception of the very few dead bodies of criminals who had been executed.*

Hirt managed to escape from the allies and hid in the Black Forest. With the assistance of a farm family, he was able to obtain food and survive. When he learned of the surrender of the Nazis in May 1945 and the revelations regarding Nazi atrocities, he informed one of the farm family members that this was not true. Hirt committed suicide on 2 June 1945 in the woods, never having stood trial for his horrendous crimes. [6-9]

Hirt's racial hygiene skull research on the 'future dead' can be considered an example of bringing medical crimes to a new extreme level of terror, where the research was performed on victims while alive and after their murder.[7]

On December 11, 2005, a memorial plaque was unveiled at the Anatomy Institute of Strasburg Hospital and the Cronenbourg Jewish Cemetery in France. The unveiling of the names of 86 of Hirt's victims was attended by relatives of the victims from Thessalonica, London, Germany, Israel and France. The plaque which includes the 86 names reads:[10]

> *Souvenez-vous d'elles pour que jamais la medecine ne soit devoyée*
> *Remember them so that medicine never be corrupted again.*

These examples of medical atrocities committed by Drs. Hallervorden, Voss and Hirt represented just a few of the many revelations that were to come. The recounting of the actions of medical professions along with their affiliated institutions are so horrific and evil, they are extremely difficult to read and perhaps more difficult to put into words. The information on the ethical transgressions of the medical profession and other institutions in Europe arising from the Nazi era has been extremely well documented, so why recount this history again? It is difficult for any sane human being to understand how a 'civilized' society with world-class academic institutions renowned for groundbreaking scientific advances in all fields of culture and science, including medicine, could stray into the depths of such absolute evil, leading to the mass extermination of innocent human beings.

My education in the 1970s-80s leading to a career as an oral and maxillofacial surgeon consisted of the basic biological sciences followed by the principals of surgery, and did not include lessons on the history of medicine. I had assumed that all doctors who took the Hippocratic Oath had no possible path to become the perpetrators of medical experimentation and murder in the name of science. There was little awareness of this dark past and its relevance to becoming an ethical doctor. With the ascent of my professional career, it was going to take over two decades before I would begin to understand the importance of this history. Unfortunately, the shocking truth was revealed to me twenty years after I had become a beneficiary of the evils of Nazi medicine.

Notes

1. W.R. Forster, *Farewell Berlin*, (Thornton, CO: Farewell Berlin, LLC, 2018), pp.27-8.
2. E. Pernkopf, 'Originalabhandlungen Nationalsozialismus und Wissenschaft,' *Wien Klinische Wochenscrift*, 51 (1938), p. 545.
3. J. Peiffer, 'Neuropathology in the Third Reich: Memorial to those Victims of National-Socialist Atrocities in Germany who were used by medical science,' *Brain Pathol*, 1 (1991), p.125.
4. W. Seidelman , 'Dissecting the History of Anatomy in the Third Reich – 1989-2010: A Personal Account,' *Annals of Anatomy*, 194 (212), p.228.
5. G. Aumüller, 'Anatomy in the Nazi Era,' in Medical Student Council of Philipps University of Marburg (ed), *Responsibility of Medicine Under National Socialism*, (Marburg: Schuren Press, 1991), pp 87-111.
6. F.H. Kasten, 'Unethical Nazi Medicine in Annexed Alsace-Lorraine: The Strange Case of Nazi Anatomist Professor Dr. August Hirt,' in G. Kent, G. Mason (eds.), *Historians and Archivists: Essays in Modern German History and Archival Policy*, (Fairfax, Virginia: University Press, 1991), pp. 173-208.
7. S. Hildebrandt, *The Anatomy of Murder – Ethical Transgressions and Anatomical Science During the Third Reich*, (New York and Oxford: Berghahn Books, 2016), pp. 304-6.
8. Kasten FH. Personal correspondence, 29 November 1994.
9. H. Lang. 'August Hirt and "extraordinary opportunities for cadaver delivery" to anatomical institutes in National Socialism: A murderous change in paradigm,' *Ann Anatomy*, 2195 (2013), pp.373-80.
10. Associated Press, 'France Honors Jewish Victims of Nazi Anatomy Professor,' *The Jerusalem Post*, 11 December 2005.
11. R. Toledano, 'Anatomy in the Third Reich – The Anatomical Institute of Reichsuniversitat Strassburg and the Deliveries of Dead Bodies' *Ann Anatomy*, 205 (2016), pp.128-44.
12. A. Breedem, 'A French University Confronts Medical Crimes and its Nazi Past,' *The New York Times*, 27 July 2022.

4

Surgical Anatomy Lessons 1977–94

Throughout my development as an oral and maxillofacial surgeon and educator, I was obsessed with the need to be prepared for the challenges and responsibilities that were going to be placed upon me. We are all human and flawed as we stumble through our lives. I believed that doctors were not allowed to make mistakes, although we do. One brief slip can result in a life that is ruined. I knew that errors were inevitable, however, I decided that this would never occur with a patient under my care due to lack of vigilance. It was my responsibility to be thoroughly versed in the management of every possible complication that can occur as a requirement for every patient encounter. Therefore, my textbooks and reading the most current literature were the foundational elements of my readiness for patient care. Within that realm, thorough knowledge of anatomy and all variations of normal are absolutely necessary. The anatomy of the head and neck is perhaps considered the most complex in the human body. A one-second false move by the surgeon or assistant can result in permanent facial paralysis, numbness, excessive bleeding, loss of taste or the ability to open one's mouth to chew, amongst a myriad of other complications. Furthermore, in the education of residents in training, the professor must instill these important concepts into one's students. Throughout a career span of four to five decades, complications were bound to occur. In my mind, this would and should never occur with me or my trainees as the result of not being thoroughly prepared for each patient encounter.

How does one go from being inexperienced, knowing extraordinarily little about taking care of patients, to becoming a skillful experienced surgeon? With the responsibilities of taking care of each individual person seeking your help and expertise, this is not an easy road. The story of my progression to become a boarded oral and maxillofacial surgeon, academician and teacher is what follows.

St. Luke's Hospital Center & the New York City Blackout of 1977

Upon graduation from Columbia University School of Dental & Oral Surgery in 1977, I entered my postgraduate training years, initially as a General Practice Resident at St. Luke's Hospital Center, Manhattan, New York. The building was old and the hospital had been constructed in stages since 1896. The location on Morningside Heights on Amsterdam Avenue and 114th Street in Manhattan, was only a block away from the Columbia University main campus. The rear of the hospital was an imposing edifice overseeing Morningside Park, a haven for drug dealers and other nefarious activities during the 1970s. The on-call room was in an apartment building off of Morningside Drive by the rear of the hospital. I felt a combination of both fear and exhilaration for this new phase of my education I was about to enter. The starched white uniforms all residents were required to wear helped to fuel these feelings. Crossing the street in one's bright white resident uniforms at 3a.m. when called to the emergency room was an adventure. On one hand, I was now a 'doctor' as evidenced by my white coat, about to learn the craft of treating patients. But in reality, although I felt comfortable with my knowledge base in the basic sciences, the practical aspects of taking care of people who were either in pain or had a problem that I had never delt with was terrifying.

I recall the first time I went to the operating room at St. Luke's Hospital Center. The operating rooms were in a wing of the hospital that was adjacent to the Cathedral of St. John the Divine, a New York City landmark and perhaps the one of the largest cathedrals in the world. The building was constantly under repair and construction, I assume due to its massive size. As I gazed out of the window before entering the operating room, I wondered if praying to G-d at that moment was the most appropriate thing to do. I spent many hours in those operating rooms and quickly learned that praying for your patient and your performance as a doctor was what was in order, particularly for me.

The one-year General Practice Residency (GPR) Program was an introduction to Hospital Dentistry, and most important for me, there was an Oral & Maxillofacial Surgery Residency Postgraduate Training Program that was a major component within the Department of Dentistry. Basically, the oral & maxillofacial surgeons, both residents in training and faculty, were the essential providers of care for head trauma, infections of the head and neck, tumors and other disease conditions of the jaws, oral cavity and surrounding anatomic structures. The GPRs were the residents that did most of the scut work for the 'higher level' oral & maxillofacial surgery (OMFS) residents at night, such as being on call for emergencies, admitting patients to the hospital, performing history and physical examinations, and obtaining medical clearance for surgical procedures that were to be performed, usually one day following admission to the hospital.

Every morning, the OMFS residents and GPRs went to check on the patients that we were responsible for who had been admitted on our service. The chief OMFS resident was the one with the most experience, and Dick was both an imposing figure and great teacher who was respected by all of the residents below him. I will never forget that first morning when we all went on rounds. The patient was a young man who had been operated on the day before by the oral & maxillofacial surgery residents. The first year OMFS resident presented the case to everyone, and in general the patient was doing well. The patient was a chronic smoker and drug abuser with a mild chronic cough. After we exited the patient's room, we all gathered around Dick to hear his final instructions. I'll never forget what Dick said to the first-year resident. 'You better get this guy discharged and out of the hospital this morning, before he really gets sick.'

The first several weeks of the General Practice Residency program involved orientation to hospital protocol, and the teaching was initiated by the more experienced oral & maxillofacial surgery residents, as well as faculty. It was a very exciting and anxiety producing time in my professional development. I was no longer taking examinations and being graded on my independent performance based on the answers to a series of questions. If I failed to obtain correct answers on an examination as a student, the only individual who suffered was me. Now, I had to have answers and provide the correct treatment, with the responsibility for the well-being of my patient. A failure on my part would cause suffering and possible harm to the patient I was responsible for. The problem was, I had no experience and felt as if I knew nothing. However, luck was going to come my way.

On July 13-14 there was a major failure of electrical power that caused the New York City blackout of 1977. The impact of this blackout on many New Yorkers was profound. There was looting of businesses with storefronts in many neighborhoods throughout the city. There were no functional air conditioners, no open movie theatres, no open restaurants and no television broadcasts to watch on these hot summer nights. There was nothing to do for most people. Others took advantage of the blackout by breaking into storefronts and stealing items. However, there were many others who were more productive in a positive way. Apparently, there was a boom in the rate of births nine months following the blackout. The impact on me was profound in another way. Here I was, two weeks into my residency without experience, but I desperately wanted to learn. I knew that the emergency rooms throughout New York City were being overwhelmed with injuries, many being related to the significant amount of looting that was taking place, with broken glass often being embedded in the tissues, requiring debridement and repair. I was not on call that night, but I just decided to go into the emergency room at St. Luke's Hospital Center to observe and learn. When I arrived in my clean white coat, which was short (indicating that I was a first-year resident, a rookie), I was overwhelmed by how crazy the emergency room was. There were so many patients to be treated, and the experienced surgical residents were exhausted, treating patients non-stop, and still not being close to treating all of those who had been injured and were in the emergency room waiting area, which had overflowed. An exhausted surgical resident pulled me over and asked me if I knew how to place sutures and if I could assist him. This was the first time I heard the expression that was common with surgical residents in training 'see one, do one, teach one.' I had placed sutures inside the mouth while I was a senior student at Columbia, but I had never sutured any other parts of the body. The surgical resident demonstrated to me in detail the steps involved in suturing any wound, which involved, placing an antiseptic on the wound, providing local anesthesia to numb the area, irrigating the wound and removal of any foreign bodies and debris, control of bleeding, removal of tissue that had no blood supply, and finally performing the repair in layers, with resorbable (melting) sutures in the deeper tissue layers, and nylon sutures for skin. The wound was dressed, patients were given Tetanus booster shots as well as oral medication and instructions. On the next case I assisted and once the surgical resident was satisfied with my performance, he allowed me to treat several patients with his careful oversight. I had made my first step toward becoming a surgeon.

As the residency progressed, I continued to learn much more, with guidance from the OMFS residents and faculty. My confidence gradually grew as I was exposed to more patients and clinical situations. When I was on emergency call, the oral & maxillofacial surgery residents were delighted, as I seemed to be seeing a high volume of patients with jaw fractures, oral infections, dislocated jaws and other unusual conditions, which kept the residents quite busy for the surgical cases that were to be performed the following day. It seemed to be sheer luck, that for some reason, when I was on call, patients with the craziest, most complex and interesting problems seemed to find their way to the chaotic St. Luke's emergency room. After my initial evaluation and preliminary care, I would admit patients to the hospital for further diagnostic testing, and ultimately surgical treatment. My reward was to be able to assist the oral & maxillofacial surgeons in the operating room, which reminded me to say my silent prayer as I looked out the window overlooking the massive Cathedral of St John the Devine. I was thankful for having the opportunity to assist in a surgery that repaired a broken jaw, drained a facial infection or treated a mysterious condition and then round on the patients the following days until they were well enough for discharge. When I wasn't busy being on call, I opened up my Pernkopf's Atlas, studied the anatomy related to the condition that was being treated by the surgeons, and I envisioned, one day, being the surgeon who would be prepared to treat these patients.

Oral & Maxillofacial Surgery Residency Program, Oral Cancer, and the 'Killer Lecture Series' 1978 –81

I was accepted into an oral & maxillofacial surgery (OMFS) training program at the East Orange Veterans Administration (EOVA) Medical Center in New Jersey. This was not a 'glamorous' or highly touted OMFS residency program, such as those at Harvard, Yale, Massachusetts General, and UCLA. However, the EOVA's program appealed to me and was tailored to areas of study that were of great interest to me. The two things that stood out for me were the OMFS schedule of weekly lectures throughout the year, and the major focus on diagnosis and treatment of oral cancer, which unfortunately was a major disease afflicted by veterans. The weekly OMFS lectures were quite different from those of other programs. There were fifty-two different topics chosen, each one presented every Thursday morning, with the OMFS residents and attendings only. Attendance was mandatory. The topics ranged from diagnosis and treatment of deep space infections of the head and neck, to fluid and electrolytes, treatment of medically compromised patients with a thorough review of conditions such as diabetes, cardiac disease, kidney disease, endocrine disorders, blood transfusions, airway management, maxillofacial trauma and many other conditions. All of the topics chosen were focused on providing the necessary information that is required of a surgeon treating patients in a hospital setting. A unique aspect of these conferences was that there were no guest lecturers, as each presentation had to be prepared by the OMFS resident. The amount of preparation that was required for each session was incredible, as the OMFS attendings who supervised the residents, were thoroughly knowledgeable and prepared to 'grill' the resident presenter if there was any missing information. The residents were not passive receivers of knowledge but were active learners who were actually teaching the material. Upon completion of the residency program, I had fifty-two folders filled with my notes on all of the presentations I had given at these conferences. At that time, I didn't realize that I would be reviewing my presentation notes for many years into the future.

The atmosphere in that small conference room lined with textbooks, journals and anatomic skulls was extremely intimidating. One of the initial conferences of my first year of residency required that I deliver a presentation on diagnosis and treatment of deep space infections of the head and neck. I arrived at 6:30 AM, one half hour prior to the start of the conference so that I can be fully caffeinated and open the windows. I was anticipating the heat that was going to be generated over the duration of my presentation. The more experienced residents, who had given this presentation in the previous years were in their easy seats, smirking, knowing how I was going to be the target of a series of questions from the faculty. They had already passed this rite of passage and now it was my turn to be in the hot seat. When the OMFS faculty entered the conference room, I began to sweat. Dr. Arthur Mashberg was the program director who was the administrator for the program and Dr. Stanley Leban was the main full-time faculty member who did most of the hands on teaching of the OMFS residents supervising most of the cases in the operating room. Stan 'The Man' Leban, was perhaps the most intimidating presence in the room. The breadth of his knowledge was incredible, and he let you know it. Stan's piercing eyes did not blink when he asked me a series of questions. I could see the repressed smiles on the faces of the other residents as they had been through this scenario many times before. If you were not able to answer to his satisfaction, he would stare at you with a stony expression on his face which let you and everyone else know what was on his mind. 'How the hell are you going to be able to take care of your patients competently if you don't know the answer to my question?' Although Stan would not embarrass you in front of the residents, you knew what he was thinking because in the privacy of his office after the conference, he would provide you with his honest assessment.

Most people are not aware of the serious potential consequences of infections originating from the oral cavity. Since the oral cavity represents the upper part of a person's airway, infections that are not resolved adequately can readily spread to dangerous anatomic spaces of the head and neck. Airway compromise with blockage may occur if the infection spreads to the spaces of the neck. Infections can also spread superiorly causing serious intracranial complications. Other infections from the oral cavity can spread rapidly inferiorly, descending into the mediastinum (chest) which can affect the heart. The source that I used for understanding the spaces of the head and neck was Hollinshead's *Anatomy for Surgeons, Volume 1, The Head and Neck.*[1] This book was fabulous in the descriptions of the relationships between the oral cavity and the various deep and dangerous spaces of the head and neck from which an infection can spread. However, this book was filled with simple diagrams and was not an atlas with detailed pictures of the true anatomy that the surgeon was going to encounter. Therefore, Pernkopf's Atlas combined with Hollinshead's descriptions were my sources for mastering this difficult and crucial subject.

By the end of that first year of residency training I had delivered many presentations in that small conference room and I learned a tremendous amount of material from being the active presenter rather than a passive listener. I spent many hours at night preparing for each lecture, diving into textbooks and journal articles. The highlight for me came at the end of the year when I was called into Stan's office. Every year, OMFS residents in the US and Canada are required to take an examination, testing their knowledge base and competencies in a variety of complex topics which are required for a satisfactory advancement in one's education and to maintain standards of excellence in the specialty. The OMSITE (Oral and Maxillofacial Surgery in-service Training Examination) is also designed to assist Program Directors and residents identify weaknesses and deficiencies in their training programs with corrections to maintain accreditation standards. On that day when I was called into Stan's office, I knew that he was going to provide me with the results of my performance on the OMSITE exam. My knees were shaking when he told me 'Howard, I have good news and also bad news.................' Stan paused for ten seconds to build up the level of tension, which all good surgeons feel, especially when they are in the operating room. 'The good news is that you did very well on the OMSITE examination........................but the bad news...(long pause)..................you will never do any better.' I had scored the highest marks possible on the exam.

There were other major benefits of my education as an oral and maxillofacial surgeon at the EOVA Medical Center. The affiliation with the New Jersey School of Medicine (currently changed to Rutgers Health New Jersey Medical School) enabled me to take the required medical school courses in pathophysiology, internal medicine and physical diagnosis. My program director made it clear to all residents that a requirement in one's OMFS training at the EOVA Medical Center was not merely to pass the course, but to excel with a grade of 'high pass.' Additionally, the OMFS service was responsible for the diagnosis and treatment of all patients with oral cancer. The program director, Dr Arthur Mashberg, was one of the leading experts in the world on the early diagnosis of oral cancer. The goal was to diagnose the oral cancer at an early stage where it was much easier to treat successfully, with higher survival rates and a greatly improved quality of life for the patients. Dr Mashberg recognized that most oral cancers were diagnosed in the later stages of the disease, where there was pain and a noticeable tumor, which had already spread to the jawbone and the lymph nodes of the neck. The emphasis on early diagnosis was significant since early oral cancer is often without any symptoms and goes unnoticed by the patient, as well as medical and dental professionals. However, being trained at the EOVA medical center, I learned what to look for and the subtle signs of the appearance of the tissues to be suspicious of cancer and obtain a biopsy to corroborate the diagnosis of an early oral cancer.

Unfortunately, many of the veterans who first arrived at the EOVA medical center for evaluation already had advanced cancers requiring major surgery to remove the tumor, as well as the affected bone and soft tissues of the neck. As an OMFS resident, I was required to be first assistant to the Head and Neck specialists who were the primary surgeons that operated on these patients with major surgery, requiring many hours in the operating room. During my direct participation in those cases as the assistant surgeon, the entire complex anatomy of the head and neck in a living human being was laid out before my eyes. This was no cadaver dissection laboratory, it was the real thing. This required intense preparation for these cases. My Pernkopf's Atlas began to show signs of great wear as I reviewed the anatomy over and over again. As an assistant surgeon, I wanted to be certain of knowing each artery, vein, nerve and vital structure that was going to be encountered, as to avoid any potential further injury that would harm these already severely compromised patients.

Academic Oral & Maxillofacial Surgery at Columbia University 1981-2000

Having successfully completed my Oral & Maxillofacial Surgery Training Program, it was time to get a job and develop a professional career. Mindy and I had our first child, and with the hope of having more, it was my turn to support the family. Although I immediately was able to obtain employment in a private oral & maxillofacial surgeon's office on Long Island, I knew that I wanted to teach, and so I joined the voluntary oral surgery faculty at Columbia University School of Dental & Oral Surgery (1981-82). The importance of teaching was paramount to me, as I had learned, early on in my OMFS residency program that you learn more by teaching than you do by being a passive learner. Furthermore, as a member of the faculty, teaching young, bright, inexperienced students, you not only are able to spread your knowledge base to others, but most importantly you often learn more from the questions and challenges of bright students.

I thrived in the academic environment at Columbia University and in 1983 I participated in the submission of a multispecialty cancer grant, with my contribution being in my area of expertise, oral cancer. Shortly thereafter, I was hired as the first full-time oral and maxillofacial surgeon, by the new Director of Oral & Maxillofacial Surgery, Steven Roser, DMD, MD. Dr. Roser was, at that time, one of the few oral and maxillofacial surgeons who had undergone OMFS training in the program at the College of Dental Medicine at Harvard University, which provided a dual degree training in the specialty of oral and maxillofacial surgery, as well as obtaining the medical degree. Under Dr. Roser's leadership, Columbia University established a dual degree OMFS residency program where, upon graduation, the resident obtained both specialty certification in OMFS and an MD from Columbia University College of Physicians and Surgeons. As the other full-time faculty member, I was responsible for the training of oral and maxillofacial surgery residents, as well as the dental students at Columbia University. It was a very exciting time and my library, which of course included Pernkopf's Atlas, was also filled with books on pathology, medicine, anesthesia, pathophysiology, surgery, trauma, cancer and orthognathic surgery, a relatively new field within the specialty of oral & maxillofacial surgery.

To continue to pursue my academic career it was necessary for me to become a boarded certified oral and maxillofacial surgeon. This was one of the most grueling and difficult periods of my life. To pass the board examinations one had to demonstrate extensive knowledge of surgery, medicine, fluid and electrolytes, anatomy, physical diagnosis, treatment of medically compromised patients, microscopic pathology, anesthesia, emergency management, microbiology, current research and a host of other topics, the list being too long to mention. I studied intensively for two years with my books at my side every night in the basement, while Mindy took care of our two young children, and attending to most household affairs.

The written examination was an all-day affair which took place in Philadelphia, which I passed. Now I became eligible for the terrifying oral board examinations which took place on an extremely frigid, windy February day in Chicago, at the historic Drake Hotel, decorated throughout with Victorian era charm. There would be two, three or four board examiners in a very opulent hotel suite with antique furniture, a carousel slide projector and a screen. Slides projected on the screen would depict a variety of patient cases, microscopic slides of certain diseases, anatomic depictions, microbiology, trauma and a variety of different scenarios. Questions were asked by the board examiners in rapid succession and you, the examinee, were required to give your answers and provide the rationale for your responses. The temperature in Chicago that day may have been 0 degrees Fahrenheit outside, but in those luxury examination suites, it felt like 100. Several months later a letter from the board arrived in my mailbox informing me that on 27 March 1985, I became a certified Diplomate of the American Board of Oral and Maxillofacial Surgery. Most important, I was now able to leave the basement, return to the land of the living and become a dad and husband again.

Orthognathic surgery became a special interest for Dr. Roser and the rest of the OMFS department, as it involved creating precise surgical cuts in the jaw bones (osteotomies) and reposition the bones of the lower face to create improved jaw function as well as facial esthetics. Prior to the development of orthognathic surgical techniques, individuals who had a significant discrepancy in the sizes of the upper and lower jaw, would have no other option than to undergo orthodontic repositioning of the teeth. However, the orthodontic specialists realized that you can only reposition teeth a certain distance and were limited by the sizes of the jawbone. An individual with a huge lower jaw would often have the lower teeth protrude much further forward than the upper teeth, creating problems with speech, chewing and giving the person a very large lower jaw appearance. The reverse problem is also common, where the lower jaw is much too small for the upper jaw, giving the patient the appearance of having 'buck teeth,' with the upper teeth in front protruding much further forward than the lower front teeth due to the presence of a small lower jaw. This scenario also creates problems with chewing and facial appearance and can create significant problems for young adults who are at an important stage in their psycho-social development. The major challenge with performing orthognathic surgery is to ensure an adequate blood supply to the bony segments. With the extremely complex vascular and nerve anatomy of the head and neck structures, orthognathic surgery is quite challenging for the surgical team and was much more challenging in those early days, where the instrumentation and the surgical planning techniques that were available were crude, as compared to what is available today. The surgeons have to make operative maneuvers in a small, dark, wet hole (the oral cavity), with great precision to avoid excessive bleeding and nerve injury. This type of operation is both technically and intellectually challenging, as well as requiring great stamina particularly in those early days. A typical case would require at least eight hours of surgery, whereas today, most surgeons can proceed in less than half that amount of time, with improvements in instrumentation, fiberoptic lighting, virtual digital treatment planning, and the fabrication of custom titanium plates and screws to provide rigid fixation of the repositioned bony segments. Precise knowledge of the anatomy of the head and neck is always crucial for the success of the surgery. Needless to say, Pernkopf's Atlas was my go-to source for every surgical procedure, with the planning and preparation that was necessary to obtain a successful surgical result and also with the need to train oral and maxillofacial surgeons for the future.

Interestingly, the surgical techniques required for orthognathic surgery were developed by a handful of brilliant and innovative oral and maxillofacial surgeons in Europe, after the Second World War. These surgeons became world-renowned and brought their knowledge to oral surgeons in America. Oral surgeons became more than just dentists who extracted teeth. The *Journal of Oral Surgery* had to change its name to the *Journal of Oral and Maxillofacial Surgery*, and the specialty changed dramatically as well. OMSs now were doing all of their complex cases in the operating rooms of medical centers becoming fully knowledgeable in all aspects of surgery, hospital and medical care. The innovators who made complex jaw surgery possible were trained in the most prestigious academic institutions in Austria and Germany. This history was going to be quite relevant much later in my career as I discovered that there were many more lessons to be learned from the Pernkopf Atlas other than anatomical relationships in preparation for surgery.

I flourished in the stimulating academic environment at Columbia University in the 1980s -90s. I received academic promotions from Assistant Professor to Associate Professor and ultimately to full clinical Professor as an educator, clinician, and researcher. As a clinician, I developed an interest and expertise in minimally invasive temporomandibular joint (TMJ) surgery using arthroscopic techniques, as I collaborated with orthopedic surgeons and researchers. The TMJ is the jaw joint that allows one to open and close the mouth to speak and chew. I received grant funding from the NIH (National Institutes of Health) through my partnership with the orthopedic research department, studying the synovial fluids of patients with arthritic temporomandibular joints. I taught courses in pain control and chronic oral and facial pain and also served a variety of administrative roles as chair of the admissions committee, chair of the curriculum committee, and served as a representative of the dental school in the Columbia University Senate. However, my most important and consistent role throughout those years was as a clinical oral and maxillofacial surgeon treating patients in need of my services. Patient care was the most important aspect of my professional career as it also enabled me to help people suffering from a variety of conditions and also contribute to the education of oral and maxillofacial surgery residents in training, who represented the future of our specialty.

Perhaps my greatest strength as an educator was in emphasizing the importance of preparation prior to each surgical procedure, no matter how complex or routine the planned procedure was expected to be. I was known by all residents to come to the operating room with my 'operation planning sheet' on paper from a yellow lined pad, which listed step by step every planned action that was necessary for a successful operative procedure, complete with anatomic diagrams, and potential complications and back up plans for any untoward events that may occur during the surgery. Each 'operation planning sheet' was created by me prior to the surgical procedure, with my Pernkopf's Atlas opened to the pages demonstrating the most relevant anatomy for the planned portions of the procedure. This strict regimen continued for twenty years with little deviation until it became necessary to stop.

Notes

1. W.H. Hollinshead (ed.), *Anatomy for Surgeons, Volume 1, Second Edition, The Head and Neck*, (Hagerstown, Maryland, New York, San Francisco and London: Harper & Row Publishers, Inc., 1968), pp. 306-29.

5

Discovery - Anatomy Lessons from a Nazi Doctor 1994

It was a very ordinary day in my academic career as an oral and maxillofacial surgeon at Columbia University. After over ten years as a full-time faculty member, I relished the multiple varied stimulating assignments and responsibilities that would encompass a typical week. Each day had a different focus which could be any combination of lecturing, overseeing a laboratory session, research, faculty practice providing clinical care, supervising patient care by residents and students in the oral surgery clinic, clinical research, administration as Chair of the Curriculum Committee, and treatment of patients with major surgical procedures in the operating room with oral and maxillofacial surgery residents. On this very typical day, I was in my academic office reviewing each step for a major surgical case that was scheduled for the operating room the following day. I was not prepared for the initial spark that was to come which would rock the foundation of my core being as a doctor, surgeon, and teacher, whose highest priority was to provide the best care possible for my patients and to eliminate or reduce suffering and pain.

The surgical procedure that was being planned for the following day required an extraoral approach, with incisions in the neck, leading to the surgical site where the problem was located in the lower jaw. I had my yellow lined pad for writing notes and my 1963 edition of the Pernkopf Atlas[1] open to a page which showed the anatomic layers of tissues that would be encountered in my approach to the surgical site.

I was adhering to my typical presurgical preparation regimen, as I had been doing since I became an oral and maxillofacial surgeon, when there was a knock on the door, as my colleague and friend, Dr. Steven Syrop entered my office, just to say 'hello.' He could see my preparations for surgery and the Pernkopf Atlas open on my desk. Dr. Syrop recognized the anatomy book, and in a very casual manner commented

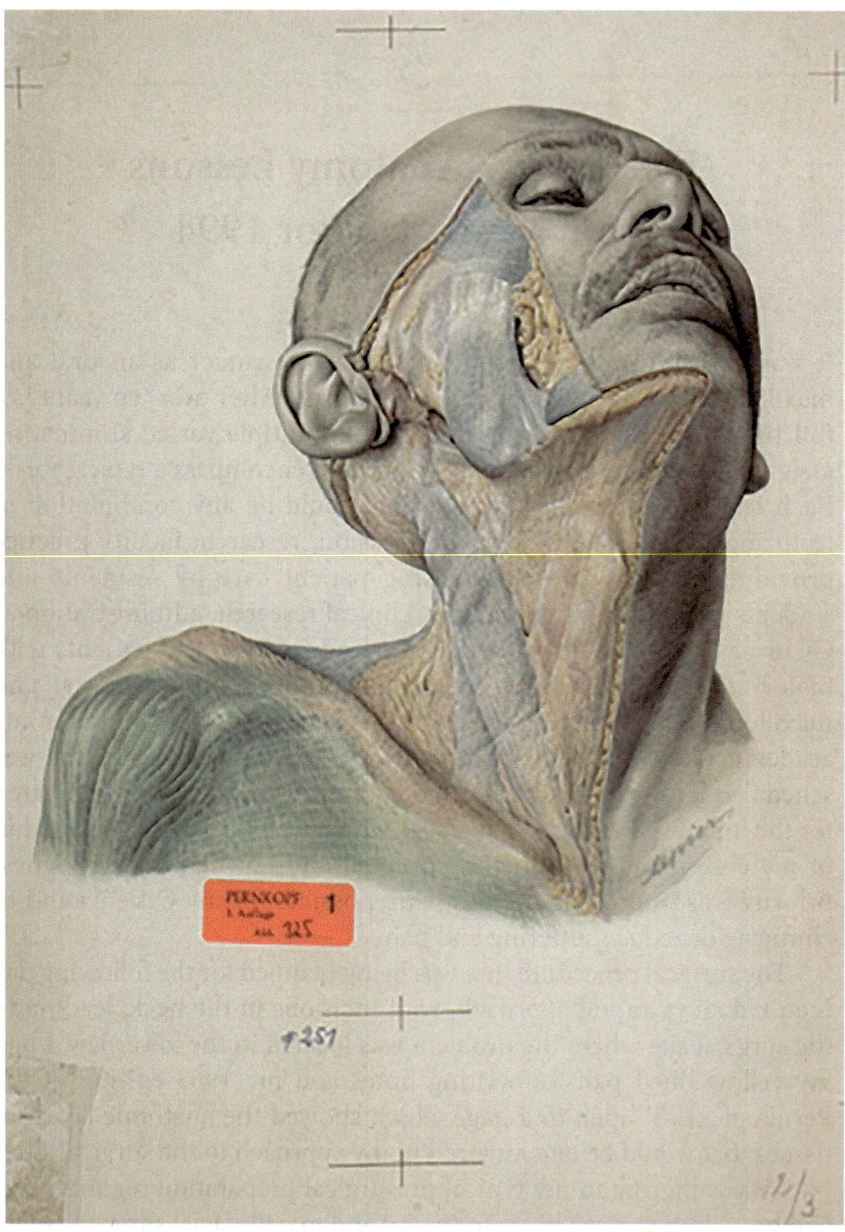

Figure 1. Anatomical illustrations from the Pernkopf Atlas are superb when preparing for surgery. I was studying the above figure from the 1963 edition[1] when a colleague suggested that Pernkopf was a Nazi. The illustration above is the original painting signed by the artist Eric Lepier, reprinted with permission from the archives of the Josephinum - Ethics, Collections and History of Medicine, MedUni Vienna.

'I see you are using Pernkopf's Atlas.........did you know that this book may have been created by Nazis?' My response was that I had never heard of this nor ever considered who Pernkopf was. I told Dr. Syrop about my regular use of this atlas for so many years as my most trusted source of the head and neck anatomy that I used in preparation for surgery.

After Dr. Syrop left my office following this very brief encounter, I stared at the anatomic picture that I was studying and had reviewed so many times, as I had done in the past. The picture showed the face of a young male, who was extremely thin with prominent bony features of his face, and with a head that was shaved. The neck structures and tissue layers which I had been studying were now completely irrelevant to me. Who was this person? How did he die? Did he know Dr. Pernkopf? Was he a victim of the Nazis? I realized that I was looking at a human being who had a life but died at a very young age. I felt totally ignorant that I was studying from my most prized book for so many years and had no idea who Pernkopf was. Had I unknowingly benefited from a creation of evil? Were my patients benefiting from lessons that I had learned from a Nazi? The foundation of who I was and the driving forces that led me to become an oral and maxillofacial surgeon, clinician, and educator, were shaken to my core. I had to find out the truth behind the origins of my most trusted book.

Notes

1. H. Ferner (ed), *Eduard Pernkopf Atlas of Topographical and Applied Human Anatomy, Volume I, Head and Neck,* (Philadelphia and London, W.B. Saunders Company, 1963), Fig. 251, p. 234.

6

Searching for the Truth and Wanderings - 1994

With this upheaval in the foundation of my professional development as an oral and maxillofacial surgeon, I was certain of only one thing. I had to find out the truth about my most precious anatomy book and its origins. My first approach was to discover as much as possible of the known facts. I had no idea as to where to go to uncover the truth nor who I should turn to for help, but I had to do something to get started. My first instinct was to see if there were previous editions of Pernkopf's Anatomy Atlas, other than my 1963 English language edition. I was fortunate to be able to search the old library stacks of books in the basement of the Columbia University Health Sciences Library. I discovered the German language editions of Eduard Pernkopf's *Topographische Anatomie des Menschen* published by Urban & Schwarzenberg, Berlin and Wien (Vienna) in 1937, 1943 and 1952. These books were very old, dusty and in poor condition. The 1943 edition included a depiction of a dissection of a pregnant woman and her fetus, with the artist, Lepier, signing his name with a swastika. Eric Lepier's signature with a swastika appears with many of his anatomic paintings created during the Nazi era (Figure 2).

Throughout this 1943 volume, there were numerous anatomic paintings with the artists signing their names adding a Nazi icon, to demonstrate their allegiance to National Socialism. Another artist, Endtresser, signed his name with the 'SS' rune, denoting allegiance with the *Schutzstaffel*, a major paramilitary organization throughout the Nazi Party which enforced mass surveillance, state terrorism, racial policy and allegiance to Hitler. Franz Batke appears to have demonstrated his loyalty to the Nazi state by signing his name with what many interpret as the lightning bolt 'SS' rune in 1944 (Figure 3).

There were numerous Nazi icons associated with the signatures of the artists throughout the German language editions. Most importantly,

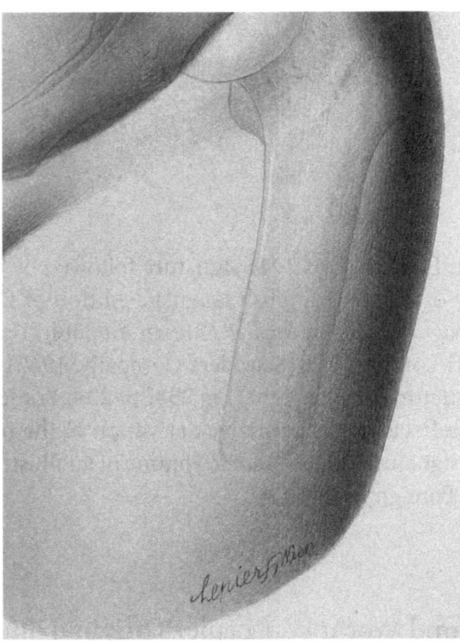

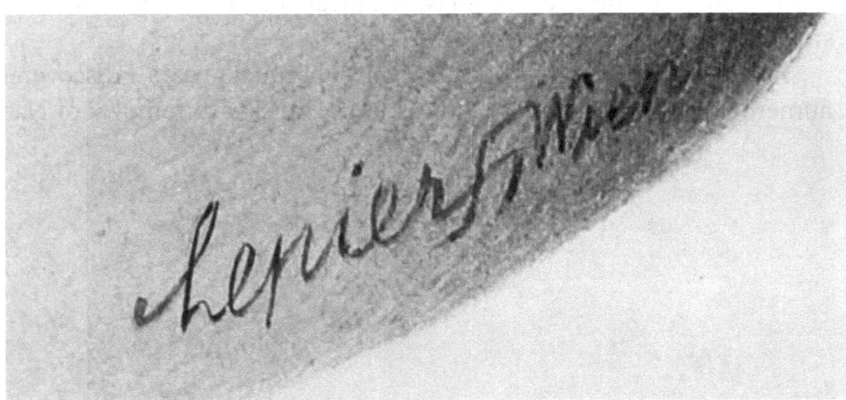

Figure 2. Signature of anatomical artist Eric Lepier with swastika demonstrating allegiance to the Nazi regime appearing in the German language edition of *Eduard Pernkopf Topographische Anatomie des Menschen* published by Urban & Schwarzenberg, Berlin and Wien. The illustration above is the original 1940 painting signed by the artist Eric Lepier, reprinted with permission from the archives of the Josephinum - Ethics, Collections and History of Medicine, MedUni Vienna.

when I searched through my 1963 English language edition of the atlas, I did discover evidence of a Lepier signature in which the swastika at the end of his name was erased (Figure 4a).

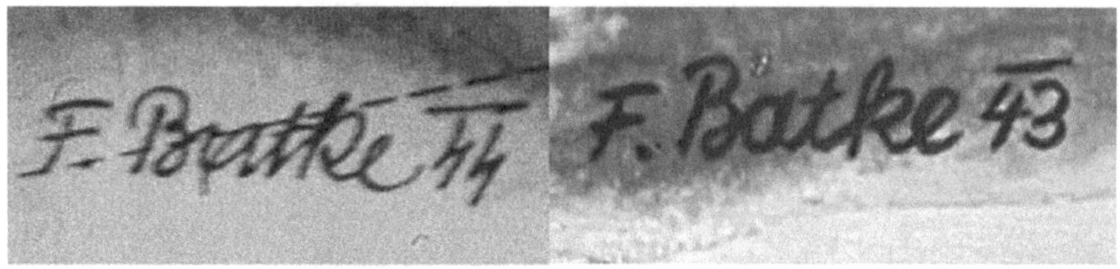

Figure 3. Above left, Franz Batke's 1944 signature followed by what resembles the SS rune, from my copy of the 1963 English language edition of H. Ferner (ed), *Eduard Pernkopf Atlas of Topographical and Applied Human Anatomy, Volume I, Head and Neck,* (Philadelphia Pa and London, W.B. Saunders Company, 1963). Signature on the left, Fig. 263, p. 254, signature on the right, Fig.254, p. 239. Some have interpreted the symbols on the left reflecting an alternative derivation of the number '4' in German. Above right, Batke's signature from the same volume of an illustration from 1943. With permission Elsevier Foreign Rights.

After the Second World War Lepier's original illustrations appeared in subsequent editions of the atlas, but evidence of signatures with the swastika were removed (Figure 4b).

As I investigated more thoroughly in subsequent years, I discovered numerous examples of later editions of the atlas with removal of Nazi

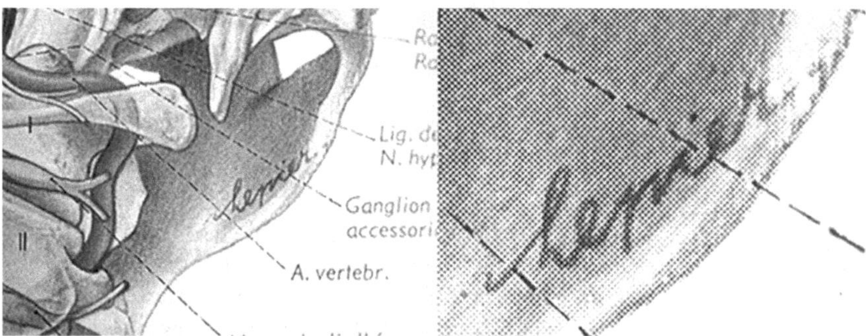

Figure 4a. Pernkopf artist Erich Lepier's signature with swastika erased from my copy of the 1963 English language edition of H. Ferner (ed), *Eduard Pernkopf Atlas of Topographical and Applied Human Anatomy, Volume I, Head and Neck,* (Philadelphia Pa and London, W.B. Saunders Company, 1963), Fig 289, p 301. Although this was in my copy of the atlas, I never noticed it until 1994. With permission Elsevier Foreign Rights.

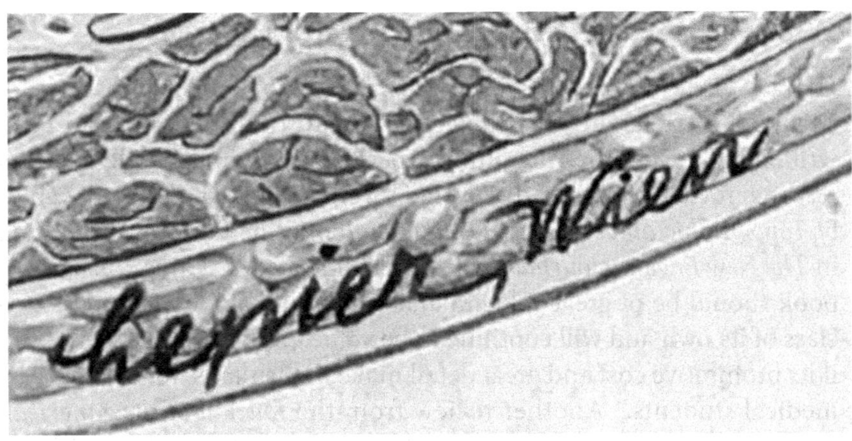

Figure 4b. The illustration above first appeared in the 1937 edition of the Pernkopf Atlas, with a swastika connecting 'Lepier' with 'Wien,' in the same format as figure 2. The illustration above is the original painting with the signature modified in 1953 to erase the swastika and was used in the publication of future editions. Reprinted with permission from the archives of the Josephinum - Ethics, Collections and History of Medicine, MedUni Vienna.

icons. More details on the cover up to remove evidence of the book's Nazi origins with alteration of artist's signatures will be described in later chapters.

There was another interesting finding while I was searching the library stacks. I found other classic anatomy atlases contained some images that were from Pernkopf's artists. Anatomy books including *Sabotta - Atlas of Human Anatomy*, *Clemente - Anatomy* and other books had included some of the illustrations that had originally appeared in Pernkopf's Atlas. With these anatomy books in medical libraries throughout the world, one wonders how many medical students, physicians, anatomists and surgeons have studied these illustrations and enhanced their medical knowledge over the spread of many years. Without acknowledgement of the background of these anatomical depictions, the unsuspecting viewer is totally unaware of the origin of these illustrations and the bioethical issues related to their use. How many of these healthcare professionals knew that they were being taught by Nazis and benefited by learning from their victims?

Who was Eduard Pernkopf? Literature Search

Having visual evidence of the Nazi affiliation and sympathies of Pernkopf's artists, my next objective was to find out what had been written in the published literature by performing an independent library research review. Initially, I discovered several reviews of Pernkopf's *Atlas of Topographic and Applied Human Anatomy.* Snell's review published in *The New England Journal of Medicine*[1] indicated that 'this outstanding book should be of great value to anatomists and surgeons' and 'is in a class of its own and will continue to be valued as a reference work even if its prohibitive cost and great detail make it unsuitable for purchase by medical students.' Another review from the *Journal of the American Medical Association* published in 1990 indicated that this atlas is a 'classic among atlases of anatomy' that 'will be most useful to otolaryngologists, plastic surgeons, head and neck surgeons, ophthalmologists, oral surgeons and orthopedists.'[2] It was clear that the volumes of Pernkopf's Atlas, present in the libraries of medical schools throughout the world were critically acclaimed as a resource that was unparalleled in its detailed depictions of anatomy. This work had made a significant contribution to the education of health care professionals and thus to the quality of care of so many patients. But the question remained, who was Eduard Pernkopf and how was this classic anatomy atlas created?

I was surprised to discover that my literature search, aside from reviews on the quality of the Penkopf Atlas, yielded only a few articles that provided insight into Eduard Pernkopf, the person. Articles by Weissman,[3,4] the *Viennese Medical Weekly (Wien Klinische Wochenschrift 1938)*[5] and an article on the history of the atlas[6] were important publications that gradually pieced together the story behind the creation of the atlas and who Eduard Pernkopf was. Dr. Gerald Weissman as Professor of Medicine and Director of Rheumatology, New York University School of Medicine in 1982 and 1985 published articles titled 'Springtime for Pernkopf' that provided insight into Eduard Pernkopf, the person. Weissman describes the changes in leadership of the editorial board of the prestigious *Viennese Medical Weekly* in the 20 May 1938 issue, after the *Anschluss,* when Hitler's campaign to annex Austria as part of the expanding Nazi empire succeeded in April 1938. Eduard Pernkopf, Professor of Anatomy at the University of Vienna was promoted to Dean of the Faculty at the prestigious University of Vienna School of Medicine in 1938. The Nazi's realized that Pernkopf was well positioned to assume the position of Dean, as he had been a devout member of the National Socialist Party who led the purge against the Jewish faculty. In the May 20th issue of the *Viennese Medical Weekly*, Dean Pernkopf's 1938 address to the Faculty of Medicine of the University of Vienna (Figure 5) was published, and summarized Pernkopf's view on the role of medicine under the new regime:[2,3,4]

> *To assume the medical care-with all your professional skill of the Body of the People (Volkskorper) which has been entrusted to you, not only in the positive sense of furthering the propagation of the fit, but also in the negative sense of eliminating the unfit and defective. The methods by which racial hygiene proceeds are well known to you: control of marriage; propagation of the genetically fit whose genetic, biologic constitution promises healthy descendants; discouragement of breeding by individuals who do not belong together properly, whose races clash; finally the exclusion*

Figure 5. The newly appointed Dean of Medicine at the University of Vienna, Eduard Pernkopf, addressing his faculty in 1938 on the role of medicine in the Third Reich to emphasize 'exclusion of the genetically inferior from future generations by sterilization and other means.' Photograph from '*Wein 1938*' Historical Museum of the City of Vienna, Documentation Archives of the Austrian Resistance. © Austrian National Library, Image rights ÖNB/Wien S 283/30.

(Ausschaltung) of the genetically inferior from future generations by sterilization and other means.

Weissman concludes that Pernkopf and the editors of the *Viennese Medical Weekly* were eminent Viennese academicians who were 'mistaken men, certain and arrogant, planned a broad racial experiment, told their students – and the world – what they planned to do, and went about doing it.' Weissman indicates that Pernkopf's address calling for the exclusion of the genetically inferior from future generations by sterilization and other means 'was the beginning of the long road to Auschwitz.' The political agenda of National Socialism was supported, rationalized and promoted by prestigious academic medical institutions, such as the University of Vienna, through the pseudo-science of racial hygiene.

No matter how many times I recount the story of who Pernkopf was as a person, I am chilled to my core. This was the man who had delivered essential anatomy lessons to me through his work.

David Williams, a medical illustrator, authored 'The History of Eduard Pernkopf's *Topographische Anatomie des Menschen*,' in 1988.[6] This article describes Pernkopf's background, rise to Dean of the Medical Faculty (1938), followed by *Rector Magnificus* (President) of the University of Vienna (1943-45) and the creation of the anatomy atlas. Pernkopf supervised and depended on very talented artists such as Erich Lepier, Franz Batke, Karl Endtresser, and Ludwig Schrott to create paintings of anatomical dissections at the Anatomy Institute. With the use of vivid colors to differentiate the various tissues, these artists were able to represent real-life anatomical relationships for study by medical professionals and served as a road map for surgeons. These artists demonstrated their support of National Socialism by signing their anatomic paintings with Nazi icons (the swastika and the '*SS*' *rune)*. This led to suspicions that the source of the cadavers depicted in the atlas were of concentration camp victims. It was well documented that many of the cadavers that were sent to the Anatomy Institute were from the *Wiener Landesgericht*, the local district court, where those who were considered enemies of the Nazi state were executed, including communists and Austrian patriots. Following the Second World War, Pernkopf spent three years in an Allied prison. When he returned to the University of Vienna in 1948, he continued work on the atlas. The artists returned following their 'denazification' processing, to continue their work. Werner Platzer, an anatomist at the University of Vienna, joined the Pernkopf group, preparing dissections for the third volume of the atlas and writing legends for the illustrations. Pernkopf died of a stroke in April 1955. Platzer became the future editor of the Pernkopf's Atlas in the 1960s and he ultimately became the Head of the Anatomy Department at the University of Innsbruck. Williams indicated that many of the dissections from the Anatomy Institute at the University of Vienna had 'survived and may be seen in the University of Innsbruck's Anatomy Institute.' Williams concludes that 'Eduard Pernkopf's *Topographische Anatomie des Menschen*....was frequently misunderstood because of the history of the time in which it was produced.' Furthermore, Williams acknowledges 'Nazi science and art of merit, regardless of its contribution to mankind, can be difficult to fully appreciate in light of the incredible cruelties the regime inflicted on Jews and others it considered its enemies. For this reason, Pernkopf's *Topographische Anatomie des Menschen* will always remain controversial and will, unfortunately, never be acknowledged by some as the masterpiece it truly is.'[6]

Yes, a 'masterpiece' from a 'master race.'

As I began to dissect through the layers of this horrific story, I became obsessed and was committed to learn as much as possible on this important history of anatomy and medicine, about which I had known nothing. I was at the very beginning of my transformation.

The Professor, Again

I contacted the eminent anatomy professor who had recommended Pernkopf's Atlas when I was a student, twenty years previously. I recounted what I had discovered about the atlas and its origins. His responses were quite discouraging and shocking to me. Initially, the professor indicated that the anatomical dissections and depictions in the atlas were done in Vienna prior to the Second World War. However, I pressed on with what I had learned from my review of the literature and the discovery of the artist's signatures with Nazi icons in the 1943 German language editions I found in the Health Sciences Center Library at Columbia University. The professor responded to me as follows: 'this is your problem,' 'what if it were true?' and 'if these were Nazi victims, so what?' (personal communication, 1994).[8]

Floundering

The gradual uncovering of Pernkopf's Nazi background from the published literature at that time, resulted in many more questions that I felt needed to be answered. Where did the bodies depicted in the atlas come from? Were there specimens from the Anatomy Institute of the University of Vienna from the Pernkopf era still being stored and used? What did the University of Vienna administration and faculty know about the creation of the atlas? Was the publisher of the atlas aware of the Nazi origins of the creation of the book as well as the removal of the Nazi icons in the more recent English language editions? In the search for answers the question remained, once the facts are known what next? How should one proceed? What was the 'end game?' I had no clue as to what the next steps should be, and I needed to find expert individuals who could help guide the course of this investigation.

Initially, I wanted to determine if Pernkopf's Atlas was still being published and was for sale in 1994. I contacted the publisher, WB Saunders Company in Philadelphia, and their customer service department indicated that the latest 1981 edition was for sale as a volume set for $355. This established that the book was still being sold and distributed. At that cost, the market for this book in 1994 was clearly not for students, but more likely to be found in medical center libraries and departments of surgery and anatomy.

I contacted the UJA (United Jewish Appeal) Federation in March 1994 with my concerns that the illustrations in the atlas may have been depictions of concentration camp victims and others who were Nazi victims. Their representative had several suggestions, including contacting two organizations: the Anti-Defamation League (ADL), a leading global organization for exposing and fighting antisemitism, with offices in New York City, and Yad Vashem, the Holocaust Research Center in Jerusalem Israel. These were suggestions that ultimately would be pursued in the future, as I continued to search for experts in this largely unknown field of study with whom I could collaborate.

In July 1994 I contacted the ADL and was informed of the work of Drs. Michael Franzblau, and Michael Thaler, who conducted a course at Stanford University titled 'Ethical Values in Health Care in 1994: Lessons from the Nazi Period.' Topics included racial hygiene, Nazi health and social policy, experiences at Auschwitz, the scientific value of medical experiments conducted at Dachau, issues of informed consent, rationing of care, euthanasia, and clinical experiments conducted by Nazi doctors.[11] Interestingly, from my communications with the ADL, Thaler and Franzblau, the name of another individual who was quite knowledgeable in this field continued to be mentioned. Dr. William Seidelman, a professor from the University of Toronto, was acknowledged to be a proactive expert in this field and he was on my list of individuals whom I should contact.

As a member of Temple Isaiah of Great Neck in New York, I turned to my fellow congregants who might be able to advise me. Mr. Harold Klein had been a communications and media specialist prior to his retirement, and he suggested that I contact publications such as the *Jewish World* and *New York Magazine.* Harold also suggested trying to connect with Professor Elie Wiesel from Boston University regarding the subject matter. I learned that another congregant and friend, Mr. Kurt Kellman, lived in Vienna during his youth until his family was forced to leave in 1938. Kurt was very familiar with the Austrian Resistance Documentation Archives under the leadership of Professor Wolfgang Neugebauer. Importantly, Kurt volunteered to provide German to English translation of any documents that I received as I probed for answers. I recall having many meetings at his home, one block from our Temple, reviewing important material and I am forever grateful for his wisdom, advice and assistance. Interestingly, I later found out that Kurt became a Bar Mitzvah at the Seitenstettengasse Temple in Vienna. This synagogue was built in 1826 and survived the Nazi era, which is an amazing story by itself, which will be reviewed in a later chapter of this book describing my experiences in Vienna in 2005 as an invited speaker at the International Conference of Oral & Maxillofacial Surgery meeting.

I asked Rabbi Bonnie Steinberg from Temple Isaiah of Great Neck for advice and direction in March 1994. She recommended that I read *Nazi Doctors: Medical Killing and the Psychology of Genocide* authored by Dr. Robert Lifton, Professor of Psychiatry and Psychology at the City University of New York.[10] Lifton studied and interviewed doctors who had been Nazis, with the goal of answering the question as to how healers could become killers. Hitler's vision centered around a biomedical explanation of the history of the Nordic race, which had previously been healthy and dominant, only to become 'infected' by the influence of the Jewish race and other genetically inferior peoples. The elimination of the 'infection' of the Nordic race to health was the rationalization for genocide. Doctors, as healers, were now charged to focus on racial hygiene, with elimination of the 'genetically' unfit, consistent with Pernkopf's address to his faculty in 1938. But how did physicians who had taken the Hippocratic Oath to heal the sick, with relative ease turn to the normalization of evil with socialized killing and mass murder?

Lifton describes a psychological pattern, he termed 'doubling: the division of the self into two functioning wholes.' This theory proposes that the Nazi doctor at Auschwitz functioned in that environment by rationalizing mass murder as part of the overall cure of racial hygiene of the Nordic peoples. This created the 'normalization of evil' for the Nazi doctors implementing Hitler's vision. The Nazi doctor's other functioning whole involved vision of his prior self as a humane doctor, husband and father with avoidance of guilt from performing the 'dirty work' for the overall cause of racial hygiene.

I found it quite difficult to truly comprehend Lifton's explanation, but I did understand certain aspects of human nature that fit within the concept of doubling. I recalled the horrors of my initial experiences in the anatomy laboratory at Columbia University, dissecting bodies of people who had at one time been breathing living human beings. Having experienced this day after day, in order for me to survive, my mind had to put these experiences in a separate 'box,' which was required for me to function and realize that this education was for the greater goal of enabling me to become a good doctor. This 'box' also permitted me to go out to dinner with my fiancé and enjoy the pleasures of life, without guilt. Of course, this type of 'doubling' if that is what this is to be called, is on no level the same as the normalization of evil described by Lifton.

Dr. Robert Lifton – A Chance Meeting or was it Bashert?*

As I pondered these things throughout my workday as an oral and maxillofacial surgeon at Columbia Presbyterian Medical Center, I came across a flyer posted throughout the medical center. Dr. Lifton was to

* Bashert (Yiddish) destiny, a fortuitous event, inevitable, preordained.

be the guest speaker at the medical center's annual Remembrance Program to Commemorate the Holocaust, on 7 April 1994 (Figure 6). This was an incredibly lucky coincidence. Perhaps this was my opportunity to meet with Dr. Lifton who could provide some direction with respect to the questions I had related to the Pernkopf Atlas.

I contacted Dr. Lifton's office on 5 April 1994 and spoke to his secretary to find out his transportation plans for getting to the medical center for the Holocaust Program, and to my surprise, I found out that he was going to take the New York City Subway system from downtown Manhattan to uptown Columbia Presbyterian Medical Center. I explained that I was a doctor on the faculty at Columbia and it would be my honor to provide transportation to pick him up and bring him back by car. Dr. Lifton accepted and now I had to figure out what was the best way to introduce him to the dilemma I was facing with the atlas. I realized that prior to any presentation, the speaker's main focus is to

Figure 6. Flyer posted throughout the Columbia University Health Sciences Campus in 1994. The program commemorated the victims of the Holocaust and featured Dr. Robert Jay Lifton, the author of '*Nazi Doctors: Medical Killing and the Psychology of Genocide,*' a book that I had just read prior to the program. Fortuitously, this enabled me to personally meet with Dr. Lifton which ultimately led to my collaboration with Dr. William Seidelman.

provide a stimulating and engaging presentation, consistent with commemoration of the victims of the Holocaust. Therefore, I did not discuss anything related to the anatomy atlas after I first met Dr. Lifton when I picked him up and traveled in my car to the medical center. I found Dr. Lifton truly engaging and friendly and enjoyed our very casual conversations during the 30-minute ride to the medical center. The Holocaust Remembrance Program on 7 April 1994 was very meaningful for me as Dr. Lifton described his experiences with the interviewing of former Nazi Doctors, the concept of 'doubling,' and how readily the medical profession under the Nazi regime changed from healers of the sick to mass murderers. The audience of medical professionals, students and residents, filled the Alumni Auditorium and we were all truly mesmerized, engaged and emotionally moved by the presentation and commemorative program.

When the program was over, I asked Dr. Lifton to give me a few minutes of his time to provide some guidance with what I had learned about my treasured anatomy atlas. I showed him my 1963 copy of Pernkopf's Atlas, along with the 1943 German language edition of *Topographische Anatomie des Menschen* with anatomical paintings signed by the artists with swastikas and other Nazi icons. I noted that the swastikas were erased in my English language edition, and I also relayed to him everything I had learned about Eduard Pernkopf through my literature review. Although Dr. Lifton was not familiar with history of this anatomy atlas, he did indicate that he had some ideas and would get back to me. I was very appreciative of his time and felt that I had 'lucked out' with this chance personal encounter with Dr. Lifton.

Dr. Lifton demonstrated his concern about the creators of the Pernkopf Atlas, and the truth behind the origins of the individuals who were depicted in the anatomical paintings. He contacted Dr. Michael Kater, Distinguished Research Professor Department of History, York University, Ontario, Canada. Dr. Kater, author of *Doctors Under Hitler*,[11] who had extensively studied the medical profession during the Third Reich, and the denial and continued abuses of Nazi doctors in the post-Second World War period. Dr. Kater, in a letter of response to Dr Lifton,[12] expressed his concern about the origins of the Pernkopf Atlas, and referred me to Dr. William E. Seidelman, an individual with considerable knowledge and research on anatomical specimens and the medical profession during the Nazi era. This introduction to Dr. William Seidelman led to a bond which would have a profound influence on the course of this inquiry into Pernkopf's work, which, after thirty years continues to evolve and have an impact today.

Before I had been introduced to Dr. William Seidelman, I felt obligated to put my thoughts on paper, so I began to write. What follows is an essay, perhaps article, which I authored between June and September 1994. Although by most standards, this essay may not be worthy of publication, it does reflect what was in my mind shortly after my discovery of the Nazi origins of my most used resource for two decades, greatly enhancing my development as an academic oral and maxillofacial surgeon. In addition, this 'essay' permitted me to communicate my concerns and the issues raised, with others who were experts in the field, such as Professors William Seidelman, Robert Lifton, Michael Kater, Michael Franzblau, Michael Thaler, and Gerhard Aumüller. This essay provided enough information to stimulate the interest of other organizations, such as the Anti-Defamation League, United Jewish Appeal, and the Simon Wiesenthal Center, which could potentially exert pressure for a thorough investigation to uncover the true origins of Pernkopf's Atlas. Excerpts from my original written essay revealing my reflections on the atlas before and after my discovery are noted below.

> *I knew that the residency program was going to be long, difficult and grueling. There would be many nights on call in the emergency room, many operations to be learned and performed and much anatomy to be reviewed again and again. But, with my pal Pernkopf at my side, how could I miss? I didn't. Thanks to Pernkopf I could stay up all night until I knew the stuff cold. Thanks to Pernkopf, I could perform the operation over and over again in my mind and on paper the night before the real thing, knowing every nerve and blood vessel I would encounter the next day.*
>
> *I advanced from Assistant Professor to Associate Professor, I taught students and residents. I would grill them on anatomy. What is the location of the temporal branch of the facial nerve when performing a temporomandibular joint arthroplasty? Pernkopf and I knew the answer but was the resident fully prepared like we were?*

Following the discovery and corroboration that Pernkopf and his artists were ardent Nazis, along with my dependence on the knowledge that I obtained from this atlas, my shock and horror were reflected in the following passages:

I stared at the page that I had been looking at. I studied the picture which I had looked at thousands of times, but this time in a different way. I saw a picture of a young man who looked emaciated. His eyes were half open but he refused to look at me. The skin of half of his face had been dissected off. The hair on his scalp was approximately one half inch long. His nose was slightly hooked. There was no look of terror on his face. Instead, he looked calm, almost happy to be dead. I looked again. He looked like Grandpa Max.

Notes

1. R.S. Snell, 'Pernkopf Anatomy: Atlas of Topographic and Applied Human Anatomy, vol. 2 Thorax, Abdomen and Extremities, 3rd ed. Platzer W (ed), Monsen H (Transl).' *The New England Journal of Medicine,* 323, 3 (1990), p. 205.
2. H.M. Hast, 'Pernkopf Anatomy: Atlas of Topographic and Applied Human Anatomy, vol1, Head and Neck, 3rd ed, Platzer W (ed), *Journal of the American Medical Association,* 263, 15 (1990), p. 2115.
3. G. Weissman, 'Springtime for Pernkopf', in *They All Laughed at Christopher Columbus: Tales of Medicine and the Art of Discovery,* (New York: Times Books, 1987), pp. 48-69.
4. G. Weissman, 'Springtime for Pernkopf,' *Hospital Practice,* (15 October 1985), pp.142-168.
5. E. Pernkopf, '*Originalabhandlungen Nationalsozialismus und Wissenschaft*' *Wien Klinische Wochenscrift,* 51 (1938), p. 545.
6. D. Williams, 'The history of Eduard Pernkopf's *Topographische Anatomie des Menschen,*' *J of Biocommunication,* 15, (1988), pp. 2-12.
7. Historical Museum of the City of Vienna Special Exhibition, '*Wien 1938,*' (Vienna: Documentation Archives of the Austrian Resistance, 11 March – 30 June 1988). pp. 196-222.
8. Personal communication, 1994.
9. M. Thaler, M. Franzblau, Personal correspondence, 1994.
10. R. Lifton, *The Nazi Doctors: Medical Killing and the Psychology of Genocide,* New York: Basic Books, 1986.
11. M.H. Kater, *Doctors Under Hitler,* (Chapel Hill NC and London: The University of North Carolina Press,19890.
12. M.H. Kater, Letter to R. Lifton and H. Israel, 21 July 1994.

7

Strategic Partnership with Dr. William E. Seidelman – History, Inquiries, Progress, Roadblocks 1994-96

In 1994 Dr. William Seidelman was Professor Department of Family and Community Medicine, University of Toronto, The Wellesley Hospital and Medical Director, HIV Ambulatory Program. On 8 August 1994 I had my first telephone conversation with Dr. Seidelman which was quite lengthy, and perhaps, one of the most important and impactful discussions I have ever experienced.[1] This phone conversation was essentially my initial introduction and first lesson on the post-Second World War years of denial of the influence of Nazi doctors and persistent use of anatomical specimens from that era. Dr. Seidelman first informed me of Drs. Julius Hallervorden, and Hermann Voss and their complicity in committing atrocities during the Nazi era, with direct involvement of formerly prestigious academic institutions. This was a world that I knew nothing about. I belonged to the baby boomer generation, and as our parents assimilated to post-war America of the 1950s and 1960s, many people could not face and would not discuss what happened to the Jews and other minorities in Europe.

And thus began my three decades of friendship and collaboration with Bill Seidelman, which continues to this day. From that first conversation with him, I learned that he had performed extensive research on the medical profession in the Third Reich. His numerous publications exposed the dark history of academic medical institutions in Europe that had remained hidden and denied by many for five decades. He informed me of scandals in West Germany that erupted in 1989 when it was discovered that anatomical and pathological collections in academic institutions in the former West Germany contained remains of Nazi victims.[1-8] Furthermore, unlike many of the few individuals who had reported on individual cases of the collection, storage and use of anatomical specimens that were the product of Nazi atrocities, Dr. Seidelman exposed, reported, lectured, and published articles on the global nature of the bioethical issues associated with the use of mortal remains of victims as specimens. He focused on the uncovering and dissemination of the truth, as well as definitive action to memorialize and honor the victims with appropriate burial of specimens and to educate future generations of the path that led doctors to change from healers to murderers. Based on my notes from our initial extensive telephone conversations, the following is a summary of the education I received from Dr. Seidelman in 1994 regarding the use of human specimens from the Hitler period derived from victims of Nazi terror:

University of Tübingen, West Germany

Medical students at Tübingen became aware of the continued use of anatomical specimens of Nazi victims in their training in 1989. Professor Jurgen Peiffer, a neuropathologist and one time director of neuropathology at the University of Tübingen became an advocate for the students. Professor Peiffer had known Professor Julius Hallervorden after the war and initially was unaware of his background. Hallervorden was a neuropathologist who exploited the murder of handicapped and psychiatrically ill individuals from the Nazi era by maintaining collections of their anatomical specimens. Ultimately, the Senate of the University of Tübingen authorized an investigation conducted by faculty and student representatives. The final 1990 report of the investigation documented the presence of cadavers of hundreds of individuals that had been executed by the Gestapo in Stuttgart. The victims were mostly Russian and Polish prisoners who were put to death for various alleged crimes and whose bodies were delivered to the Anatomy Institute at the University of Tübingen. The anatomical specimens were buried in a special section of the Tübingen cemetery specifically to honor and memorialize subjects who had become victims of the Nazis and used at the Anatomical Institute.[1,2,6,7]

Dr. Seidelman provided my first introduction to the history of the complicity of medicine and academic institutions in the atrocities perpetuated by the Third Reich in their quest to create a master race. He informed me of the numerous examples of the medical profession and academic institutions using pathoanatomical specimens for their collections and research originating from victims of Nazi murder. Examples included the Max Planck Institute, Julius Hallervorden, Herman Voss, Herman Stieve and Henrich Gross. I learned for the first time about how a profession of healers became murderers who abused and tortured victims in the name of science.[1] I was now armed with this introductory education on the horrific atrocities perpetuated by Nazi doctors and with my newfound collaboration with the world's expert on such affairs, I felt confident that my partnership with Bill Seidelman would lead to a successful path toward the truth, exposure to the public and appropriate memorialization and commemoration of the victims.

Bill Seidelman became my first dedicated e-mail friend, with our frequent communications which began in 1994 and continue to this day. My files now include thirty years of notes of telephone conversations, faxes and e-mails between Bill and myself and upon retrospective review, one could see that a complex strategy was being developed, to ultimately achieve the goals of uncovering the truth, conveying these discoveries to the world, acknowledgement rather than denial of the continued influence and use of specimens of Nazi victims in academic and other institutions.

It was extremely important to acknowledge the victims and the unfathomable horrors they went through. This required appropriate dignified burial of mortal remains that were in the collections or being used for teaching purposes in academic institutions. Memorialization and commemoration of the victims by academic medical institutions was essential. Of great importance was to teach this dark history to students so that future health professionals became aware of their power and to prevent the slippery path that can lead doctors to perform unethical experiments and murder. What I did not know in 1994, was that we were about to embark on a lengthy arduous journey and encounter significant resistance to exposing the truth. We conducted many inquiries of the leaders of prestigious academic institutions, faculty, anatomists and publishers and their initial responses were cement roadblocks. I learned that denials and obfuscation of the truth about the complicity of the medical profession in mass exterminations were common and represented a major barrier to conducting investigations to reveal the truth.

Professor Gerhard Aumüller University of Marburg 1991

During that initial telephone conversation with Bill, he indicated that the academic medical community in Germany was not prepared to take on the challenge of revealing the truth from the past. I discovered that Dr. Michael Kater had not only introduced me to Bill Seidelman, but he also had the foresight to introduce the issues related to the Pernkopf Atlas to an academician from the University of Marburg, Germany. Professor of Anatomy Gerhard Aumüller was one individual from Germany who was willing to reveal the truth and investigate the origin of anatomic specimens at the University of Marburg from the Nazi era, as well as other institutions throughout Germany. I corresponded with Professor Aumüller in August 1994, and received a copy of his 1991 presentation titled 'Anatomy in the Nazi Era' at the University of Marburg, which was included in a publication from the Medical Student Council of Philipps University of Marburg, 'The Responsibility of Medicine Under National Socialism.'[8] This landmark presentation by Dr. Aumüller provided an introspective review of the Gestapo victims that had been brought to the anatomy department at the University of Marburg and had been used for teaching, and included a scathing review of similar instances at other academic institutions, in which Nazi victims were used in anatomy departments throughout the Third Reich. Furthermore, Dr. Aumüller reported on the resistance of the German scientific community and academic institutions to confront their past history and complicity in committing murder, torture and horrific medical experiments on the "unfit and defective" as an essential part of the Nazi era's racial hygiene agenda. This resistance to uncovering the truth was frequently encountered by Dr. Seidelman and myself in our preliminary queries to reveal the origins of the Pernkopf Atlas and had to be considered as we developed strategies to achieve the goal of a thorough independent investigation.

Professor Aumüller indicated in 1991, that there was a significant hidden history of the medical profession, including anatomists, and academic institutions during the Third Reich which had yet to be uncovered. He recounted the horrendous crimes related to Nazi victims of anatomists and medical physicians such as August Hirt, Johann Paul Kremer, Hermann Voss, Sigmund Rascher and Herman Stieve. Examples of such crimes included experiments infecting camp prisoners with typhus, studying the results of human starvation, exposure of concentration camp prisoners to poison gases such as phosgene and hypothermia, and developing collections of Jewish skulls.

Dr. Aumüller was a student of Herman Voss and knew him as a popular Professor Emeritus of Anatomy at Greifswald University and contributed to a commemorative publication dedicated to him on the occasion of his 90th birthday in 1984. However, this was prior to Aumüller's knowledge of Voss's background as a devout supporter of National Socialism whose diary demonstrated a hatred of Poles and Jews. Voss, as an anatomist at the University of Posen, used executed Polish resistance fighters and Jewish persons for teaching and profit, developing a brisk trade in the sale of skeletons and skulls. Voss had an acclaimed academic career following the end of the Nazi regime similar to Dr. Herman Stieve.[8]

Dr Herman Stieve

Herman Stieve, an anatomist at the University of Berlin, published research on the effects of stress on the female reproductive system, with the stress being the victim's imprisonment or impending execution. This extended Nazi research into the realm of 'the future dead' as described by Hildebrandt.[9] Dr. Aumüller provided a quote from Stieve's 1952 publication:

> *Some of these people were completely healthy; I was able to establish facts in them that were previously completely unknown. All of these examinations expanded our knowledge of human reproductive activity, they can benefit many sufferers and thus all of humanity. In this way, the deaths of all these victims of a confused time have certain meaning even in retrospect.* [8]

After the war, Stieve's academic career continued, as Head of the Department of Anatomy at Humboldt University in East Berlin. The Charite Hospital in Berlin erected a bust of Stieve and named a lecture hall after him to memorialize the 'master anatomist' who performed research on the reproductive organs of women who were executed by the Nazis.[10]

Professor Edzard Ernst, University of Vienna Medical Faculty Member Reveals Vienna's Nazi History

Edzard Ernst MD, PhD became Chair of the Department of Physical Medicine and Rehabilitation at the University of Vienna in 1990. Dr. Ernst gradually became aware of the history of the Medical School during the Nazi era. Similar to Dr Aumüller, his ethical values moved him to investigate further and expose the results of racial hygiene pseudoscience policies in his article titled 'A Leading Medical School Seriously Damaged: Vienna 1938.'[11] Ernst indicates that the formerly prestigious medical school, which included a faculty that had four Nobel prize winners, lost all prominence following the 1938 annexation of Austria by Germany. Within a few days, Eduard Pernkopf was installed as Dean of the Medical School and the purge of racially unfit faculty members was severe, with the dismissal of 153 of the faculty's 197 members. Most of these faculty were of Jewish origin, who, if fortunate were able to emigrate, but many died in concentration camps or committed suicide. The remaining faculty were required to sign an oath of loyalty to Hitler. In May 1938 Pernkopf submitted to the authorities the list of faculty members who refused to sign the oath of loyalty to Hitler, and these individuals were transferred into retirement. Within weeks of the Anschluss, new legislation for the 'restoration of professional civil servants' prevented Jews and those married to Jews to work as civil servants in Austria. The Medical Faculty was cleansed of 'undesirables' and replaced with lower ranked faculty who were much less qualified than their predecessors but were loyal to National Socialism and the concept of racial hygiene. The medical school now focused on forced sterilization, euthanasia and the use of executed victims of the Nazis for teaching and research in the Anatomy Institute. The medical profession in Vienna followed a similar downhill course, with the number of practicing physicians prior to 1938 being 5000; and by 1942 the number of physicians decreasing to 730. Similarly, the curriculum of the medical school listed 491 courses at the University of Vienna before 1938, which been reduced to 259 courses after the purge of faculty who were 'undesirables.' Following the end of the Second World War, those faculty members who had been dismissed and survived, in general, did not return. They no longer wished to live in Vienna. Many of the faculty who had participated in Nazi crimes, eventually returned to their previous positions in the medical school. Ernst concludes that the true story of the demise of the previously prestigious medical school must be exposed, to honor the victims, and to prevent academic medicine from allowing political ideology from influencing medical faculty and physicians as healers.[11]

Ernst's article in the *Annals of Internal Medicine* was followed by an editorial from doctors at Columbia University.[12] The authors, Lerner and Rothman, recount the history of denial by the German medical profession after the Nuremberg trials. Many German doctors proposed that the atrocities committed by the medical profession were committed by a handful of evil Nazi physicians in the concentration camps. Thus, the narrative from the German medical establishment was that extermination, torture and sadistic experiments performed on victims of the Nazis were largely perpetuated by a limited number of fanatical Nazi doctors. This narrative went largely unchallenged for several decades following the Nuremberg trials as there was a conspiracy of silence in Germany and Austria in the medical profession and academic institutions. The authors conclude that Ernst's reporting of the atrocities committed by the medical profession and medical faculty from Vienna, along with the use of anatomical specimens from victims of Nazi executions, with specimens that 'still remain' and are 'in use' must be exposed as a matter of professional medical ethics.[12]

In response to Ernst's revealing article, there was very strong criticism from the Medical Faculty at the University of Vienna. In July 1995, the Dean of the Medical Faculty of the University of Vienna authored a letter in response to Ernst's article which was submitted to the *Annals of Internal Medicine.*[13] There is acknowledgment of the Medical School's notorious Nazi past resulting from official Austrian policy between March 1938 and April 1945. However, the Dean indicates that Ernst ignores the new generation in Austria, with universities and science in a free democratic country that was 'liberated' by allied forces. This response denies the complicity of Austria which for the most part welcomed Nazi ideology. For many years after the war the narrative of Austrian authorities was that their country was a victim of the Third Reich, rather than an active participant in National Socialism. The author also criticizes Ernst for deliberately indicating that he is not Jewish, and that he ignores the new post war generation in Austria, while adhering to his own prejudicial beliefs. Again, this response to Ernst's article reflects the denial of Austria's active role in promoting Nazi ideology, particularly in academic medicine. Another response to Ernst's article was authored in November 1995 by a Professor of Anatomy[14] who had been dismissed by the Anatomy Institute in Vienna for refusing to follow Nazi ideology and was imprisoned from 1940 –42. However, this professor returned to the University of Vienna following the war and in 1995 was a member of the faculty of the Anatomy Institute. He criticizes Ernst for reporting on the research of others and not doing primary research on his own. The author indicates Ernst's negligence resulted in 'a dangerous defamation of the present staff of Vienna's Anatomical Institute,' and requests that the editors of the *Annals of Internal Medicine* publish a clarification. These written responses to Ernst's article attack Ernst for exposing the truth about Pernkopf's purge of 'undesirable' faculty and represent the typical resistance that was encountered when someone spoke out. It is not surprising that Ernst left his position as Chair of the Department of Physical Medicine and Rehabilitation at the University of Vienna in 1993, to assume the Chair at the University of Exeter in the United Kingdom.[8]

Developing Strategy to Discover the Truth

The more I learned about this unknown history, the angrier I became. Why didn't I know about this important history? Initially, I had become obsessed with reaching my potential to become the most ideal oral and maxillofacial surgeon possible. However, with this obsession, there was no consideration of the origin of the knowledge I had learned. If I was to become an ethical healthcare provider, was it acceptable to use scientific information created through the suffering of victims? This realization had shaken the foundation of my education and who I was as a doctor and person. Therefore, I became increasingly focused on finding the truth, learning from this past history, and sharing the importance of this knowledge with others in the health professions. I had no experience or understanding how to accomplish this, but I was confident that with Bill Seidelman as my passionate colleague and friend, there was a chance that these goals would be achieved.

Dr. William Seidelman is internationally known for his research on uncovering the anatomical evidence of crimes of Nazi medicine which continued to be used by medical institutions. Additionally, he was acutely aware of the political issues associated with the call for investigations, and the denial by many in the medical profession, academic institutions and publishers. Clearly, Dr. Aumüller, a German anatomist had attempted to enlighten anatomists, physicians and academicians from those institutions whose policies and actions were controlled by the political power of the Third Reich between 1938 and 1945. The question for Bill and myself was how to come up with a successful plan, with us as academicians, from Canada and the US, and additionally both of us being of the Jewish faith. We didn't realize that our religious background would become an obstacle to our goal of uncovering the truth, since many erroneously thought that we were only concerned with Jewish Holocaust victims. Bill clearly had a plan and readily convinced me that as individuals, we were unlikely to accomplish anything close to what our goals were:

- to uncover the truth about the origin of Pernkopf's work with a thorough independent investigation,
- to appropriately memorialize and commemorate victims of Nazi murder,
- to provide appropriate and dignified handling of human remains of Nazi victims still in use or storage according to the religious beliefs, if determined, of those victims, and
- acknowledgment in the Pernkopf Atlas of the origin of the anatomic specimens depicted in the book, so that the individual user could make one's own ethical decision regarding whether to use the atlas.

This was truly going to be an uphill battle for these two Jewish 'baby boomers!' The strategy which we developed to uncover the truth about the anatomical specimens at the Anatomy Institute under the directorship of Pernkopf included:

- Publish articles in peer reviewed journals.
- Give presentations at major professional meetings.
- Provide information to the media to promote articles informing the public.

- Continue to investigate, each of us individually with interviews, communication and follow up on leads provided by people who either had firsthand accounts of the events in Vienna between 1938 and 1945, or those who had performed significant research on this subject.
- Most importantly, to provide the evidence and additional information to one or two major international organizations to exert pressure on the Universities of Vienna and Innsbruck, the publisher of the atlas and Austrian government authorities:
  - to investigate and report findings,
  - to support appropriate commemoration of Nazi victims,
  - to ensure proper dignified handling and burial of anatomical specimens that were in use for teaching or in storage and
  - to acknowledge the Nazi origin of the atlas in each volume of the book for sale or present in medical center libraries.

As I have reviewed my extensive volume of notes and e-mail correspondence with Dr. Seidelman today, I can more clearly see the brilliant strategy that evolved from his experience dealing with the hidden past and continued horrific legacy of academic anatomy and medicine during the Nazi era. An important component of this strategy was to report on the facts and raise questions and concerns, as we knew them in 1994 which were:

- Pernkopf and his artists were ardent Nazis.
- Nazi icons were used in their signatures in the 1937 and 1943 editions.
- Subsequent editions contain the same illustrations with most of Nazi icons eliminated.
- Anatomical specimens from Nazi victims at the *Wiener Landesgericht* were sent to Pernkopf's Anatomy Institute.
- Anatomical specimens from Pernkopf's collections were reported to exist at the University of Innsbruck.
- The exact names and cause of death of subjects in illustrations were unknown.

Dr. Seidelman had years of experience and research in the arena of uncovering the truth about academic medicine during the Nazi era. He indicated that to make any significant progress in this area, we, as individual academicians from Canada and the US, would not likely be successful in pressuring academic institutions in Austria to conduct investigations to uncover and report the truth. Therefore, Dr. Seidelman informed me that it would be essential for a major international organization to exert pressure on the Austrian institutions, publisher and government to conduct an appropriate investigation and publish a report on the findings. Dr. Seidelman arranged to meet with officials at the Israel Holocaust Martyrs' and Heroes Remembrance Authority, Yad Vashem in Jerusalem and I was going to meet with representatives from the Anti-defamation League (ADL) in New York.

Meetings with the Anti-defamation League

I was nervous. Surgeons are not supposed to get nervous for fear that their hands might begin to shake. My hands were perfectly fine, but the pulse rate had increased considerably, and my knees were knocking against each other that chilly day on 2 December 1994. The fluorescent lights in the room where I was sitting at the ADL headquarters in New York, located at United Nations Plaza seemed to make the room even colder as I was about to meet the Assistant National Director and plead my case for them to request investigations at Austrian institutions. The ADL is a global leader in combating antisemitism, countering extremism and battling bigotry wherever it occurs. Just a few of the past investigations the ADL had supported were exposing extremism and violence by the Ku Klux Klan, challenging Henry Ford's antisemitic propaganda on the 'International Jew,' and the denouncement of Senator Joseph McCarthy who led the anti-Communist fervor in the 1950's with false character assassinations. The room was getting much hotter as the ADL officials gathered around me.

I had been able to secure a meeting with officials at the ADL after several phone calls and correspondence which included my essay 'Nazi Anatomy Lessons Today.' I sat in the middle of the room with my files, anatomical pictures and other documentary evidence. Gathered around me were Kenneth Jacobson, Assistant National Director, and other high level officials of the ADL. I steadily presented my case to the group while my blood pressure must have risen considerably. Following the presentation of the evidence, the meeting was focused on several key questions:

- How should the Nazi origins of Pernkopf and his artists be exposed?
- How to determine if the cadaveric illustrations in the atlas were Nazi victims, regardless of whether they were of Jewish or non-Jewish origin?
- How to exert pressure for an investigation in Austria?

The ADL officials were 'blown away' by the discovery of the Nazi origins of an internationally acclaimed anatomy atlas that continued to be published and used in medical centers throughout the world. I also informed them that my colleague, Dr. William Seidelman from the University of Toronto was a leading expert on the issues raised, and he was going to attempt to enlist Yad Vashem to provide the official requests for an investigation. The ADL officials agreed to help with these efforts. Their assistance in obtaining Pernkopf's dossier, from the Berlin Document Center, was an important additional step in uncovering the truth. This dossier was a massive document written in German. The translation provided details on Pernkopf's quest to obtain more cadavers to meet the needs of the Anatomy Institute of the University of Vienna. Furthermore, the information in the dossier would assist us in determining if the initial responses of the Austrian institutions were consistent with the truth.

The ADL was convinced that an investigation into the origins of the Pernkopf Atlas had significant merit, with the evidence that was available at the time. On 7 March 1995, the Assistant National Director of the ADL sent letters to the Presidents of the Universities of Vienna and Innsbruck, requesting an investigation to determine whether Nazi victims were depicted in the book.[15]

A Critical Meeting- Dr. William Seidelman and Officials from Yad Vashem

By the end of 1994 Dr. Seidelman and I had been collaborating for five months, and we had collected much information. We were still two individuals from academic institutions in North America, in pursuit of uncovering Nazi crimes within prestigious Austrian Academic Medical Institutions. Faculty at these Austrian institutions had previously demonstrated resistance to investigations into the past, as Austria publicly viewed itself as victims, not perpetrators of National Socialism between 1938 and 1945. Furthermore, evidence of these crimes included specimens that still existed and were being used, thus, there was continued abuse of and profit from the victims, over fifty years later. Denial was no longer an acceptable outcome, but as we had learned from previous attempts at uncovering the truth about the essential role of medicine in promoting the Nazi political agenda, individual efforts were not powerful enough to effect change, particularly in Austria. Dr. Seidelman's correspondence and meetings with Yad Vashem representatives were critical in making this internationally recognized organization the official party requesting the Austrian Institutions to conduct an investigation that would be in the public record. Ultimately this would lead to a change in the perception of Austria as a victim, to that of an active and willing participant in the crimes of the Nazi era.

Upon his return from Jerusalem, Israel, Dr. Seidelman reported to me the results of his meeting with Yad Vashem officials on December 29, 1994.[16] The representatives from Yad Vashem in attendance were Brigadier General Avner Shalev, Chairman of the Directorate, Ambassador Reuven Dafni, Vice Chairman, and Yaacov Lozowick, Chief Archivist. Dr. Seidelman informed them of his experience in dealing with human pathoanatomical specimens from Nazi victims in the collections of several German universities (e.g. University of Tübingen) and research institutes (e.g. Max Planck Institute). Dr Seidelman provided the evidence we had collected regarding the continued use of pathoanatomical specimens of Nazi victims at the Anatomy Institutes of the Universities of Vienna and Innsbruck, and the likelihood of anatomical depictions of these victims in Pernkopf's Anatomy Atlas, present in medical school libraries throughout the world, with no acknowledgement to the unsuspecting user of the book. Furthermore, Dr. Seidelman's letter to me indicated their response:[16]

> *The Yad Vashem officials agreed to assume a responsibility and to undertake the initiatives required to bring this matter to a proper resolution and it was agreed that the initial approach should be private with a public approach to be reserved if the private efforts prove unsuccessful.*

This was fabulous news, bringing hope that with Yad Vashem as the official responsible organization requesting an investigation, that the truth would eventually be uncovered with appropriate actions to follow. It was agreed that Yad Vashem would present the evidence and make requests for an investigation to the Institutes of Anatomy at the Universities of Vienna and Innsbruck, Urban and Schwarzenberg, Inc., the publisher of the Pernkopf Atlas, and the Chancellor of Austria. Furthermore, Yad Vashem requested that Dr. Seidelman and I assist in the formulation of the letters to be sent. Over the following three months, the correspondence between Dr. Seidelman and I was extensive. Drafts of letters along with evidence were formulated and eventually we agreed on a draft that would be sent to Yad Vashem for their review. Ultimately this draft needed to be hand delivered to Ambassador Dafni, who would review, finalize, and send to the Austrian institutions and the publisher. Why was it important to hand deliver these letters? Dr. Seidelman and I agreed that if the content of these letters were lost and fell into the wrong hands, the entire strategy and effort could potentially be disrupted or thwarted.

The Clandestine Drop Off Operation (Spy craft? Bashert?)

A relatively humorous side note of these efforts leading to investigations of the atlas took place in February 1995, when Bill's daughter, Rhona, and I had the opportunity to play the game using spy craft. The collapse of communist Soviet Union several years earlier, along with the well documented operations of clandestine operations during the very 'hot' cold war that played out in the 1980's was very fresh in one's memory. That was the era of Aldrich Ames, the CIA (Central Intelligence Agency of the U.S.) agent who became a double spy and betrayed the names of CIA agents operating in the Soviet Union. One of the many agents that Ames exposed was the famous, Oleg Gordievsky, a KGB (Soviet Union intelligence organization) operative who became double agent, working for the British Secret Intelligence Service (MI6) from 1974-85. Fortunately, Gordievsky was able to escape from the Soviet Union and a likely execution and flee to Great Britain, unlike many of the other agents who were exposed by the traitorous Aldrich Ames.[17] Having read about the techniques of spy craft and clandestine exchanges of important information (drop offs), we figured that we could learn from those techniques which had been common during the cold war era.

Bill Seidelman was extremely concerned that the very sensitive material and evidence included in the letter that we drafted for use by Yad Vashem, may not reach Ambassador Dafni. If the material contained in this letter were to fall into the wrong hands, the entire strategy in search of the true origins of the Pernkopf Atlas, could potentially fail. Therefore, Bill and I devised a plan for this draft letter containing evidence of Pernkopf's use of Nazi victims to be delivered directly into the hands of Ambassador Dafni, in Jerusalem. It was quite fortunate that at that time, Bill's daughter, Rhona, who had been studying at Hebrew University in Jerusalem, was on a student break, staying with a friend at Barnard College in Manhattan, New York, located on the West side of Broadway, across the street from the main campus of Columbia University. At that time, I was on the full-time faculty of Columbia University School of Dental & Oral Surgery, just a few minutes away by car. I had in my possession the draft letters and all of the evidence that was required for Ambassador Dafni. Bill arranged for what spy craft may consider a 'drop off,' a rapid and secret exchange of information that would not be noticed by an observer. I received information on the exchange from Bill, indicating that Rhona, was a 5 foot 4 inches tall 19-year-old woman, with dark hair, who would meet me just outside of the gate of Barnard College, by Sulzberger Hall on Broadway. The exchange of the parcel with Rhona was arranged to take place on 13 February 1995 at 6:15 pm. I have a vivid memory of that cloudy day, with the parcel containing these important letters on the passenger seat of my car, moving the car to the curb in front of Sulzberger Hall on Broadway, and noticing a young, dark-haired woman waiting to meet me. No, we didn't have any code phrases, but our eyes met in acknowledgement, I rolled down the passenger window and in a very quick exchange, she identified herself as Rhona, I confirmed that I was her dad's colleague, and in a moment, the parcel was in her hands. The drop off operation was successful and upon her return to Israel, Rhona hand delivered this very special parcel directly to Ambassador Dafni, Vice Chairman of Yad Vashem.

Today Dr. Rhona Seidelman is currently Director of the Schusterman Center for Judaic and Israel Studies at the University of Oklahoma and is world-renowned as a leading scholar on the history of immigration, medicine, and public health in Israel. Her many accomplishments are not surprising as 'the apple does not fall far from the tree.'

Every time I think of this initial clandestine meeting with Rhona, the music from the 1960's television show 'Mission: Impossible' plays inside my head. This spy themed music can readily be found on an internet search of 'The Theme from Mission: Impossible.'

Yad Vashem's Initial Requests for Investigation, Report and Appropriate Commemoration and Acknowledgement, 23 March 1995

The initial phase of 'Mission: Impossible' was accomplished with the delivery of the letters Bill and I had drafted directly into the hands of Ambassador Dafni, Vice Chairman of Yad Vashem. Ambassador Dafni approved and signed the official letters from Yad Vashem that were sent to the Presidents of the Universities of Vienna and Innsbruck, and the publisher Urban and Schwarzenberg Inc.'s President. Copies of these letters[18] were also sent to the Chancellor of the Federal Republic of Austria, Israel's Ambassador to Austria, as well as Dr. Seidelman and me (Appendix I). The most important excerpt from each of these letters indicates the requirements for the requested investigations:

> *Our expectations for such an investigation are:*
>
> 1. *There be proper documentation copies of which should be deposited in the archives of Yad Vashem.*
> 2. *Upon the completion of the investigation there should be an official published report in the public domain.*
> 3. *If it is established that some of the subjects had, in fact, (or could possibly have) been victims of the Nazis, there should be a public acknowledgement and commemoration to the victims by the institutions and organizations concerned.*
> 4. *Specimens shown to have been derived from Jews, which are larger than glass slides, must receive a proper burial in a Jewish cemetery.*
>
> *The University of Vienna and the University of Innsbruck may wish to consider a joint investigation.*

Given the public and political sensitivities involved we are informing the Chancellor of Austria of this matter and copying this letter to him.

We trust that the collections and the documentations will not be in any way disturbed until such time as the examination can be properly completed.

We could request also that all correspondence on this matter be copied to all those whose names and addresses are attached.

Yours sincerely,
Ambassador Reuven Dafni
Vice Chairman

The letter addressed to Professor Moser, President of the University of Innsbruck is exactly the same as the letter that was sent to President of the University of Vienna, Alfred Ebenbauer. The inclusion of the University of Innsbruck was extremely important because the Williams publication in 1988 on the history of the atlas indicated that many of the dissections from the Anatomy Institute in Vienna survived and 'may be seen in the University of Innsbruck's Anatomy Institute.'[19] The letter was also sent to the publisher's President, Michael Urban of Urban and Schwarzenberg, with the following additional requests:

1. *The original paintings from the Pernkopf Atlas, which was in the publisher's collections, were important in the history of anatomical illustration and should be preserved. These paintings should not be altered, destroyed or suppressed.*
2. *The original Nazi icons should be included in future publications of the atlas with an acknowledgement in a special foreword of each book of the ardent National Socialist agenda of those who created this work.*
3. *If it is determined that the illustrations originate from victims of the Nazis, then all future volumes, in every language edition should include an acknowledgement with memorialization of these subjects.*
4. *The publisher is urged to support and participate in the investigation and support a public commemoration.*
5. *Permission is requested of the publisher to make color reproductions of the relevant illustrations to facilitate the investigations.*

Once the letters from Yad Vashem, as the official organization were sent, Bill Seidelman and I were elated, and we felt that this was an important turning point in the 'ballgame.' I was compelled to send the following e-mail message to my esteemed colleague, demonstrating my ecstatic reaction to the direct involvement of Yad Vashem:

> *Hi Bill,*
> *As you know I am a real baseball fan. I grew up in the Bronx on Gerard Avenue, one block from Yankee Stadium. You could see the games from the roof of our house. The reason why I bring this up is that the only response I could think of to your e-mail was related to baseball, so here it goes:*
>
> ***Where does it mention Baseball in the Bible???????***
> *(In the BIG INNING)*
> *Your e-mail has now made it impossible for me to take off my baseball cap.*
>
> ***Regarding the Atlas saga, let's put it this way……***
> *It was one of the most important games to be played. I was 0 for 3, striking out with Columbia University, the Anti-Defamation League, Williams, Weissman and many others. We were losing 5-3 in the bottom of the ninth. You were on the team, but I didn't know you. You were responsible for the other 3 runs in the 5th inning having hit a home run with 2 men on base (Lifton & Kater). The blast went so far it reached Tübingen. I was up in the bottom of the 9th facing the University of Vienna's best pitcher, Werner Platzer. With 2 outs, 2 strikes, I hit a screaming double You followed with another home run to make it 5-5. We are now in extra innings, and the game has gone on for quite a while, but now we have the new members of the team taking over and making great plays every inning.*
>
> *Yes, this is quite a strange letter.*
> *But, thank you so much for your passion and friendship.*
>
> *Howie*

Notes

1. W. Seidelman, Personal communication with H. Israel, 8 August 1994.
2. S. Dickman, 'Scandal over Nazi Victims' Corpses Rocks Universities,' *Nature* 337, (1989), p. 195.
3. W. Seidelman, 'In Memoriam: Medicine's Confrontation with Evil,' *Hastings Center Report*. (November/December 1989), pp5-6.
4. W. Seidelman , 'Medspeak: for Murder: The Nazi Experience and Culture of Medicine,' in A. Caplan (ed), *When Medicine Went Mad: Bioethics and the Holocaust,* (Totowa, New Jersey: Humana Press 1992), pp. 271-9.
5. M. Kater, 'Unresolved Questions of German Medicine and Medical History in the Past and Present,' *Central European History*, 25, 4 (1993), pp. 407-423.
6. J. Peiffer, 'Neuropathology in the Third Reich: Memorial to those Victims of National-Socialist Atrocities in Germany who were used by medical science,' *Brain Pathol*, 1 (1991), pp. 125-31.
7. W. Seidelman, 'Dissecting the History of Anatomy in the Third Reich – 1989-2010: A Personal Account,' *Annals of Anatomy*, 194 (2012), p. 228-36.
8. G. Aumüller, 'Anatomy in the Nazi Era' in Medical Student Council of Philipps University of Marburg (ed.), *Responsibility of Medicine Under National Socialism*, edited by the Medical Student Council of Philipps University of Marburg (Marburg: Schuren Press 1991), pp 87-111.
9. S. Hildebrandt, *The Anatomy of Murder – Ethical Transgressions and Anatomical Science During the Third Reich*, (New York and Oxford: Berghahn Books, New York and Oxford, 2016).
10. W. Seidelman,'Nuremberg Lamentation: For the Forgotten Victims of Medical Science.' *BMJ* 313, 7070 (1996), pp.1463–67. https://doi.org/10.1136/bmj.313.7070.1463.
11. E. Ernst, 'A Leading Medical School Seriously Damaged: Vienna 1938,' *Ann Intern Med*, 122, 10 (1995), pp. 789- 92.
12. B.H. Lerner, D.J. Rothman, 'Medicine and the Holocaust: Learning More of the Lessons,' (Editorial), *Ann Intern Med*, 122, 10 (1995), pp. 793-4.
13. H. Gruber. Letter (unpublished) sent to the Editor *Ann Intern Med*, 12 July 1995.
14. H. Krause. Letter (unpublished) sent to the Editor *Ann Intern Med*, 9 November 1995.

15. B. Jacobson, Letters from the Anti-Defamation League to the Presidents of the Universities of Vienna and Innsbruck, cc H. Israel, 7 March 1995.
16. W. Seidelman, Letter to H. Israel upon return from meeting with Yad Vashem, 10 January 1995.
17. B. Macintyre, *The Spy and the Traitor: The Greatest Espionage Story of the Cold War*, (New York: Broadway Books, 2019).
18. R. Dafni, Letters from Yad Vashem to Presidents of Universities of Vienna, Innsbruk, Urban and Schwarzenberg, cc. H. Israel, 23 March 1995.
19. D. Williams, 'The history of Eduard Pernkopf's *Topographische Anatomie des Menschen*,' *J of Biocommunication*, 15, (1988), pp. 2-12.

8

Willful Amnesia

Responses from the Universities and Publisher Hiding the Past

Due to the extremely rapid flurry of letters, correspondence, replies and meetings, numerous significant landmark events in our quest for the truth took place simultaneously. Therefore, some of the documentation of events to follow may not be in exact chronological sequence but should provide the reader with an understanding of the gradual change in attitudes of the Austrians, from that of a victim, to acknowledgment of its past history as a major supporter of National Socialist ideology and active participant in Nazi crimes. In general, the initial responses were defensive and filled with obfuscation. However, as our team, Yad Vashem, Dr. Seidelman and I pushed forward with correspondence that included further corroborating evidence, and refutation of the claims of the Austrian respondents, a little progress was made toward the ultimate goal of an appropriate investigation to uncover the true origins of Pernkopf's cadavers from the Anatomy Institute at the University of Vienna. Some of the newer faculty members began to question the veracity of the responses from the faculty from the 'old guard' who worked at the Anatomy Institute during the Pernkopf era. Unfortunately, the University of Innsbruck continued to resist any inquiry, indicating that their anatomic collections had no specimens from Jewish concentration camp victims or from the Anatomy Institute at the University of Vienna during the Nazi regime.

University of Vienna Initial Responses 1995 – Disappointing

As a result of the requests from Yad Vashem, the Presidents of the Universities of Vienna and Innsbruck both asked members of their respective medical faculty and anatomy institutes to respond. The

University of Vienna's Rector (President) Professor Alfred Ebenbauer contacted faculty from the Anatomy Institute, Professors Wilhelm Firbas (Director of the Anatomy Institute), Alfred Gisel, Walter Krause (Gisel and Krause both worked at the Anatomy Institute under Pernkopf) and the university archivist, Professor Kurt Muhlberger for further detailed information regarding the questions raised by Ambassador Dafni from Yad Vashem, regarding the origin of the specimens obtained by Pernkopf during the Nazi era and used in the creation of the atlas. Firbas[1] denied that there were any specimens at the Anatomy Institute from the Pernkopf era. He indicated that the institute's museum of displayed specimens was damaged during an air raid in 1945 and that the only remaining specimens on display were from the 19th century. Firbas also indicated that all corpses of executed victims from the regional court during the Nazi era were buried in 1945. This information directly contradicted the background evidence that we had uncovered.

Alfred Gisel returned to the Anatomy Institute as a faculty member in 1949. He had questioned Erich Lepier, the artist who signed his name with a swastika to his anatomic paintings that appeared in Pernkopf's Atlas. Lepier indicated that the swastika 'was just a frivolity' and 'nobody objected to it.' Gisel indicated that when Werner Platzer became editor of the atlas in the 1980's the signatures were 'cleaned up.' Gisel's response also indicated that the artist, Endtresser who incorporated lightning bolts 'SS' to his signature may have represented a parody as a counterpart to Lepier's swastika; and that Batke's incorporation of the lightning bolts to his signature in 1944 should not be blamed. Gisel concludes that Pernkopf succeeded in contributing a great, significant and valuable anatomical book with abundant illustrations which were second to none.[2]

Walter Krause, an anatomist who refused to pledge loyalty to Hitler in 1938 and had been imprisoned during the war years for this, returned as a member of the faculty in the Anatomy Institute in 1946. Although he claimed to have no knowledge of the ongoings of the Anatomy Institute during the Nazi period, he recalled what had been told to him from his colleagues when he returned as a faculty member in 1946. In his response, Krause mistakenly assumes that the inquiry is only concerned with the corpses of Jewish victims from concentration camps. He indicated that his Jewish wife had been imprisoned in the

Theresienstadt and Auschwitz and he concludes that it was very unlikely that the corpses from the far away concentration camps would be requested and used by the Anatomy Institute. Executions from the regional court in Vienna were much more practical and he assumed with 99% likelihood that if there were Jewish corpses that were received by the Anatomy Institute, these would have been used for dissection studies and not for Pernkopf's book. Regarding the question of circumcision of a dissection depicted in the atlas, his response was that the Jewishness of a corpse could not be proven, as he worked on over one thousand corpses and never looked to see if anyone had been circumcised.....'what for?' Krause also confirmed that there had been a bombing of the Anatomy Institute with all of the specimens from the upper floors being totally destroyed and concludes that it is unlikely that there were any remaining specimens remaining for burial. Finally, Krause dismisses the presence of Nazi icons in the atlas indicating 'I cannot understand the importance of the fact that some illustrator's swastika in his signature has anything to do with all of the other questions' posed by the Yad Vashem letter.[3]

Muhlberger, the University of Vienna archivist indicated that prior to 1938, there were inadequate numbers of corpses for the Anatomy Institute, and in particular, the corpses of children. He also responded that the archives do not indicate any connection between concentration camp victims, as a source of material for the Anatomy Institute at the University of Vienna between 1933 and 1945. Muhlberger also indicated that the current (1995) presence of anatomical specimens in Vienna and Innsbruck cannot be found in the archives.[4]

Clearly, these initial responses from faculty at the University of Vienna did not reflect any support for a detailed investigation to answer the questions posed by Yad Vashem regarding the history of the Anatomy Institute during the Nazi era.

University of Innsbruck Responses 1995 – Refusal and Denial

The Rector of the University of Innsbruck, Dr Hans Moser, in a similar fashion to Ebenbauer, transmitted the inquiry from Yad Vashem and the ADL to his faculty. Moser requested a response from Professor Werner Platzer, Head of the Institute of Anatomy at the University of

Innsbruck who had worked under Pernkopf after the war. Platzer, who had become editor of Pernkopf's Atlas in 1980, responded with a very revealing letter, indicating 'The Institute of Anatomy in Innsbruck does not have any specimens that could have come from people executed between 1938 and 1945 or who were prisoners in a concentration camp.'[5] Platzer also indicated that he was aware of the swastikas in the signatures of one of the artists and 'I urgently insisted that these signatures be destroyed.' His response to the Yad Vashem letter concluded that the anatomical depictions of corpses with hair shaved, and circumcisions do not provide any evidence that these were concentration camp victims. Platzer also indicated that cadavers of circumcised men were exclusively from voluntary estates, and that the hair from all cadavers must be shaved for hygienic reasons. Platzer concluded that he had no knowledge of what happened in connection with Pernkopf prior to 1949, as he did not study under Pernkopf during the war. In addition, Platzer 'emphatically' denied that there are any cadavers or anatomical parts from human beings who died under inhumane conditions in the collections the Institute of Anatomy of the University of Innsbruck.[5]

Dr. Esther Fritsch, Vice Chairperson, Department of Radiotherapy and Radiation Oncology at the University of Innsbruck, and a leader in the Jewish community, communicated with the Vice Chairman of Yad Vashem in a letter dated 29 September 1995.[6] The letter indicated that she had known Professor Platzer for a very long time and held him in very high regard, also indicating that there was never any insinuation that he was sympathetic or involved with Nazi ideology. Fritsch did report that Platzer, according to his own statements 'took only two anatomic specimens with him to Innsbruck....prepared by himself... .and cannot possibly have been taken from Jewish persons.' She added that although Professor Platzer as a young anatomist, assisted Pernkopf in the final stages of completion of the atlas after the war, he was not involved with the preparation of any anatomical specimens during the Nazi regime. This letter written by a Jewish professor at Innsbruck mistakenly assumed that the concerns of Yad Vashem were solely the presence of corpses of murdered Jews in the Pernkopf Atlas,[6] ignoring the ethical transgressions of the use of executed victims, irrespective of their religious faith.

Countering Willful Amnesia - Providing More Evidence

Ambassador Johanan Bein, Vice Chair Yad Vashem

In 1995, Johanan Bein became the newly appointed Vice Chair of Yad Vashem, succeeding Reuven Dafni and Dr. Seidelman wanted to ensure that he was up to date on the Pernkopf atlas investigation and would be supportive of these efforts. Dr. Seidelman provided Ambassador Bein with a detailed summary of his meeting with Ambassador Dafni and other Yad Vashem officials on December 29, 1994, and the letters sent by Yad Vashem to the Austrian Universities and the publisher. Additionally, Dr. Seidelman sent Ambassador Bein a copy of his presentation titled 'Complicity, Complacency and Conspiracy: The Enduring Legacy of Medicine in the Third Reich' delivered at the US Holocaust Memorial Museum, in January 1996.[7] Ambassador Bein forwarded this presentation to the Presidents of the Universities of Vienna and Innsbruck (Ebenbauer and Moser respectively) in February 1996. Dr. Seidelman had a very important face to face meeting with Ambassador Bein, Vice Chair of Yad Vashem in Jerusalem, in April 1996, which further solidified and coordinated these efforts.

Professor Esther Fritsch, as a representative of the University of Innsbruck responded in a letter dated 26 February 1996, to Yad Vashem's Ambassador Bein. Fritsch indicated since there are no remains of anatomical specimens from the Nazi period at the University of Innsbruck, the investigation must be conducted at the Anatomy Institute of the University of Vienna.[8]

Unlike the University of Innsbruck's refusal to participate in an inquiry, the University of Vienna's Rector, Alfred Ebenbauer, was not satisfied with the initial responses of his faculty. Ambassador Bein continued to provide Rector Ebenbauer with more evidence and documentation supplied mostly by Dr. Seidelman. Ebenbauer probed further into his faculty and additionally obtained reports from Wolfgang Neugebauer, an Austrian historian who was the Director of the Documentation Archives of the Austrian Resistance, and faculty from the Institute of Contemporary History at the University of Vienna, Gustave Spann, Michael Hubenstorf and Peter Malina. Their overall conclusions in their response to Ebenbauer were that the corpses sent to the Anatomy Institute at the University of Vienna were from persons executed in the local district court, and that although improbable, the possibility of executed Jewish persons as a source of cadavers could not be excluded. Rector Ebenbauer sent this information to me, Ambassador Bein and Dr. Seidelman in March 1996 and it appeared that he was going to be supportive of an investigation.[9]

Pernkopf requested cadavers from executions in Poland

Also included in the attached documents from Rector Ebenbauer was a master's thesis from 1990 titled 'The Faculty of Medicine of the University of Vienna 1938 – 1945' by Martina Lehner.[10] The dissertation was written in German, however, I discovered that I had previously received a copy in October 1995. The English translation of this dissertation indicates that prior to 1940, there was a shortage of corpses for the Anatomy Institute at the University of Vienna. Pernkopf knew there were many executions taking place in Poland and in other regions outside of Vienna and he repeatedly made requests for more corpses. However, the Berlin authorities refused his request for permission to use bodies of executed persons in German occupied Poland. Apparently, the cost of transportation of bodies from a great distance was a factor in this denial. However, by 1940, the wave of executions in Vienna resulted in a massive increase of bodies for Pernkopf's Anatomy Institute. By 1942, there was such an oversupply of corpses that executions in Vienna had to be delayed, and delivery of cadavers cancelled. Other buildings at the University of Vienna Vienna, such as the Institute for Race Research had accumulated hundreds of heads in their storage rooms. Lehner's dissertation included information refuting the claim that the specimens from the Anatomy Institute were destroyed in an allied bombing raid at the end of the war. Lehner provided documentation that some subjects from the Anatomy Institute had been identified after the war.[10] Since this dissertation was written in 1990, it was clear to us that there was much more information that was probably hidden in the University of Vienna Archives.

On 17 December 1996, a letter from Rector Alfred Ebenbauer to Ambassador Johanan Bein, Vice Chairman of Yad Vashem indicated that an inquiry with a detailed research project plan at the University of Vienna was going to be formed.[11] Ebenbauer indicated that the Department of Contemporary History would be involved, with the inclusion of Wolfgang Neugebauer, Peter Malina and Gustav Spann.

Publisher Urban & Schwarzenberg

The publisher of Pernkopf's Atlas responded to Yad Vashem in August 1996 indicating that they would support an investigation at the University of Vienna and would be willing to make a financial contribution toward that effort.[12] In a letter to the editor of the *Journal of the American Medical Association*, in November 1996[13] the publisher provided further details of their response, indicating that although they would support an investigation at the University of Vienna, they would continue to publish Pernkof's Atlas because of its scientific merit and lack of concrete evidence that Pernkopf used 'cadavers originating from Nazi concentration camp victims.' In addition, the publisher's reply indicates 'while we renounce his abhorrent views, we separate Pernkopf, the man from the work because of the lack of evidence as to the true origin of the cadavers used in the atlas.'[13] The reply indicates if an investigation provided evidence, the publisher would provide an appropriate acknowledgement in future editions with commemoration of the victims.

Review of the Initial Responses and Denials– 1996

As we had expected, there were significant denials in the responses of the University of Innsbruck and initially in the responses from the University of Vienna. A consistent and very troubling theme we found was the claim that the cadavers in the atlas and at the Anatomy Institutes at the Universities of Vienna and Innsbruck did not depict Jewish concentration camp victims. This response was reiterated by many of the individuals who replied to the letters from Yad Vashem and the ADL. I was absolutely outraged at this recurrent theme, as if we would only be concerned about victims of the Nazis who were of the Jewish faith. Did the respondents believe that our ethical values were such that we would find it acceptable to forgo any investigation of those who were non-Jewish victims? By indicating there was no evidence of Jewish concentration camp victims, did the respondents believe this was a satisfactory position to placate our horror at discovering that one of the most acclaimed anatomy books throughout the world was the product of Nazi victims? Furthermore, the book continued to be published for profit while hiding the fact that it was created by ardent Nazis from unsuspecting users of the atlas such as doctors and students, eliminating any possibility of allowing those individuals to make their own decisions on the ethics of using a highly acclaimed anatomical resource that was likely created through the inhumane suffering of nameless innocent victims. There was no dignity, memorial or honor for these nameless victims depicted on the pages of Pernkopf's Atlas.

The publisher's response indicated that they would support an investigation to determine the truth. However, the publisher's mistaken focus appeared to assume that we were concerned only with Jewish concentration camp victims. Additionally, the decision to separate 'Pernkopf the man from his work' implies a lack of concern for each user of the atlas to determine if their moral compass permitted the use of such a resource. The entire ethical dilemma surrounding the Pernkopf's Atlas was taken out of the hands of the individuals who were using and purchasing the book. Although the initial University of Vienna faculty responses were consistent with denial and cover up, the moral leadership of Dr. Ebenbauer and other members of the faculty ultimately led to the decision to conduct a thorough investigation. The University of Innsbruck refused to consider an investigation and placed the focus of this issue on the University of Vienna.

Dr. Seidelman and I concluded that the first phase of the strategy to have Yad Vashem make a formal request for a proper investigation would potentially be successful with the University of Vienna. However, the responses from the University of Innsbruck were disappointing with denial and a lack of sensitivity to the profound medical ethical issues that the Pernkopf Atlas raised. It was important to move forward with another phase in the pursuit of the true origins of the Pernkopf Atlas, as discrete political diplomacy was still being met with resistance to fully uncover the truth.

Overcoming Roadblocks to the Truth with Public Exposure

Following the initial responses from the Universities of Vienna, Innsbruck and the publisher in 1996, it was clear that it was necessary to aggressively pursue another component of the strategy which involved reporting our existing findings to the medical establishment and the general public. With the information that we already had uncovered regarding Eduard Pernkopf, his artists and the Anatomy Institute, along with the concealment of the original signatures of the artists in the more recent editions of the atlas, we were hopeful that pressure from the medical community outside of Austria, as well as the general public would ultimately result in investigations that would lead to the truth. Dr. Seidelman and I agreed that the next phase would involve publishing our findings in peer reviewed medical journals, delivering presentations at major professional meetings, and notifying major media outlets to stimulate interest by journalists to inform the general public, and hopefully exert enough influence that would result in investigations by institutions that had used pathoanatomical specimens of victims of the Nazi regime.

In 1996 Dr. Seidelman and I authored a manuscript titled 'The Swastika and the Cadaver: Eduard Pernkopf and Anatomy in the Third Reich,' that was submitted to the *New England Journal of Medicine*, which had published a glowing review of the Pernkopf Atlas in 1990.[14] Interestingly, the response we received from the editor was not very encouraging '...........this is not the sort of article we typically publish.....we therefore decided not to have the manuscript evaluated by any external reviewers.' Following this rejection, we submitted the article to *The Lancet*, and again, the manuscript was rejected, with the editor indicating that there were previous publications on the same material. However, we were not discouraged and when Professor William Seidelman was invited to give a major presentation at The US. Holocaust Memorial Museum Conference titled 'Hippocrates Betrayed: Medicine in the Third Reich' in January 1996 this was a major opportunity. Dr. Seidelman's powerful presentation 'Complicity, Complacency and Conspiracy: The Enduring Legacy of Medicine in the Third Reich' introduced the details of the Pernkopf Atlas controversy, amongst those crimes of Nazi medicine which had previously been well documented.[15] Furthermore, Dr. Seidelman informed the audience that the Israel Holocaust Martyrs' and Heroes Remembrance Authority, Yad Vashem had agreed to become the official organization to make the requests for a thorough investigation.[15]

Following Dr. Seidelman's powerful presentation at the US Holocaust Memorial Museum, the evidence that had been presented was 'published exclusively for the first time' in an article titled 'The Corpses That Won't Die' in *The Jerusalem Report* in February 1996.[16]

The National Public Radio became aware of the issues raised in *The Jerusalem Report* and I was interviewed in February 1996 for a 15-20 minute segment on their popular show '*All Things Considered*,' which was regularly broadcast on Saturdays and Sundays from 5-6 pm on WNYC to the New York Greater Metropolitan area.[17] We were hopeful that public awareness was going to be raised to counter the willful amnesia that existed.

Notes

1. W. Firbas, Letter to Rector of the University Professor Alfred Ebenbauer, 30 March 1995.
2. A. Gisel, Letter to Rector of the University of Vienna Professor Alfred Ebenbauer, 26 April 1995.
3. W. Krause, Letter to Rector of the University of Vienna Professor Alfred Ebenbauer, 13 April 1995.
4. K. Muhlberger, Letter to Rector of the University of Vienna Professor Alfred Ebenbauer, 3 April 1995.
5. W. Platzer, Letter to Rector of the University of Innsbruck Professor Hans Moser, 3 April 1995.
6. E. Fritsch, Letter to Ambassador Johanan Bein, Vice Chairman Yad Vashem, 29 September 1995.
7. W. Seidelman, 'Complicity, Complacency and Conspiracy: The Enduring Legacy of Medicine in the Third Reich,' Presented at the Conference 'Hippocrates Betrayed: Medicine in the Third Reich,' The U.S. Holocaust Memorial Museum, Washington, D.C. 24 January 1996.
8. E. Fritsch, Letter to Ambassador Johanan Bein, Vice Chairman Yad Vashem, 26 February 1996.
9. A. Ebenbauer, Letter to Professor H. Israel, Columbia University with attached documents, letters, reports from faculty of the University of Vienna and additional experts, 18 March 1996.
10. M. Lehner, 'The Medical Faculty of the University of Vienna 1938 – 1945 (Dissertation),' University of Vienna, May 1990.
11. A. Ebenbauer, Letter to Ambassador Johanan Bein, Vice Chairman Yad Vashem, 17 December 1996.
12. E.B. Hutton, President and CEO Waverly, Inc. Letter to H. Israel, Columbia University School of Dental & Oral Surgery, 29 August 1996.
13. E.B. Hutton, 'In Reply Pernkopf Anatomy,' *JAMA*, 276, 20 (1996), p. 1634.

14. R.S. Snell, 'Pernkopf Anatomy: Atlas of Topographic and Applied Human Anatomy, vol. 2 Thorax, Abdomen and Extremities, 3rd ed. Platzer W (ed), Monsen H (Transl).' *The New England Journal of Medicine*, 323, 3 (1990), p. 205.
15. W. Seidelman, 'Complicity, Complacency and Conspiracy: The Enduring Legacy of Medicine in the Third Reich,' Presented at the Conference 'Hippocrates Betrayed: Medicine in the Third Reich,' The U.S. Holocaust Memorial Museum, Washington, D.C. 24 January 1996.
16. J. Broder, 'The Corpses That Won't Die,' *The Jerusalem Report*, 22 February 1996.
17. D. Zwerdling, 'Interview of Dr. Howard Israel regarding the Nazi Origins of the Pernkopf atlas controversy,' *All Things Considered*, National Public Radio Broadcast, February 1996.

9

Major Turning Points – 1996

The New York Times, Journal of the American Medical Association and Eyewitnesses

How Did a Fractured Tooth Facilitate Pressure on the University of Vienna?

There are times in one's life that you have a goal to pursue, and you do everything within your power to achieve the desired result, only to be met with failure. But there are also times when you just get plain lucky.

Early on in my discovery of the Nazi origins of the atlas that I had used for two decades, I concluded that most reasonable people would be outraged when the story was told. Therefore, on 24 October 1994, I wrote a letter to the assistant managing editor of *The New York Times* revealing my discoveries to date and included the initial essay that I had composed 'Nazi Anatomy Lessons Today.' I appealed to *The New York Times* for assistance in publishing an article. Unfortunately, I did not receive a response.

Fast forward through the efforts with my colleague Dr. Seidelman, the meetings with Yad Vashem and ADL officials, the letters to the Austrian Universities and the responses which met with resistance to conducting investigations to uncover the truth and let us go to the date 8 November 1996. As an oral and maxillofacial surgeon, I would occasionally have patients erroneously seek consultation with me for a routine dental problem, rather than a complex oral facial pain disorder or one requiring surgery. On that date, a patient with a broken front tooth without pain sought my advice, and at that time, I informed her that the appointment was made by mistake, but that I would assist her by referring her to an excellent dentist. I spoke to that dentist, informed him of the urgent nature of her problem since a fractured front tooth presents a significant esthetic issue, particularly for someone who has an important administrative position in midtown Manhattan and deals with the public. I was successful in arranging for her to have an early appointment with an excellent restorative dentist. She was incredibly grateful for my assistance and in the course of our conversation I discovered that she worked for *The New York Times*. I informed her of the issues raised with the Anatomy Atlas which greatly piqued her interest, and she requested more detailed information. I faxed to her a copy of the article in *The Jerusalem Report*, as well as the unpublished manuscript Dr. Seidelman and I had authored titled 'The Swastika and the Cadaver: Eduard Pernkopf and Anatomy in the Third Reich.' Over the next several days, there was more correspondence between us via telephone, fax and e-mail and she was greatly moved by the story, agreeing to assist us in getting this information to the public. Nicholas Wade, a leading journalist who authored articles for the Science Times Section of *The New York Times*, was introduced to this material through my patient with the 'chipped tooth,' and he became quite interested in writing an article on the controversy surrounding the Pernkopf Atlas. After I had spoken to and met with Mr. Wade, he indicated that this was

Doctors Question Use Of Nazi's Medical Atlas

By NICHOLAS WADE

A CLASSIC anatomy atlas, famed for the beauty and fine detail of its paintings, has come under attack because of some none too metaphorical skeletons in its past. A letter appearing in tomorrow's issue of The Journal of the American Medical Association says that the author of the atlas was a leading Nazi who purged the University of Vienna medical faculty of Jews and that the cadavers portrayed in the paintings "may have been victims of political terror."

The book is known as the "Pernkopf Anatomy," and it is still in use among specialists. Although there have long been rumors of its dubious origins, the evidence now emerging seems not to be widely known to anatomists, despite their general admiration for the book.

An effort to publicize the background of the atlas is being led by Dr. Howard A. Israel, an oral surgeon at Columbia University, and Dr. William E. Seidelman, director of an AIDS unit at the University of Toronto, who wrote the letter to the journal. They want the University of Vienna to inquire into the identity of the cadavers portrayed in the atlas and for the publisher to include in the next edition a historical account of the atlas so readers can then decide whether it is ethical to make use of the material.

Edward B. Hutton, president of Waverly Inc., the American publisher of the atlas, agreed that the University of Vienna should undertake an inquiry into the identity of the cadavers shown in the paintings, and said his company would contribute to its cost. If the cadavers depicted should be found to be from concentration camps, the victims would be commemorated in future editions of the book, Mr. Hutton said.

"But there isn't one shred of evidence to date that the cadavers used in this atlas came from concentration camp victims, and in fact there is circumstantial evidence to the contrary," Mr. Hutton said. Without such a finding, a new preface would not be justified since "we separate the man from his work," he said, referring to the author, Eduard

Continued on Page C10

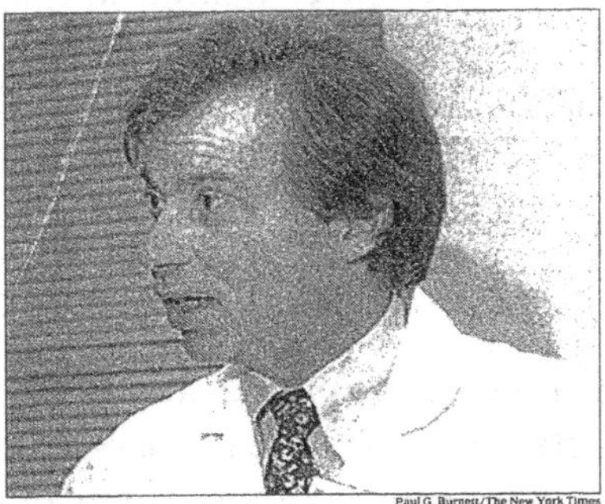

Paul G. Burnett/The New York Times

Dr. Howard A. Israel of Columbia University has questioned the continued use of "Pernkopf Anatomy," whose author, Eduard Pernkopf, was a leading Nazi. One of the book's artists, Erich Lepier of Vienna, signed his name with a swastika.

Pernkopf Anatomy/Waverly Inc.

Figure 7. Nicholas Wade's article exposes the Pernkopf Atlas controversy to the public. From The New York Times, November 26, 1996, The New York Times.

a fascinating story, and he was provided all of the important evidentiary documentation which Dr. Seidelman and I had accumulated. On November 26, 1996 on the front page of the Science Times section of *The New York Times*, an article titled 'Doctors Question Use Of Nazi's Medical Atlas' by Nicholas Wade was published.[1] The article refers to a publication 'appearing in tomorrow's *Journal of the American Medical Association*' authored by myself and Dr. Seidelman, revealing the Nazi origins of the creators of the Pernkopf Atlas and with cadavers portrayed in the book suspected of being executed victims. Wade describes the reactions of the publisher, a professor of medical illustration and academic anatomists to the exposure of a world-famous anatomy atlas created by ardent Nazis, with the possible depiction of cadavers who were victims. Some of the responses indicated that there were no Jewish concentration camp victims depicted in the book, and the source of cadavers most likely were derived from execution of prisoners who were enemies of the Nazis. Anatomists and illustrators praised the unique quality of this 'phenomenal, very complete and authoritative book.' However, I indicated that the atlas posed an ethical 'problem if Pernkopf used victims of Nazi terror, whether or not they were Jewish.' The call for further investigation and appropriate responses by the Austrian Universities and the publisher was now in the general public domain via the extensive readership of *The New York Times* (Figure 7).

Personal Letters Received in Response to The New York Times Article

Following the publication of the Science Times article, I received many letters, addressed to me personally, with a wide variety of reactions. Most respondents were supportive of our efforts to uncover the truth. Some that were supportive cautioned against banning the book, while others supported the continued use of the atlas by enabling doctors to perform more skillfully, thus creating good from evil. Other letters focused on commemoration of the victims, while others indicated that the book should be banned, indicating that by using the atlas one can potentially justify a repeat of history as the Nazi medical profession proceeded to go from healers to killers.

In February 1996 I had written a letter to Holocaust survivor and Nobel Peace Prize laureate, author, Elie Wiesel, Professor of Humanities

Boston University. I informed him of the efforts of Dr. Seidelman, Yad Vashem's Vice Chairs Dafni and Bein, and myself to uncover the truth regarding the source of material for the creation of the Nazi Anatomy Atlas. Professor Wiesel responded by thanking me for the information and requesting that I continue to keep him informed of our progress. Immediately following the publication of the article in The New York Times, I received a letter from Professor Wiesel dated November 26, 1996, with the following words:[2]

> *Dear Dr. Israel*
>
> *Bravo for the important article in the Times! See what the persistence of one man can do?*
>
> *All best*
> *Elie Wiesel*

Although Professor Wiesel and I both knew that this effort involved the persistence and passions of Bill Seidelman, Ambassadors Dafni and Bein and others, these words of encouragement from this Holocaust survivor and Nobel laureate were extremely important to me then, and I continue to be touched, motivated and persistent to this very day. At this very moment, I am looking at the original framed letter from Elie Wiesel, which has a permanent place in my study.

However, there was another letter that I received which was immediately frightening and it haunts me still. As I now re-read this letter twenty-eight years later, I am inconsolably sad, especially for my children and grandchildren, that there are people in this world with such venom, prejudice, and hate. It is difficult to repeat the words used in the letter that was written directly to me, but nonetheless, it is important to document them. I honestly believe that most people are good, care for each other and in their hearts are not prejudicial. However, one must be aware that this is not necessarily true for everyone. The following are some verses which came from this hateful communication:[3]

> *....your protest is obviously based upon politics, namely part of the continuing battle of one group of people against another, and in your special case, part of the battle of the Jews against Aryans.*

> *....according to today's judgment every single person who was executed by 'the Nazis' was innocent....just as every Black who had been lynched in the US a hundred years ago was innocent...*
>
> *....you probably wondered why you (Jews) are (after a while) always disliked in your host countries......turns into hate, and eventually results in expulsion.*
>
> *... Jews view themselves in general as being an essential and beneficial part of the society in which they live....*
>
> *Do you seriously believe that most of your Christian colleagues... ...American doctors....agree with you, or am I right in assuming that most of them will complain about that ubiquitous Jew named Howard Israel who can't leave well enough alone? Will the next ... .step by you and your coreligionists be to have Pernkopf's Anatomy being put on the index of forbidden books and see it replaced by a similar, albeit never as good work by a Jew?*
>
> *I can just hear you: 'but six million Jews were exterminated under the swastika!' I do not want to destroy your belief in this fairy tale... ....the real Jewish losses were probably fewer than one million.*
>
> *Finally, I do believe that you and your fellow Jews ought to begin to view the Third Reich as that which it was: the very legitimate German Government at a time when the German nation was in a desperate battle against the internationalist forces, of whom International World Jewry was one........I pity all Jews, like you who still cannot find peace.*

I am aware that such hateful speech is quite common on social media today and so the average reader may not be shocked by this letter. Words do matter, as history has repeatedly told us. The repetition of lies, ultimately can lead individuals to be convinced that these 'alternative facts' represent the truth. I believe that this was one, amongst many other complex factors, which can partially explain how human beings, including doctors of healing became killers during the Third Reich.

The JAMA Letter Reports on the Nazi Origins of the Atlas to the Medical Profession

On November 27, 1996, the *Journal of the American Medical Association* (JAMA) published a special issue on research ethics commemorating the fifty years since the Nuremberg Trial and the Nuremberg Code. Dr. Seidelman and I authored a detailed letter to the editor titled 'Nazi Origins of an Anatomy Text: The Pernkopf Atlas'[4] which was published in this special issue. This publication revealed that Pernkopf and his artists were ardent Nazis and that Pernkopf, as the Director of the Anatomy Institute and Dean of the Faculty of Medicine (1938) of the University of Vienna, led the purge of Jewish faculty. The artists signed their names to the anatomical paintings depicted in the atlas with Nazi icons, which could be seen in the German language editions of the book, but many were erased in later editions of the atlas published after the Second World War. Nazi victims from the Vienna district court were executed and sent to the Anatomy Institute, which was the source of the dissections depicted in the atlas. Specimens from that era were likely still in use at the University of Vienna. The book was being used and present in medical libraries throughout the world, without any knowledge of the tainted origins of the book to the unsuspecting user. The article indicated that with this information, Yad Vashem had contacted the University of Vienna, other Austrian institutions suspected of having pathoanatomical specimens of Nazi victims, and the publisher of Pernkopf's Atlas for a thorough investigation, acknowledgement in the book, commemoration and an appropriate and dignified handling of any specimens that may have originated from victims of the Nazi era. The revelations included in this publication finally did have a major impact on the events that were to occur in the future.

The responses to the *JAMA* letter and *The New York Times* article, both from November 1996 reflected the diversity of opinions regarding the bioethical issues raised when an outstanding scientific resource is published, which can improve medical knowledge and save lives. However, if that valuable resource was created by unethical means through the inhumane suffering of others, should the book be used? The Pernkopf controversy represented just one of many instances where this bioethical dilemma was raised.

In a response to the editor of *JAMA*, Richard Panush, MD, a physician from Saint Barnabus Medical Center in New Jersey, indicated that the medical staff decided to expunge Pernkopf's atlas from their library. Additionally, Panush's moral convictions and conscience, made him decide to withdraw editorial responsibilities he had held with the publisher, Williams & Wilkins, and canceled his subscriptions of the publisher's journals.[5] Urban and Schwarzenberg, the publisher of Pernkopf's Atlas was a subsidiary of Williams & Wilkins, a major publishing company in 1996.

A letter to the editor of *The New York Times* in response the November 26, 1996, article by Wade, supported the continued use of the atlas as there was benefit to doctors in training and ultimately in patient care. Yaros, the letter's author, was against censorship and indicated that the atlas could serve as a memorial for Nazi victims.[6] Dr Michael Franzblau's letter to the editor of *The New York Times* indicated that Pernkopf, the creator of the atlas was evil and the book should have no place in any medical library.[7] Dr. Franzblau, Clinical Professor of Dermatology at the University of California, and member of the World Medical Association had led the campaign which resulted in the forced withdrawal of Dr. Hans Joachim Sewering as President of the World Medical Association, due to Sewering's past as a member of the Nazi party and links to patient murder programs.

The revelations regarding the Pernkopf Atlas controversy has stirred great interest in both the US and throughout the world from 1996 and to this day. Between 1996 and 1997, journalists published articles related to the controversies surrounding the anatomical atlas in the *Philadelphia Inquirer, The Washington Post, Michigan Live Ann Arbor, The British Medical Journal, Science and Technology – Frankfurter Rundschau* and *Tempo Medico, The Toronto Star* and the *Baltimore Sun.*[8-13] The aforementioned publications are just a small sample of the many early publications representing the intense interest in the controversy surrounding the atlas.

CNN

In 1997, Henry Schuster, a producer of CNN and Time's weekly television newsmagazine, titled 'IMPACT CNN,' contacted me and Bill Seidelman. He was planning to produce a segment on Nazi medicine and the Pernkopf Atlas controversy. After numerous telephone conversations and e-mails I eventually met with Henry Schuster for dinner, discussing the focus of the segment. There were interviews with numerous individuals, including Dr. William Seidelman, Wolfgang Neugebauer (Documentation Archives of the Austrian Resistance Director), Werner Platzer (Professor and Chair of Anatomy University of Innsbruck and editor of the atlas), Walter Krause (Professor of Anatomy University of Vienna), Rector Alfred Ebenbauer University of Vienna, Michael Urban (publisher) and myself. The final segment was shaped by all of these interviews, although not everyone appeared on camera for the documentary that was aired on 19 October 1997.[14]

The CNN reporter, Art Harris indicated that there were approximately 100,000 English language editions in print and tens of thousands more German language editions. Very shortly after my discovery of the Nazi origins in 1994, I had found out that a two-volume set of the English edition of Eduard Pernkopf's Atlas of Topographical and Applied Human Anatomy was priced at $355. Although I had no knowledge of the sales statistics for the book, I was, and still am quite surprised by the total value of the inventory for the English language editions being in excess of $35 million dollars in 1997. A visually shocking component of this broadcast included the 1943 drawings of Austrian artist, Leopold Metzenbauer of the heads and headless bodies that were stored in the Anatomy Institute at the University of Vienna. These drawings were obtained from the Documentation Archives of the Austrian Resistance, when Henry Schuster, the producer, met with Dr. Neugebauer. These graphic pictures provided viewers just a small glimpse of the horrific acts of terror and murder committed during the Nazi era, which incredibly involved what had formerly been a prestigious academic institution. Rector Ebenbauer made it clear that the University of Vienna's investigation would focus on the presence of Nazi victims, whether Jewish or non-Jewish. He also indicated that if Nazi victims were discovered to be depicted in Penkopf's atlas, he would not want the book expunged, as that would be analogous to 'book burning,' a policy of suppression of the truth which was common during the Nazi regime. Professor Werner Platzer was interviewed as the editor of the book, as well as Chair of Anatomy at the University of Innsbruck. Platzer worked directly with Pernkopf after the Second World War and helped in completion of the third edition of the atlas. He was asked if any of the specimens at the University of Innsbruck's collections included those of Nazi victims. Platzer indicated that he did not know but was convinced that there were no Jewish victims. Platzer wasn't bothered by the use of bodies from executed individuals being used at the Anatomy Institute of the University of Vienna, indicating that this was the law at that time. Platzer also said that he would support using Pernkopf's Atlas, as the medical profession must always be for the 'saving of lives.' The last portion of the segment involved a question posed to me as to whether I still had used the Pernkopf Atlas after the discovery of its Nazi origins. I indicated that since learning about the true origins of the creation of the atlas, I had not used the book in preparation for surgeries. However, if my son needed a surgery and the knowledge gained from Pernkopf's Atlas would make me a better surgeon, then my final response about the use of the book was 'maybe I would.' The ethical issues surrounding the use of this atlas are just one example of many similar cases which continue to be debated to this day.

The media blitz was on. Thus, the bioethical debate was now open to the general public and the medical profession.

Discovering More Evidence 1996-97 and Eyewitnesses: Drs. George Hindels, Gertrude Schneider and G.E.R. Gedye

The political efforts continued with correspondence, meetings, document exchanges involving Yad Vashem, the Universities of Vienna and Innsbruck, the publisher of the atlas, Dr. Seidelman, myself, and a growing number of other concerned parties. However, we continued to search for more information and documentation on the true origins of Pernkopf's creation. The more evidence that we were able to gather, with documentation, the stronger the pressure would be for serious, academically driven investigations in Austria, hopefully, resulting in a report in the public domain to reveal the truth.

In this regard, I was lucky, as I had been in the past, with my direct encounters with Dr. Robert Lifton, and becoming colleagues and friends with Bill Seidelman, the world's expert on issues dealing with pathoanatomical specimens at academic institutions in Europe from the Nazi era. Without the chance encounter with the patient who had a 'chipped tooth,' it is likely that *The New York Times* article would never have been published. Was this 'bashert,' destiny, inevitable? Interestingly, this theme of 'bashert,' associated with luck and chance encounters resulted in many opportunities and has continued with regularity throughout this journey. There must have been a guiding force beyond our comprehension that was 'pulling the strings.' The following two individuals that I had the opportunity to meet with and interview, George Hindels, D.D.S. and Gertrude Schneider, PhD provided valuable information in our quest to discover what exactly happened in Vienna during the Nazi era. Both of these individuals were direct eyewitnesses to the events in Vienna before and after the Anschluss and were able to survive to reveal the truth. Having the opportunity to meet with them must have been 'bashert.'

As an Associate Professor in the Division of Oral & Maxillofacial Surgery at Columbia University, I also had many hospital responsibilities at New York Presbyterian Hospital, both located in the Health Sciences Campus on 168th Street and Fort Washington Avenue in uptown Manhattan. On 23 August 1996, upon making routine morning rounds checking up on my patients, I found out that a fellow faculty member's wife was a hospital inpatient. Even though I had never met George Hindels, DDS or his wife, it was always appropriate to conduct 'courtesy rounds' so that patient could see a friendly face in a white coat to offer support, conversation and to see if there was anything one could do to make their hospital stay more comfortable. When I arrived at Mrs. Hindels' room, she wasn't there, but Dr. Hindels was present, informing me that she was transported for more testing. Dr. Hindels informed me that he was a Prosthodontist at Columbia University's dental school who taught students how to make removable dentures during the 1960s. As the conversation progressed further, I was astonished to find out that he had been a medical student at the University of Vienna from 1932-38. In Austria one had to go to medical school prior to specializing in stomatology and dentistry. I informed Dr. Hindels of my use of the Pernkopf Atlas for twenty years until I had discovered that he was a Nazi. He informed me that he was quite familiar with the notorious Dr. Pernkopf as there were two anatomy departments, one under the directorship of Dr. Julius Tandler and the other under Dr. Eduard Pernkopf. Tandler was Jewish and all of the Jewish students in the medical school, including Hindels, studied anatomy under him. Pernkopf, being an ardent Nazi, had medical students who were

National Socialists, and taught them both anatomy and the concepts of racial hygiene. Hindels informed me that the National Socialist students fought with and beat up the Jewish students all of the time. In 1938, after Germany annexed Austria, Hindels, in his senior year and about ready to graduate, was taken by the Nazis and deported to the Dachau concentration camp. Dr. Hindels did not describe his experiences in the concentration camp but went on to tell me that he came to the US in the 1940s after the war, completed his dental education and became a member of the Prosthodontics Department at Columbia University School of Dental & Oral Surgery.[15]

Shortly after my spontaneous encounter with Dr. George Hindels, I was able to obtain a copy of the publication titled '*Wien 1938*' which had been a special exhibit of the Historical Museum of the City of Vienna in 1988 from the Documentation Archives of the Austrian Resistance.[16] Although written in German, there were numerous photographs documenting the encounters that Hindels suffered through when he was a medical student at the University of Vienna (Figure 8).

Dr. Gertrude Schneider was President of the PhD Alumni Association at the City University of New York, a Holocaust survivor and author of *Exile and Destruction: The Fate of Austrian Jews, 1935 – 1945,* published in 1995.[17] When I found out that she lived in Harrington Park, New Jersey,

Figure 8. During an attack by National Socialist students on the Anatomical Institute at the University of Vienna, Jewish students are forced to escape to safety, in 1933. © Austrian National Library, Image rights ÖNB/Wien 435.956-B.

just miles away from the George Washington Bridge in upper Manhattan, I was determined to contact her and find out if she had any information that could be of assistance in the uncovering of the origins of the atlas. Again, luck intervened and I was quite fortunate to have the opportunity to meet with her in her New Jersey home on 6 December 1996. Dr. Schneider was born in Vienna Austria in 1928 and experienced the Nazi annexation of Austria in 1938 along with the antisemitic attacks, violence, and taunting of the Jewish community under National Socialism. Although she and her family were deported to the Riga Ghetto in Latvia, Dr. Schneider did not discuss the horrors and terror that she and others experienced there with me. Instead, while sitting in her living room, she listened carefully to my story regarding the origins of the Pernkopf Atlas. Dr. Schneider exuberantly indicated that she was quite familiar with the history of Vienna under the Nazis, along with the *Wiener Landesgericht* (the Vienna district court), Eduard Pernkopf, and the fate of the Jews in Vienna. She informed me that in performing further detailed research on her book on the fate of the Austrian Jews, she received much information from Dr. Wolfgang Neugebauer the Director, and Herbert Exenberger, the Chief Librarian of the Documentation Archives for the Austrian Resistance. Upon further questioning, Dr. Schneider corroborated many things which had been described previously and provided additional new important information.[18] She knew that the local district court served essentially as a notorious prison where death sentences were readily given for those who expressed anti-Nazi political views, communists and individuals who were charged with being in the Austrian resistance. The *Wiener Landesgericht* served as a court and execution chamber where Nazi dissenters were routinely guillotined. This court is listed on an Austrian memorial monument to the victims of National Socialism standing with Auschwitz, Bergen-Belsen, Theresienstadt and other Nazi execution centers.

Dr. Schneider confirmed that the *Landesgericht* supplied corpses to the Anatomy Institute located only several blocks away. She also confirmed that in the early years of the Nazi reign over Austria, Pernkopf requested more corpses for research and teaching of medical students from the hierarchy in Berlin. He requested corpses originating outside of Vienna, such as Poland, where the supply of cadaveric material for the Anatomy Institute would greatly facilitate Pernkopf's work. Dr. Schneider told me that the Berlin authorities denied Pernkopf's request for executed individuals from Poland. I asked her about the fate of the Jews in Vienna, and in particular, those that were sent to the *Wiener Landesgericht*. Dr. Schneider asserted that if a Jewish person were sent to the *Landesgericht*, they would likely be deported to the concentration camps and the court's final disposition of each individual would be documented in the records of the *Wiener Landesgericht*. Dr. Schneider indicated that she would search through Pernkopf's lengthy dossier, which was written in German, to determine if she could get any more information that would be of assistance to the investigation of the source of Pernkopf's cadavers. I left Gertrude Schneider's living room knowing that I had just interviewed a very passionate person who had directly witnessed the Nazi horrors and was persistent about uncovering the truth.[18]

Figure 9. The basement of the notorious *Wiener Landesgericht* (Vienna District Court) where Communists, members of the Austrian Resistance, homosexuals, gypsies, and those who expressed any political dissent contrary to Nazi doctrine received harsh punishment, which was frequently death by the guillotine. The corpses of fresh, young, healthy guillotine victims were prioritized for dissections to be depicted in the Pernkopf Atlas. © Austrian National Library, Image rights ÖNB /Wien H 12083.

Dr. Schneider contacted me the following day on the telephone having just reviewed in detail, Pernkopf's dossier. She was unable to find anything in the dossier relevant to the questions I had posed to her the previous day. However, Dr. Schneider indicated she would be giving a presentation in Germany and was also traveling to Vienna, where she lived for the first ten years of her life. Dr. Schneider said that she would seek the assistance of Neugebauer and Exenberger from the Documentation Archives of the Austrian Resistance to determine if there was any archival material that could possibly shed light on the Jews in Vienna and those who were sent to the court following arrest. Her plan was to find names and dates of Jewish persons who were sent to the notorious *Wiener Landesgericht.*

Gertrude Schneider spoke with me in June 1997 upon her return from Europe and indicated that she had a list of Jewish people who had been sent to the *Landesgericht.* She sent me photocopies of documents, which had been in the archives of Yad Vashem. These documents, written in German, were the records of the Secret State Police in Vienna, the Gestapo.[19] They included the names of ten male persons that had been arrested by the Gestapo and sent to the *Wiener Landesgericht* between 1940 and 1943. This included 3/10 non-Jewish and 7/10 being Jewish persons who had been charged with various 'crimes/allegations.' Of the three non-Jews, one was released, one was sentenced to two years in prison for violating the Treachery Act, and the records of the third individual indicate that 'the investigation is ongoing.' See Table I for further details and English translation of Gestapo records.

Although the documentation sent to me by Dr. Schneider did not provide direct roof of the ultimate fate of all of those arrested and sent to the *Wiener Landesgericht*, the brief accounts of the alleged crimes and likely disposition of these individuals is quite chilling. This new information with the names and ultimate fate of the victims, clearly demonstrated the horrific experiences of those sent to the *Landesgericht* under the laws of the Nazis. It is well known that there was meticulous record keeping during the Third Reich and the absence of documentation of an individual leaving the *Landesgericht* is very highly suspicious that they never left. There was a record of deportation for one of the Jews arrested, which demonstrates that the disposition of the prisoners was documented. The phrase 'protective custody requested' without any further information is suspicious and may reflect the fate

Gestapo Records of 3 Non-Jewish Males Arrested and Brought to Hearings at the *Wiener Landesgericht*

Name	**Date of Birth**	**Date of Hearing(s)**	**Alleged Crime/Violation**	**Final Disposition**	**Comment**
Johann Strobel	9/24/1891 Age 49.6	6/2/1941	Illegally stayed in a guest house occupied by members of the German army	Released after several days in prison	
Heinrich Pawlicek	6/15/1893 Age 47.9	5/6/1941	Violation of Section 2, Paragraph 1 of the Treachery Act	Sentenced to 2 years in prison	The nature of the violations not specified
Alois Brebec	6/27/1899 Age 42	6/17/1941	Told workmates that there was a planned military coup in the near future	Investigation is ongoing	Status not documented

Gestapo Records of 7 Jewish Males Arrested and Brought to Hearings at the *Wiener Landesgericht*

Name	Date of Birth	Date of Hearing(s)	Alleged Crime/Violation	Final Disposition	Comment
Kurt Israel Feuer	2/22/1924 Age 17.2	6/7/1941	Made derogatory and untrue statements about the conditions and treatment of Jews in 'retraining' camp located in Doppl, Austria	No disposition in the record	No record of leaving Landesgericht
Adolf Israel Weiss	4/1/1903 Age 38.9	6/6/1941 6/8/1941 2/21/1942	Violation treachery act, falsified discharge papers from Dachau, spread news on treatment in German concentration camps, fraudulent actions and propaganda	After 8 months in prison was sentenced to 15 years incarceration	No record of leaving Landesgericht
Hans Joachim Israel Albu	9/26/14 Age 18.2	1/5/1943	Concealment of his Jewish heritage, Had 3 year old child with German woman	'Protective custody requested'	Had been a decorated member of the Hitler Youth. No record of leaving Landesgericht
Max Israel Steiner	6/24/1887 Age 55.4	1/6/1943	Illegally returned from Hungary to Vienna, was homeless when arrested	'Protective custody requested'	No record of leaving Landesgericht

Gestapo Records of 7 Jewish Males Arrested and Brought to Hearings at the *Wiener Landesgericht*					
Name	**Date of Birth**	**Date of Hearing(s)**	**Alleged Crime/Violation**	**Final Disposition**	**Comment**
Friedrich Israel Kudorna	10/25/1895 Age 47.7	6/19/1943	Had been married to a German woman, fled Vienna in 1939 to Romania, Spread false rumors in Romania on the German empire	No disposition in the record	No record of leaving Landesgericht
Rudolf Israel Grunhaus	8/15/1875 Age 67.8	6/12/1943	Had been former Governor of Cernowitz (Ukraine), concealed his Jewish ancestry	Evaluate for transport	Evaluate for transport, likely deported to concen-tration camp
Rudolf Israel Woinor	4/17/1905 Age 38.2	6/17/1943	Concealed Jewish ancestry refrained using his first name 'Israel,' falsified work documents to obtain employment as horse drawn carriage operator, endangered public safety and fraud	'Protective custody requested'	No record of leaving Landesgericht

Table I. Records from the Archives of Yad Vashem obtained by Dr. Gertrude Schneider, were directly sent to me by her. Details of the names and records of 10 males arrested by the Gestapo and sent for hearings at the *Wiener Landesgericht* 1940-43 are shown. Documentation of the punishments of the 7 Jewish males compared to 3 non-Jewish males reveals their ultimate fate. Data from Yad Vashem Archives, 0.51/78, with permission.

of those who never left the *Landesgericht* alive. Gertrude Schneider was very confident in informing me that if there was no documentation that the prisoner left, they were sentenced to death and directed to proceed to the execution chamber in the basement. At that time, there was no proof that any of these individuals who left the prison of the *Landesgericht*, ultimately wound up as corpses of executed prisoners that were guillotined in the basement and then sent to Pernkopf's Anatomy Institute. However, from the overall evidence that has been recovered, there is strong circumstantial evidence this indeed took place. Further confirming evidence was yet to come since these freshly executed human bodies from young and relatively healthy individuals, were considered ideal for inclusion in an anatomical atlas.

G.E.R. Gedye: Another Eyewitness Account

In 2018 I received an e-mail from the woman whose grandfather was a medical student at the University of Vienna School of Medicine in 1938. She indicated that her grandfather had to flee from Vienna immediately to survive following the Nazi annexation of Austria. This was just one of many letters, e-mails, and correspondence I have received over the years, but this communication had come with something special. She asked if I had ever heard of G.E.R. Gedye, the author of a book titled *Fallen Bastions, The Central European Tragedy* published in 1939.[20] I had never heard of Gedye or his book, which I found on Amazon and purchased it immediately. This book was a treasure, and I was lucky to find another direct witness to the events in Vienna in 1938, through the eyes of the author, G.E.R. Gedye.

George Eric Rowe Gedye was a British journalist who reported for leading British and American newspapers on the events in Central Europe during the rise in Nazism. He was a direct witness to the events that unfolded as he was stationed in Vienna on 11 March 1938, the day that Hitler's troops marched into Vienna as Germany annexed Austria. Following this major upheaval in affairs, Gedye had to decide on one of two courses of action:

> *Either I suppressed all the worst features of the Nazi terror in the hope to be able to stay on indefinitely, or I gave the full truth without the least modification, in which case my days in Vienna would be very few.*

On 18 March 1938, Gedye was summoned by the Austrian police who informed him that there was an order from the Gestapo requesting that he politely leave Vienna. After thirteen years of residence in Austria, he was given no reason for the expulsion. Later, on the same day, Gedye received another phone call that he was to report to the Gestapo Headquarters in Vienna, located at No. 7 Herrengasse, at 11 AM the following day. Gedye reflected:

> *What would have happened had I the privilege of having Jewish blood in my veins when I presented myself next day at the Gestapo I do not know, as the first question asked me by the guard at the entrance was: 'Are you Aryan'?*

The Gestapo officer indicated that the reason for the expulsion was as follows:

> *You were among the journalists confined in the Chancellery on the day of the Fuhrer's visit. On that occasion you sent a message that a German officer had threatened to give an order to fire on Austrian staff officers unless they retreated into the building. What impression do you imagine the publication of such a message made in Berlin?*

To which Gedye replied to the Gestapo officer:

> *I realized at the time that your Government would be furious at publicity being given to such a shameful incident, but my duty is to my newspaper, not to the rulers of the Third Reich.*
>
> *Had the threat merely been made to the journalists, it would have been worth reading but of secondary importance only. The fact that it was made to Austrian officers in uniform threw a very valuable light for the world on the actual position between the German and Austrian armies, which were supposed to be celebrating a fraternal reunion. That is why I sent it; the story was true and I stand by every word of it.*

At the end of the interview with the Gestapo officer, Gedye was shocked when he was informed that the order for his expulsion would be cancelled. Apparently, the Berlin authorities wanted to force Gedye out of Austria without the unpleasant publicity attached to being expelled. The Nazi regime in Austria wanted the Berlin authorities to control the press, and so a host of Gedye's journalist colleagues had been forced out of the country. One of the journalists who had been transferred to Prague, had a 2-year-old daughter who the Nazis held in Austria as a hostage. Although Gedye knew that he had to leave Austria, he planned to stay as long as possible:

> *to see and hear all the horrors and bestialities of the new regime and publish them to the world, though every hour and every day were an agony. Anything too, that could be done to help the victims had to be done.*

By August 1938, Gedye had fled to Prague where he worked tirelessly to complete his book documenting his experiences in Austria before and after the Anschluss.

Gedye reported events of major significance regarding the fate of the Jews of Vienna. I was stunned when I read a passage on page 349 of my copy of '*Fallen Bastions*' in the chapter titled 'Austria – What Now?' This passage read as follows:[20]

> *Here is another true picture. Outside a house in Leopoldstadt stands the cart of the Anatomical Institute. Into it are being loaded the bodies of a whole Jewish family. Around the door lounge grinning storm-troopers. Over it hangs a large sign they have just put up – 'Neighbours, please copy.' Perhaps this incident among many more within my personal experience is worth recording. Friends of a well-known Jewish merchant in Vienna seriously planned getting him denounced and arrested in the hope of saving his life, so near was he to suicide every time the doorbell rang. And this-a chemist told me that his sales of poisons in compact form had quadrupled in a few days of the Nazi regime. He violated the law constantly in handing them out to the ashen-faced applicants. Firstly, he knew the Nazis would make no trouble for him over this, for the customers were all Jews; secondly, he had a great heart and was doing the kindest thing he knew. The poisons, be it noted, were rarely for immediate consumption-they accompanied the purchaser by day and night, ready for the call.*

Gedye's account of the bodies of an entire Jewish family being loaded in a cart to be sent to the Anatomy Institute is so horrific and revealing. If this Jewish family died by committing suicide in fear of the terror specifically aimed at Jews, shouldn't we consider these individuals Nazi victims whose corpses were transported to Pernkopf's Anatomy Institute?

Notes

1. N. Wade, 'Doctors Question Use Of Nazi's Medical Atlas,' *Science Times, The New York Times,* 26 November 1996.
2. E. Weisel, Letter sent to Dr. Howard A. Israel, in response to Nicholas Wade's 1996 article 'Doctors Question Use of Nazi's Medical Atlas, *Science Times, The New York Times,* Personal letter dated 26 November 1996.
3. Anonymous. Letter sent to Dr. Howard A. Israel, in response to Nicholas Wade's 1996 article 'Doctors Question Use of Nazi's Medical Atlas, *Science Times, The New York Times,* Personal letter dated 29 November 1996.
4. H. Israel, W. Seidelman, Letter to the editor, 'Nazi origins of an anatomy text: The Pernkopf Atlas,' *JAMA*, 276, 20 (1996), p. 1633.
5. R. Panush, Letter to the editor. *JAMA*, 276, 20 (1996), p. 1633.
6. K.A. Yaros, 'Don't Censor Atlas, However Odious Its Origin,' letter to the editor. *The New York Times, Editorials/Letters Section,* 3 December 1996.
7. M. Franzblau, 'Throw Away Evil Atlas,' letter to the editor, *The New York Times, Editorials/Letters Section*, 3 December 1996.
8. S. Vendantam, 'Anatomy of Horror,' *The Philadelphia Inquirer Health & Science section*, pD1, 18 August 1997.
9. D. Wahlberg, 'Medical Book Stirs Controversy, Nazi Ties to Anatomical Illustrations Create Ethical Dilemma,' *Michigan Live: Ann Arbor Edition*, 14 April 1997. https://www.mlive.com/ann-arbor/medbook
10. F. Charatan, 'Investigation of the Nazi Anatomy Textbook to Start,' *BMJ*, 70, (February 1997), pp. 335-6. https://www.bmj.com/archive/7080n.htm
11. V.C. Piotrowski, 'An Anatomic Classic with Swastikas,' *Science and Technology, Frankfurter Rundschau*, 53, 113/20 (January 1997), p 8.
12. E.M. Paroli, 'The Atlas Portrays the Horrors of the Reich,' *Tempo Medico*, 6 March 1996.
13. C. Schoettler, 'Do Surgeons Use Images of Nazis' Victims?' *The Toronto Star and Baltimore Sun,* August 1997.
14. H. Schuster, A. Harris, 'Nazi Medicine,' IMPACT CNN and Time's weekly broadcast newsmagazine, 19 October 1997. https://youtu.be/B4-FrCrio0w

15. G. Hindels, Personal interview, 23 August 1996.
16. Historical Museum of the City of Vienna Special Exhibition titled 'Wien 1938,' Documentation Archives of the Austrian Resistance, Vienna, Austria, 11 March-30 June 1988.
17. G. Schneider, *Exile and Destruction The Fate of Austrian Jews 1938-1945.* (Westport Connecticut and London: 1995).
18. G. Schneider, Personal interview, 6 December 1996.
19. Yad Vashem Documents from their Central Archives titled 'Secret State Police Vienna State Police Control Office' Records of ten males arrested by the Gestapo and sent for hearings at the *Wiener Landesgericht* 1940-1943, Obtained by Dr. Gertrude Schneider with copies sent to Dr Howard Israel in 1997 July. Data from Yad Vashem Archives, 0.51/78, with permission.
20. G.E.R. Gedye, *Fallen Bastions, The Central European Tragedy,* (London: Victor Gollancz LTD Publisher,1939).

10

The University of Vienna 1997-98

Public Acknowledgement and Investigation: A Triumph or Just the Beginning?

Press Conference of the University of Vienna

With further documentary evidence, publications in the medical literature and increasing public awareness from the media, our efforts leading to acknowledgment and investigation were eventually realized. Dr. Ebenbauer was not satisfied with the initial responses of his faculty at the University of Vienna to the letters from Yad Vashem requesting a thorough investigation of Pernkopf's Anatomy Institute and the sources of cadavers from 1938 to 1945. On 12 February 1997 Dr. Alfred Ebenbauer, Rector of the University of Vienna held a press conference along with Dr. Wolfgang Schutz, Dean of the Medical School, University of Vienna, Paul Grosz President of the Jewish Federation of Vienna, Dr. Karl Holubar, Director of the Institute for Medical History, University of Vienna, Dr Gustav Spann, Institute for Contemporary History, University of Vienna, Dr Wolfgang Neugebauer, Director, Documentation Archives of the Austrian Resistance, and Bernard Matouschek, Press Agent University of Vienna.[1] At that press conference, it was officially announced that the Rector and the Senate of the University of Vienna formed a committee to investigate the sources of cadavers that were sent to the Anatomy Institute of the University of Vienna during the Nazi regime, the origin of the individuals depicted in the Pernkopf Atlas, and to determine if anatomic specimens from likely victims of the Nazis were still present at the Anatomy Institute and other departments of the University of Vienna. The scope of the investigation was also expanded to determine the presence of anatomical specimens from Nazi victims in the collections of other institutions in Vienna, including the Museum of Natural History and Dr. Henrich Gross's brain specimens of children from the psychiatric hospital in Vienna, Am Spiegelgrund. Additionally, any association with the University of Vienna's Anatomy Institute with the corpses of Jewish victims and/or those from concentration camps was to be ascertained. The University Research Project was named 'Investigations of Anatomical Science in Vienna 1938-1945' with Dr. Ebenbauer, the University's Rector, and Dr. Schutz, the Dean of the Medical School serving as Chairs, and the historian Gustav Spann leading the research committee as the Project Manager.[1]

Dr. Seidelman and I celebrated this great news. The University of Vienna was now conducting an official investigation. It was clear that Ebenbauer was confronted with and disturbed by the repeated denials of the University of Vienna's active role in pursuing National Socialism. The ethical fortitude and bravery of Dr. Alfred Ebenbauer was demonstrated by his pursuit of this investigation, apparently a course of action that some of his faculty from the Anatomy Institute wanted to avoid. It was unfortunate that the University of Innsbruck was not going to be a part of this investigation comprised of academic historians, archivists and additional experts. On 24 September 1997, I received a letter from Rector Ebenbauer[2] with an enclosed document from the University of Vienna titled '*Information for the Users of the Pernkopf Atlas*.'[3] This letter was specifically for the purpose of acknowledging the National Socialist agenda of Pernkopf and informed users of the atlas that the 'possibility cannot be excluded' that the anatomical depictions in the atlas originated from victims of the Nationalist Socialist regime. The document also indicated that the source of the corpses was from the *Wiener Landesgericht*, but the possibility that some were delivered from concentration camps was a 'slight possibility'

The investigation committee was at that time in the early phases of performing research to find answers to the questions that were raised. The major purpose of Ebenbauer's letter was to inform medical libraries throughout the world. Enclosed with the letter was a list of libraries of major academic institutions in Europe and the US that had received '*Information for the Users of the Pernkopf Atlas*,' and Professor Ebenbauer indicated that the University of Vienna would send this acknowledgement to any medical library not on their list if provided with this information. I immediately forwarded the letter of acknowledgement to the head medical librarian at Columbia University Health Sciences Campus to be inserted into every copy of the Pernkopf Atlas.

INFORMATION FOR THE USERS OF THE PERNKOPF-ATLAS

In the beginning of 1997 an official scientific project team was commissioned by the University of Vienna to investigate still opaque questions concerning the origin of several anatomic illustrations in the so-called Pernkopf-atlas: the aim is to clarify if some of the anatomic reproductions were produced on the basis of corpses or parts of corpses of victims of the National Socialist despotism.

Eduard Pernkopf's „Topographische Anatomie des Menschen (...)" ('Topographic Human Anatomy') was published between 1937 and 1960 in four volumes (with several parts) by the publishing house Urban und Schwarzenberg, the volumes 1 to 3 before 1945. In the following decades the Pernkopf-atlas was republished several times in different variants (different forewords, retouched captions [without swastika or stylized SS-runes]). The Pernkopf-atlas was also published in several editions in English, a Spanish translation followed in 1953.

Professor Eduard Pernkopf (1888–1955) was a high-ranking Austrian National Socialist. Between 1938 and 1945 he was dean at the Medical Faculty of Vienna and between 1943 and 1945 rector of the University of Vienna.

At present, the possibility cannot be excluded that individual preparations, which were used for drawings in the anatomical atlas published by Eduard Pernkopf, originate from (political) victims of the National Socialist regime. These were delivered by the Wiener Landesgericht (District Court of Vienna). There is also a slight possibility that corpses were delivered from concentration camps to the Anatomical Institute of the University of Vienna.

It is therefore the ethical responsibility of the individual user to decide whether and in what way he uses this work until the investigation results are published.

The investigation committee will probably publish a detailed account of the results in the second half of 1998.

m.p. Bernd Matouschek
Liason Office; University of Vienna

Vienna, August 1997

Figure 10. Letter of acknowledgement from the University of Vienna indicating the Nazi origins of the Pernkopf Atlas, sent to medical school libraries to inform the users of the atlas. This letter was sent prior to the completion of the 'Investigations of Anatomical Science in Vienna 1938-1945.'

The change in the position of the University of Vienna to now focus on an investigation into the Anatomy Institute and the source of specimens while under Pernkopf's leadership was a reflection of the University's commitment to uncover its dark past during the Nazi era and respond appropriately to honor those who were victims. In April 1997 this landmark change in the attitudes and responses of the University of Vienna was documented in the Journal of the American Medical Association, *JAMA*.[4] Ebenbauer and Schutz in reply to the editor wrote:

> *...because of increasing pressure from abroad.....our university began to concern itself with the shameful period of the Anschluss and its aftermath.........this rethinking process has emerged against the general political trend following former Chancellor Vranitzky's public recognition of the responsibility of Austria for the events of 1938 to 1945.*
>
> *We soon recognized that the complexity of the subject requires extensive systematic analysis and, hence, a research project titled 'The Anatomical Sciences 1938-1945' has been initiated under our joint chairmanship.*
>
> *This belated investigation by the university aims to provide an objective assessment of the interconnection with atrocities perpetrated under National Socialist rule. Nevertheless, we fear that many questions will remain unresolved, in particular the identity of the persons depicted in Pernkopf's Atlas and whether people of Jewish origin (according to the Nuremberg race laws) were used for anatomical purposes. However, it is mandatory that everything in our power is undertaken to elucidate the period.*

Results of the University of Vienna's Investigation of Anatomical Science in Vienna 1938-45

An interim report on the proceedings of the 'Pernkopf Commission' was published in the *Wien Klinische Wochenschrift* (Vienna Clinical Weekly), the *Middle European Journal of Medicine*, in 1997 by Dr, Peter Malina, from the Institute of Contemporary History at the University of Vienna and a member of the advisory board of the research project.[5] This interim report indicated:

> *There is no doubt that the Viennese school of anatomy used bodies of NS victims for scientific purposes, as was only recently presented in a thesis by Martina Lehner based on the files in the Archive of the University of Vienna. It must be assumed with considerable certainty that Pernkopf used these preparations to illustrate his atlas, but currently it is impossible to prove this conclusively, nor is it to determine the identity of the subjects shown and to answer the question of whether they included Jewish victims.*

Malina reports on the efforts of Dr. Seidelman, Dr. Israel, the letters from Yad Vashem and the publications in *The New York Times* as well as the *Journal of the American Medical Association* as having a major influence on the University of Vienna to conduct a proper investigation. The article indicates that the Pernkopf Atlas is repeatedly referenced in the medical literature, most often based on the 1963, 1964 and 1980 editions in which the Nazi icons have been eliminated. However, Malina also indicates that the Nazi emblems present in the 1941, 1943 and 1952 editions, nor Pernkopf's Nazi past caused any reaction whatsoever by the academic medical community, and thus, these older editions had been used as references in the literature as well. The author concludes with the importance of maintaining ethics in the pursuit of scientific knowledge.[5]

> *National Socialism as a system of misanthropy and human derogation offered medicine the chance to exploit the human body in a way hitherto not feasible.'........ 'All those who had become "worthless" in the NS system were exposed to this anatomical exploitation: those misused as human guinea pigs in the concentration camps, just as much as the victims of NS "euthanasia" or those murdered in prisons.'......... 'We cannot ignore the possibility that there was a similar scientific enthusiasm about the "beautiful" preparations provided by the Vienna District Court at the Vienna Institute of Anatomy.*

Upon completion of the Senate Project of the University of Vienna titled 'Investigations of Anatomical Science in Vienna 1938 – 1945' Dr Gustav Spann, the Project Manager sent me a copy of the results in November

1998, which was signed 'With best regards Gustav Spann.'[6] The report indicated that the research project had the following aims:

1. To clarify as thoroughly as possible whether Nazi victims were a source of anatomical specimens used for research and teaching at the University of Vienna during the Nazi era in Austria.
2. To publish the findings of the research without any reservation.
3. To ensure that any anatomical specimens that were still in the collections of the University of Vienna which may possibly have been derived by unethical means during the Nazi era, were removed and given an appropriate and honorable burial.

The report indicates that the research investigation was challenging in that many of the important source materials were no longer available and that 'the burden of proof here was inverted to fall on the accused, rather than the plaintiff: it was often only the publication of such suspicions which led to systematic investigations.' Additionally, the research project found connections between the Department of Anatomy at the University of Vienna and institutions outside of the university, including the Natural History Museum of Vienna and the Baumgartner Hohe Psychiatric Hospital of the City of Vienna, Am Spiegelgrund.[6] Therefore, this landmark investigation into the anatomical sciences at the University of Vienna led to further important revelations of the abuses perpetuated by other individuals and institutions under the Nazi regime.

The following is a summary of findings of the research project:

Bodies sent to the Anatomy Institute of the University of Vienna from 1938-1945

1. The estimated minimum number of bodies of executed persons assigned to the Department of Anatomy was 1377, although the report indicated that this number may increase with subsequent research.
2. The 18 February 1939 decree dictated that the bodies of executed persons were to be assigned to the Department of Anatomy of the nearest university for teaching and research purposes.
3. There were 8 individuals executed at the *Wiener Landesgericht* who were Jewish according to the Nuremberg racial laws. Of

these 8, one individual was buried and not sent to the Anatomy Institute.

4. There were 3964 bodies sent to the Anatomy Institute from deceased persons whose relatives did not or could not provide for a burial and therefore were assigned to the Institute of Anatomy. The research project did not consider these bodies as victims of the Nazis, and thus categorized them as 'free' bodies, defined in the report as 'deceased persons from hospitals or geriatric homes whose relatives did not , or could not, provide for burial' and 'those whose last will bequeathed their bodies' to science.
5. There were 1118 bodies of children that arose from premature births, still born infants and miscarried fetuses. The research project did not count these as Nazi victims.

This investigation apparently was hampered by the destruction of records, including the department's important 'Corpse Book,' from an air raid on 7 February 1945. Additionally, there were many Gestapo executions that took place secretly and the report indicates these individuals were buried immediately and thus did not arrive at the Anatomy Institute.[6]

Registration of Persons Executed in Vienna 1938-1945

Since the research project was hampered by the destruction of records, they had to rely on many diverse sources with lists that were incomplete. Therefore, the number of executed individuals, sent to the Anatomy Institute is likely to be higher. Of the **1377 persons executed**, at least half were executed for crimes of resistance and disobedience towards the Nazi regime. The justice system under the Nazis was disproportionately severe, with the death penalty for slaughter of animals, black-market trading, listening to enemy broadcasts, and petty theft crimes. These were considered crimes of high treason, resulting in a very high rate of execution.[73] Simply put, any conversation in which one expressed a pessimistic view of the progress of the war (e.g. German army's failures in North Africa and the Soviet Union, allied bombings of German Cities), if reported to the Gestapo, would often result in arrest, a quick trip to the court, followed by immediate execution.[6]

Specimen Collections at the University of Vienna 1997-1998

The specimen collections at the Institute of Anatomy in which Nazi provenance could not be excluded were removed. There were **96 specimens** removed and were planned for burial in a 'grave of honor' provided by the City of Vienna. The investigation found no proof that the Anatomy Institute received bodies from the Mauthausen concentration camp complex. However, they reported that they had discovered circumstantial evidence that such deliveries were made to the Anatomy Department at the University in Graz.[6]

The University of Vienna Department of Histological Embryology had **98 specimens** fixed in formaldehyde, which originated from persons executed in the *Wiener Landesgericht.*[6]

The Department of Forensic Medicine at the University of Vienna had one skullcap.[6]

The Department of Neurology of the University of Vienna had **6 specimens** fixed in formaldehyde as well as histological slides. These specimens were donated by Dr. Heinrich Gross and were brain specimens of children who had been executed as part of the Nazi regime's euthanasia program at the Psychiatric Hospital, Am Spiegelrund, in Vienna. Although Gross donated the specimens between 1953 and 1957, they were in the collections of the University of Vienna Department of Neurology.[6] The results of this investigation were soon to have a significant impact on Dr. Gross, who would eventually be put on trial for murder.

The Department of Medical History of the University of Vienna had **2 specimens** fixed in formaldehyde, **1 skeleton** and **100 histological slides.**[6]

All specimens in which a Nazi origin could not be excluded were to be removed from the University collections and eventually given a proper burial.[6]

Eduard Pernkokpf's Atlas of Topographical Human Anatomy

The research project confirmed the Nazi sympathies of the artist Lepier, who signed his name to anatomical paintings with a swastika. However, they did not conclude that the artists Endtresser and Batke signed their names with an 'SS' that can conclusively be interpreted as a sign of Nazi sympathies.[6]

The investigation report indicated that they were not able to prove or disprove suspicions that there were Jewish victims depicted in the atlas. The report also indicates that the illustrations of cadavers with short hair, cachectic figures or a circumcision were based on bodies 'from concentration camps, possibly from victims of Jewish faith, could not be confirmed.' The report adds that the 'possibility that bodies from concentration camps were given to the University Department of Anatomy can, as indicated above, almost certainly be excluded.'[6]

Other Austrian Institutions

The investigation discovered connections between the Anatomy Institute and other institutions in Vienna. Archival research showed an association between Pernkopf and the Vienna Museum of Natural History as well as the Psychiatric HospitalAm Spiegelgrund, which had an active child euthanasia program. The project report indicated that they would be supportive of further investigative research to be performed at these other institutions.[6]

The report also indicates that the investigation did not include the Universities of Graz or Innsbruck, and that these institutions 'have the machinery and the competence to investigate their own histories.'

Most important, the report concludes:

'It is, therefore, at least probable that many of the illustrations were indeed made on the basis of anatomical specimens derived from Nazi victims.'[6]

Dr. Heinrich Gross - Psychiatrist

In 1998 there was intense public interest in the brain specimens donated to the University of Vienna by Dr. Heinrich Gross from 1953 to 1957. In 1941 Gross, was a physician at the Vienna Psychiatric Hospital Am Spiegelgrund, a designated euthanasia center. He was trained in the techniques of euthanasia and following this, 336 children died under his care. After serving in the military Gross returned to the Am Spiegelgrund after the war. Gross published articles (1952) on histopathology based on the brain specimens of 'euthanized' children that had been stored for years after the war. He gave some of his brain specimens to the Department of Neurology at the University of Vienna. Gross had become a respected and highly decorated neuropsychologist and forensic expert, who was awarded the prestigious Austrian Honorary Cross for Science and Art in 1975. Following the discovery of further documentary evidence in 1999, Gross was charged with murder associated with deaths of children at Am Spiegelgrund between 1941-43. The case against Gross was suspended by the judge, due to a psychiatric expert indicating that he had dementia. In 2003 Gross was stripped of the Austrian Honorary Cross for Science & Art Medal. Dr Heinrich Gross passed away at the ripe old age of 90, never having received punishment for his crimes.[6,7,8,9,10]

Comment

The preceding pages which summarize the results of the University of Vienna's investigation felt like a triumphant result, especially at that time. The University of Vienna, under the leadership of Rector Ebenbauer and the individuals on the investigations committee were able to acknowledge its dark past under the Nazi regime when medical ethics was lost and doctors became perpetrators of unthinkable crimes in total violation of their Hippocratic Oath. The University of Vienna, as well as Austria, were beginning to acknowledge its complicity in Nazi crimes rather than bury it. That was twenty-seven years ago, and as I re-read this report today, and review all of the files I have accumulated, I am left with further questions and thoughts. Having reviewed my interactions with Dr. George Hindels, Dr. Gertrude Schneider and after reading Gedye's *Fallen Bastions,* I am forced to ask more questions:

What is the definition of a Nazi victim? There were many people in Vienna who were so terrorized they decided to commit suicide to avoid the torture and atrocities of the Gestapo. Shouldn't they be considered Nazi victims? If the bodies of families committing suicide are taken by a cart and delivered to the Anatomy Institute, as witnessed by Gedye[11] should these individuals be counted amongst those of executed Nazi victims, even though they did not originate from the *Wiener*

Landesgericht? It has been well documented that there were a substantial number of suicides in Vienna after the Anschluss. Jews who were not able to leave Austria purchased poisons to provide them with the option of suicide, before being arrested by the Gestapo, followed by a certain death, as witnessed by Gedye.[11] Aside from the differences between the massive scale of executions in the concentration camps, compared to the *Wiener Landesgericht*, they were both institutions of Nazi terror designed to execute 'the unfit.'

Regardless of these questions, the Senatorial Project of the University of Vienna essentially fulfilled most of our initial requests as indicated in the Yad Vashem letters. The published conclusions and results of the investigation were:

1. The illustrations in the Pernkopf Atlas included anatomical illustrations that were from cadavers of executed Nazi victims.
2. The specimens in the collections of the University of Vienna in 1997 and 1998 in which the possibility or probability having originated from Nazi victims, were removed and planned for an honorable and dignified burial.
3. The University of Vienna acknowledged and apologized for the unethical practices that occurred between 1938 and 1945 at the Institute of Anatomy and other departments. Additionally, they publicly indicated their regret in the delay in the investigation and the previous denials of its Nazi past.
4. The University of Vienna provided medical school libraries with an acknowledgement of the Nazi origins of the Pernkopf Atlas, to be inserted as an additional forward for users of the book.

Unfortunately, the issues raised regarding the origins and grossly insensitive mishandling of anatomical specimens from the Nazi era did not include investigations from the Universities of Innsbruck, Graz or other academic institutions in Austria.

The questions related to the potential origin of specimens from individuals of the Jewish faith that may have been sent to the Anatomy Institute and possibly been illustrated in the Pernkopf Atlas, were never resolved. The archives did reveal that Pernkopf had requested the delivery of corpses from executions in Poland, which were denied by the Berlin authorities. To be clear, Pernkopf wanted to get bodies from the massive numbers of executions taking place in Poland, but apparently the cost of the transportation of the corpses resulted in the denial of his request. The report of the investigation indicated that the evidence provided regarding the potential use of Jewish bodies at the Anatomy Institute was circumstantial. A main point that needs to be emphasized is that determination of the presence of Jewish remains is based primarily on the importance of proper handling of mortal remains under Jewish law. However, the primary bioethical issues that we raised were based on the abuse of Nazi victims, regardless of their religious faith, with appropriate acknowledgment and commemoration of their sacrifice. All of the executed Nazi victims had the same human anatomical structures, whether Jewish or not.

A member of the senatorial research project, Dr. Daniela Angetter, authored a summary of the findings of the investigative committee in the 22 April 2000 issue of *The Lancet*.[12] In response to this paper, there were some minor criticisms of inaccuracies and omissions that were subsequently published.[10,13] Apparently there was a 1500 word limit imposed on the author and it is probable that this contributed to some important findings of the investigation which had been left out of Angetter's article.

Upon completion of the investigative report, all specimens of suspected Nazi provenance that had been collected were removed from use for teaching and research purposes at the University of Vienna. These specimens were then stored in coffins located in the basement of the Anatomy Institute, where five decades previously, stacked corpses from executed victims of the Nazis had been stored. On 22 March 2002, the specimens of suspected Nazi provenance from the University of Vienna were given a dignified burial in a 'grave of honor' in the Vienna Central Cemetery. In attendance at the memorial service were an interdenominational group of clergy, including the Chief Rabbi of Vienna. Since it was determined that some of the mortal remains may have come from Jewish victims, the burial took place in the Jewish section of the cemetery (Figure 11).

Following the completion of the Senatorial Project's investigation, the University of Vienna became a leader in confronting the role of academic institutions during the Third Reich in the implementation of the National Socialist agenda through the medical professions. Dr. Karl Holubar from the Department of Medical History of the University of

Figure 11. Burial of anatomical specimens of suspected Nazi provenance from the University of Vienna. An interdenominational group of clergy and others honored the victims in the Jewish Section of the City of Vienna's Central Cemetery, 22 March 2002. With permission. Photo by Ronald Zak/Associated Press.

Vienna sent me program information for two symposia that were scheduled. The program titled 'A Period of Darkness, The University of Vienna's Medical School and the Nazi Regime'[14] was conducted under the auspices of the Federal Chancellor and the Minister of Science and Research of the Republic of Austria and organized by the World Congresses of Gastroenterology. This conference took place on 6 September 1998 at the Society of Physicians in Vienna. Following the program, a memorial plaque in the courtyard of the main building of the University of Vienna was unveiled, which read:

> *In commemoration of the teachers and students of the Medical Faculty of the University of Vienna, who were persecuted, exiled, murdered during the Nazi regime for 'racial' or political reasons. In acknowledgment of shared responsibility, dedicated by the Faculty of Medicine, 1998.*

On 7-8 October 1999 the University of Vienna conducted an International Symposium titled 'Doctors Under Scrutiny.' Dr. William Seidelman was the invited keynote speaker and delivered his presentation titled 'Academia Under Scrutiny: An Agenda for the Next Century.'[15] The official program for this symposium had a finding which sparked my curiosity. Dr. Wolfgang Greisenegger was listed as the Rector of the University of Vienna, with Dr. Alfred Ebenbauer being listed below him as the Vice-Rector. Professor Ebenbauer's tragic death by suicide in August 2007 really shocked me with the loss of this courageous great man.[16,17]

Overall, the University of Vienna's research project 'Investigations of Anatomical Science in Vienna 1938–1945' must be considered a defining event in the documentation of the exploitation of the bodies of Nazi victims that routinely took place at universities and other institutions throughout the reign of the Third Reich in Europe. Much gratitude is deserved for the individuals on the research project of the University of Vienna twenty-six years ago. They performed an excellent investigation hampered with many obstacles in their quest to discover the truth. Their investigation represented an important change in emphasis from denial of the past to confrontation and recognition of the truth of the complicity of academic institutions and medicine in crimes against humanity during the dark era of the Nazi regime. Ultimately, the investigations of the Universities of Tübingen and Vienna uncovering the truth of their use and abuse of the mortal remains of Nazi victims in the past, helped lead to many changes with renewed emphasis on the importance of bioethics in medical education which continues today. And, as with any groundbreaking research investigation, more questions are raised stimulating more research.

Twenty-six years following the University of Vienna's Senatorial report on the anatomical sciences, more revelations regarding the origins of the corpses appearing in the Pernkopf Atlas illustrations have been uncovered. The report indicated that the Anatomy Institute received 3964 unclaimed bodies of adults from public institutions in addition to 1377 bodies of executed victims. A 2024 article by Hildebrandt and Krebs 'From body image – Pernkopf's anatomical gaze and eyewitness accounts on the process of creating images from Nazi victims' bodies,'[18] emphasizes the legacy of the atlas reflecting a medical gaze with erasure of the humanity and individuality of the victims, authoritarianism, domination, scientific ambition, systemic violence and dehumanization. Of the many corpses that were obtained by the Anatomy Institute, those obtained from executions were prime specimens for the atlas, since these represented younger, healthier and fresher specimens that were ideal for anatomical illustrations. Furthermore, the estimated 400 illustrations that appeared in the atlas created during the Nazi period required many more than 400 corpses. Each individual anatomical illustration was based on several bodies or body parts. These anatomical specimens were maintained in the morgue of the Anatomy Institute until the 1960s. Therefore, the 1963 edition of Pernkopf's Atlas that I had used, depicting the anatomy of younger and healthier persons, is very likely to be based on executed victims. The tragedy and dehumanization of this approach, combined with concealment by the editors and publishers represent ethical transgressions that are beyond comprehension.

Notes

1. University of Vienna Press Conference regarding the origins of 'Topographic Human Anatomy' by Eduard Pernkopf' announcing the research project initiated for this purpose 'Investigations into the Anatomical Science at the University of Vienna 1938-1945.' 12 February 1997.
2. A. Ebenbauer, Letter to Professor Howard Israel, Columbia University with attached documents from August 1997 titled 'Information for the Users of the Pernkopf-Atlas.' 24 September 24 1997.
3. University of Vienna. Document titled 'Information for Users of the Pernkopf Atlas.' August 1997.
4. A. Ebenbauer, W. Schutz. 'Origins of the Pernkopf Anatomy Atlas - In Reply,' *JAMA*, 277, 14, (1997). p.1122.
5. P. Malina, 'Eduard Pernkopf's atlas of anatomy or: The fiction of pure science,' *Wien Kinische Wochenschrift*, 109, (1997), pp. 935-201.
6. G. Spann, et. al., 'Investigations of Anatomical Science in Vienna - Results of the Senate Project of the University of Vienna,' B. Matouschek Editor (November 1998), pp 1-12.
7. W. Seidelman, 'Dissecting the History of Anatomy in the Third Reich – 1989-2010: A Personal Account,' *Annals of Anatomy*, 194 (2012), pp. 228-36.
8. S. Hildebrandt, *The Anatomy of Murder – Ethical Transgressions and Anatomical Science During the Third Reich*, (New York and Oxford: Berghahn Books 2016), pp.1-327.

9. W. Seidelman, 'From the Danube to the Spree: Deception, Truth and Morality in Medicine,' Documentation Archive of the Austrian Resistance (ed.), Vienna. *Yearbook* (1999), pp.15-32.
10. M. Hubenstorf, 'Anatomical science in Vienna, 1938-45 (Commentary),' *Lancet*, 355 (2000), pp. 1385-6.
11. G.E.R. Gedye, *Fallen Bastions, The Central European Tragedy*, (London: LTD Publisher, 1939).
12. D.C. Angetter, 'Anatomical science at University of Vienna 1938-45,' *Lancet*, 355 (2000), pp. 1454-57.
13. W. Seidelman, H. Israel, 'Anatomy in Vienna,' *Lancet*, 356, (2000), p.343.
14. Symposium Program. 'A Period of Darkness: The University of Vienna's Medical School and the Nazi Regime,' World Congresses of Gastroenterology, Society of Physicians, Vienna, Austria, 6 September 1998.
15. W. Seidelman, 'Academia Under Scrutiny: An Agenda for the Next Century' presented at Symposium 'Doctors Under Scrutiny,' The University of Vienna, 7-8 October 1999.
16. Symposium Program. 'Doctors Under Scrutiny,' The University of Vienna, 7-8 October 1999.
17. Alfred Ebenbauer, 1945-2007 o. Univ.-Prof. Dr. phil, University of Vienna. https://geschichte.univie.ac.at/en/persons/alfred-ebenbauer
18. S. Hildebrandt, C. Krebs, 'From body image – Pernkopf's anatomical gaze and eyewitness accounts on the process of creating images from Nazi victims'bodies,' *Anat Sci Educ*, 18, 3 (2025), pp.277-288. https://doi.org/10.1002/ase.70001

11

A Surreal Trip to Vienna 2005

Following the memorialization of Nazi victims and burial of specimen collections of the University of Vienna in 2002, my personal involvement and activities in this arena slowed down considerably. There continued to be public interest in the Pernkopf controversy, with articles in magazines, newspapers and professional journals.

I continued to remain in close contact with Bill Seidelman, mostly through e-mail correspondence who would keep me updated on progress related to these matters, such as those involving the Museum of Natural History in Vienna and the unveiling of a sculptured bust honoring Dr. Herman Stieve at the Charite Hospital in Berlin. Stieve was the anatomist at the University of Berlin during the Nazi era who conducted and published research on the effect of stress on female reproductive organs from women who were imprisoned or scheduled for execution. Dr. Seidelman always provided me the latest information on the continued crusade for exposure of the complicity of academic institutions and medicine during the Nazi era. However, my intense involvement in this arena returned when I submitted an outline for a presentation at the 2005 International Conference of Oral & Maxillofacial Surgeons (ICOMS) Annual Meeting, titled 'The Nazi Origins of Pernkopf's Atlas of Topographic and Applied Human Anatomy: A Lesson in Biomedical Ethics' on the relevant and disturbing issues raised by the Pernkopf Atlas.[1] The ICOMS conference executive committee and the Rector of the University of Vienna were informed, and my presentation on the Pernkopf Atlas was accepted for the 2005 meeting. I should also mention that the meeting was to be held in, of all places, Vienna Austria. This is where the events involving the creation of the anatomy atlas took place. I was going to enter the 'Wolf's Lair.'

The presentation took place in September 2005 in a jam-packed auditorium filled with an international group of fellow oral and maxillofacial surgeons who were unknown to me. The presentation recounting the events of 1994 to 2002 leading to the investigation by the

University of Vienna up to the burial of specimens were revealed for the first time to the great majority of attendees, and to just a few perhaps retold. My impression from the reactions and questions of the audience was that the presentation was well received, and that this had been the first these colleagues had heard of the bioethical issues raised by this famous anatomy atlas. Before I exited the lecture room, a contingent of oral and maxillofacial surgeons from Israel came up to me and indicated that they had used the Pernkopf Atlas all the time in preparation for their surgical procedures. They were shocked to learn, as I had been in 1994, of the Nazi origins of the creation of this 'masterpiece' anatomy book. With great irony, oral and maxillofacial surgeons from Israel had no idea that they were preparing for their surgeries using an anatomy atlas created by Nazis and depicting their executed victims. It had already been seven years since the University of Vienna's investigation and report revealing that Pernkopf had used Nazi victims as cadavers. The Israeli oral and maxillofacial surgeons were unsuspecting users of the atlas, just as I had been for 20 years.

After I left the lecture hall, I noticed that there was a large crowd around one of the more elderly, but elegantly dressed, oral and maxillofacial surgeons. Who was this doctor with a captive audience, surrounded by admiring surgeons asking him questions or just feeling honored to shake his hand? This was one of the most famous and influential oral and maxillofacial surgeons in the history of our specialty. He had developed many innovative surgical procedures and taught oral and maxillofacial surgeons throughout the world these new techniques that had a tremendous positive impact on the lives of so many patients. As fate would have it, I was in the presence of a famous professor whose name I shall keep anonymous, 'Professor Z,' who I found out many years later, had been a member of the Nazi party in the early years of his career. There is no suggestion here, nor is there any documentation that he did anything other than treat patients to the best of his abilities throughout his entire life. Retrospectively, I do find it quite a coincidence that I met him at that international conference in Vienna, following my presentation on the legacy of the Pernkopf Atlas. Interestingly, the mention of 'Professor Z' would come up later in this journey, in an unexpected way.

The old cliché 'a picture is worth a thousand words' is the most accurate and authentic way to describe the incredible story of my trip to Vienna. Was it some incomprehensible force, a divine intervention perhaps, an inevitable destiny, 'bashert,' that was to guide my legs exposing me to significant historical sites in Vienna in September 2005? This travel log of my surreal journey through the streets of Vienna which follows will tell the story.

Vienna is truly a beautiful city with old world charm, filled with gardens, flowers, music that can be heard as people stroll along the cobblestone streets. The ICOMS meeting was held in the Hofburg Palace that today serves as a museum and cultural center for conferences, events and concerts. The Hofburg Palace was built in the 13th century which served as the imperial palace of the powerful Habsburg dynasty that ruled Austria for many years. As my bus approached the palace, I noticed that the center of the palace had a large sign when translated was 'The Victims of National Socialism.' Apparently, the central wing of the palace had a museum exhibit focused on the evil history of Nazism in Austria. I was shocked, to discover that there was a significant change in the attitudes of the leadership in Austria to confront its past, not as victims, but as a country that had embraced National Socialism's ideology and were perpetrators of Nazi crimes. The Hofburg Palace faces the *Volksgarten* (Figure 12), a beautiful park with gardens and horse drawn carriages.

I did not know any of the oral and maxillofacial surgeons at this international conference and I decided that since this beautiful city was not like anything I had ever seen, I would tour the city by jogging through the streets of Vienna. This was going to be a haunting jogging tour to burn off those calories from Vienna's delicious pastry shops and to take some time off from my routine hectic schedule, relax and give myself a treat.

The reader may recall that the German anatomist, Professor Herman Voss sold death masks and skulls of Jewish victims to the Vienna Museum of Natural History as 'Jewish artifacts' for their 'racial gallery' collection during the Nazi era. The Jews were soon to be an extinct race. I was really enjoying myself on this beautiful day until I became aware of the contrast between my surroundings, and the truth about what really happened here more than six decades prior to my 2005 visit (Figure 12).

The next arbitrary stop on my random jogging tour miraculously found me in front of the campus of the Medical School of the University

Figure 12. The Museum of Natural History of Vienna, *Volksgarten* park gardens in the foreground 2005. During the Nazi era German anatomist, Professor Herman Voss sold death masks and skulls of Jewish victims to the Museum as 'Jewish artifacts' for their 'racial gallery collection,' depicting Jews as a soon to be extinct race. Photograph taken by H. Israel.

of Vienna. Before 1938, this prestigious institution had reached the pinnacle of academic medicine, serving as the model for medical education and research throughout the world. The campus was very open and quiet with few people around and unlike today, there was no security at the entrance. As I began to jog through the entrance, just being curious, I noticed a campus map to my right. This showed the location of the various buildings housing the basic and clinical sciences. To my astonishment, there was a building on this map labelled 'synagogue.' What was a synagogue doing on this campus? Now my curiosity had greatly heightened as my jogging legs directed me to this structure which had recently been built.

On the sidewalk in front of this monument were words commemorating the victims of the Nazis, written in German, Hebrew and English. As I investigated further, a memorial plaque revealed there had been a sacred Jewish prayer room in front of the entrance to the hospital, which had been destroyed by the Nazis in 1938, along with all of the Jewish houses of worship that were free standing buildings. This structure was a monument to commemorate the Jewish victims of the

Nazis in Austria and had been labelled on the campus map as a synagogue. I was shocked to see this memorial building, but I was glad to find active efforts to confront the complicity of Austria during the Third Reich and to commemorate the victims (Figure 13).

As I was staring at the memorial prayer room, and the inscriptions on the sidewalk, I turned my head to the building immediately to the left, just a few yards away from the new monument. Incredibly, the Jewish 'synagogue' memorial building stood just to the right of the building for Oral Surgery. Here I was, an oral surgeon, standing between a memorial to Nazi victims on the right, and the building for Oral Surgery immediately to the left, on the campus of the University of Vienna Medical School, which had been the center of the controversies and investigations into the Pernkopf Atlas. I was shaken by this coincidence, but my jogging feet were obliged to take me to my next random stop, just a few blocks away.

The local district court of Vienna, *Wiener Landesgericht*, was not like any court building I have seen in the US (Figure 14). This immense structure appeared like a fortress, encompassing an entire city block. This is the building where innocent victims were sentenced to death or sent to concentration camps for the most innocent of infractions, but

Figure 13. University of Vienna Medical School 2005. Top right, Jewish memorial prayer room. Bottom right, inscription on sidewalk memorializing the victims of the Nazi regime. Top left, the Oral Surgery Clinic building. Photographs taken by H. Israel.

according to the Nazi system of justice required harsh punishment and often execution by guillotine (Figure 9).

I noticed that although the building was massive, the sign on the main entrance was very small, and disproportionate to this massive complex.

It was extremely hot on that day, and I had forgotten to take water to replace my fluid needs, so the next stop on my random jogging journey was purposeful, to find a place to get a cold drink as close by as possible. Once I relieved my thirst purchasing a refreshing ice-cold drink at a shop across the street from the *Wiener Landesgericht*, I resumed my random jog. Within a few minutes I found myself immediately in front of the Institute of Anatomy of the Medical School of the University of Vienna. This was where Pernkopf did his work with dissection of corpses, artists painting anatomic pictures and the creation of his 'masterpiece' atlas (Figure 15).

As one ascends the stairs of the Anatomy Institute, a statue of Galenus can be seen in the center of the lobby. Galenus (born 129 C.E. – died 216 C.E.) was a Greek physician, anatomist and philosopher who revered

Figure 14. The *Wiener Landesgericht*, Vienna District Court 2005. During the Nazi era many people were sentenced to death by the guillotine in the basement. The human bodies of young, healthy individuals served as a source for dissections and illustrations by Pernkopf's artists for the anatomy atlas. Photograph by H. Israel.

Hippocrates the father of medicine and author of the ethical responsibilities of the healing professions, the Hippocratic Oath. Galenus believed that anatomy was the foundation of medical knowledge and became famous for his public demonstrations of anatomy. Ironically, his dissections were of animals, as he was not permitted to perform dissections on human beings.[2] Once I reached the top of the steps I noticed the distinct smell of formaldehyde and discovered the anatomy dissection rooms. Was this where Pernkopf had the corpses of executed Nazi victims dissected for teaching purposes as well as for inclusion in the atlas he was creating? As I left the building, I looked back toward the rear portion of the Anatomy Institute, which revealed a tall smokestack. This was an appropriate symbol which left a lasting impression for me, as I recalled the use of ovens in Nazi concentration camps.

I jogged back toward the front of the anatomy building as there was a store across the street with a familiar name that caught my eye. This was the Urban and Schwarzenberg medical bookstore. Urban and Schwarzenberg was the original publisher of Pernkopf's Atlas and I could not resist going into the bookstore to see which anatomy atlases they were selling to students (Figure 16). The main part of the bookstore had many anatomy books, but Pernkopf's was nowhere in sight. I was about to leave when I saw a small sign with an arrow pointing to their antique book collection. On the main shelf were twelve assorted volumes of the German language1943 edition of Pernkopf's Atlas. The cost of these antique volumes was rather high, each book being well over 100 Euros, with the exception of one book. For some reason, this volume, which was in good condition sold for only fifty Euros, and since Mindy had purchased my original 1963 English language edition as a gift in 1973 for fifty US dollars, I felt compelled to purchase this one book.

Following this day of random jogging, I returned to my hotel room, both physically and emotionally drained. I contemplated what I had seen with my eyes and my ability to comprehend what had taken place in those very same buildings I had entered over six decades earlier. A person who had lived in Vienna during the years 1938–45 who had been reported to have made a remark construed to represent anti-Nazi sentiment, communist loyalties, Austrian resistance sympathies, homosexual orientation or just happened to have a certain percentage of 'inferior genetics', or Jewish heritage would be picked up by the Gestapo police, sent to the *Wiener Landesgericht* where the Nazi justice

Figure 15. The Anatomy Institute of the University of Vienna 2005. Top left is the street entrance, top right is the statue of Galenus in the lobby. Bottom right is the rear of the Anatomy Institute building. Photographs by H. Israel, with the exception of the bottom left showing a recent picture of a dissection room, photograph courtesy of Dr. Wolfgang Weninger, Anatomy Institute, Medical University of Vienna.

system would commonly sentence that individual to death by guillotine in the basement of the building. After one's head was chopped off, the mortal remains were carted a few blocks away to the Anatomy Institute, where Pernkokpf's artists would create 'masterpiece' anatomical paintings, which would ultimately be published in a book from the publisher, Urban and Schwarzenberg, located across the street. The factory-like production of Pernkopf's 'masterpiece' took place within just a few square blocks.

Figure 16. Urban & Schwarzenberg medical bookstore across the street from the entrance of the Anatomy Institute of the University of Vienna 2005. Copies of the 1943 edition of the Pernkopf Atlas were on the shelf in the antique book section of the store. The *Wiener Landesgericht*, Anatomy Institute and Urban and Schwarzenberg were all within a few square blocks, facilitating the creation of the 'masterpiece'. Pernkopf's Atlas of Anatomy. Photographs by H. Israel.

Needing a mental break from this first day of jogging, I decided to choose certain destinations that were of particular interest to me on the next day. I recalled that my fellow Temple member and friend, Kurt Kellman, who was of immense help with translation of German language documents, had attended the Seitenstettengasse Temple for his Bar Mitzvah studies. I found out that this Temple still existed, so that was my first destination on the following day. The security for entering this building was extremely tight, and I recall being interviewed by a young security guard who was steely eyed and stared into my face. Once I had passed through security, I was inside a magnificent sanctuary which was surprising, since this this Temple was essentially an interior space which was housed within a large gray granite building complex. The only external clue that there was a Jewish house of worship inside was the Hebrew lettering above the door to the entrance of the Temple.

Once inside the sanctuary I sat down and listened to a fascinating twenty-minute presentation given by a tour guide on the history of the Jews of Vienna. He retold the history of a repeating cycle where Jewish people would flourish, contribute to society and be well accepted, followed by other periods where antisemitism prevailed, resulting in expulsion or execution. Apparently the Seitenstettengasse Temple was constructed in the early part of the nineteenth century at a time when

Figure 17. The Seitenstettengasse Temple 2005, the only synagogue in Vienna that survived destruction by the Nazis. Photographs by H. Israel.

Jews were tolerated, but not well accepted. As a result, this synagogue was built within a large building complex with minimal exposure to passersby outside, essentially unrecognized by most as a Jewish house of worship. Toward the mid to latter part of the nineteenth century and the beginning of the twentieth century the Jewish community flourished and became an important part of the culture and scientific excellence that Vienna had been known for. Sigmund Freud (psychiatry), Gustav Mahler (composer, conductor, pianist) and Theodor Herzl (considered the visionary behind modern Zionism) are just of few of the giants from that era who have had a monumental influence on the world, lived in Vienna at that time. As antisemitism increased in the 1930s with increasing power and influence of National Socialism, Jews were forced to leave Vienna in large numbers or stay and be subject to deportations to concentration camps or extermination. All of the magnificent, opulent synagogue buildings in Vienna were destroyed by the Nazis, except for one. The Seitenstettengasse Temple could not be destroyed, or burned to the ground, because it had been built within this huge building complex. This Temple survived because of the repression and antisemitism that had existed when it had been constructed, to be hidden from the outside world. When the guide finished his presentation, I marveled at the beauty of the inside of this temple with all of the walls lined by hundreds, maybe thousands of memorial plaques. I decided to view these memorials on the wall more closely, but my eyes could not get past the first one I read. Immediately to the left of my seat was the memorial for 'Chaim Ben Israel,' which happens to

Figure 18. The memorial plaque of Chaim and Chana Ben Israel, one of the many memorial plaques surrounding the sanctuary at the Seitenstettengasse Temple, 2005. Photograph by H. Israel.

be my name in the Hebrew language (Figure 18). Was this just another haunting coincidence, random event, or just 'bashert?'

From that point on, I assumed that anything that I would label as a random event through the streets of Vienna was somehow, just meant to be.

My next stop was the Judenplatz, which had been a center of the Jewish community in Vienna before the Anschluss. I entered the Jewish Museum which housed many exhibits including further details of the history of the Jewish people in Vienna. I learned that there had been an influx of Jews to Vienna in 1360, which resulted in the expansion of their temple building. The Jewish community flourished until 1421, when the synagogue was demolished under the orders of Duke Albrecht V, along with extermination of the Jews. The exhibit showed a model of the synagogue that had been destroyed and noted that some of the stones from that temple were used in the construction of the Vienna University. I find this quite fascinating since this was the same institution where Pernkopf had purged the Jewish faculty and used executed corpses of Nazi victims for his atlas. The foundation of the University of Vienna included stones from a synagogue! Incredible.

In the center of the Judenplatz is a Holocaust memorial, which provides the names of the many concentration camps where mass exterminations had taken place (Figure 19). This memorial stands above the remains of the synagogue that had been destroyed in 1421.

Figure 19. The Holocaust Memorial in the center of the Judenplatz, Vienna 2005. The memorial was built above the remains of the Viennese synagogue of a flourishing Jewish community, destroyed in 1421 due to a wave of antisemitism. Stones from the demolished synagogue were used in the construction of the University of Vienna. Photograph by H. Israel.

There is plaque on a wall facing the Holocaust memorial. The words on the plaque revealed an Austria that had changed dramatically since the 1990s acknowledging its history of antisemitism from the Middle Ages through many centuries leading to exterminations during the era of National Socialism. Inscribed on this plaque were the following words:

> *"Kiddusch HaSchem" means "Sanctification of G-d." With this awareness, Jews of Vienna in the synagogue here on Judenpatz-the center of a significant Jewish community-chose a voluntary death at the time of persecution of 1420/21, in order to escape the forced baptism they feared. Others, about 200, were burned alive at a stake in Erdberg.*
>
> *Christian preachers at that time spread superstitious anti-Jewish ideas and agitated against Jews and their faith. Under this influence Christians in Vienna accepted the crime without resistance, they approved it and became perpetrators. In this way, the destruction*

of the Viennese "Jewish City" in 1421 was already threatening concern for the events that took place in all of Europe at the time of the National Socialist tyranny.

Medieval popes turned without success against this anti-Jewish superstition, and individual believers fought in vain against the racial hatred of the National Socialists. They were too few.

Today, Christianity regrets its share in responsibility for the persecution of Jews and realizes its failure. For Christians today, "Sanctification of God" can only mean asking for forgiveness and hoping in God's saving action.

Perhaps the main lesson to be learned from my stay in Vienna was, indeed, history does repeat itself. This is something to keep in the forefront of our minds when we contemplate the future.

Throughout the city of Vienna, there were numerous indications that a new generation of Austrians were determined to acknowledge the past and attempt to repent for the sins of those from previous

Figure 20. Memorial sculpture of a bearded elderly Jewish man scrubbing the cobblestone streets of Vienna. © Werner Spremberg/Shutterstock.

Figure 21. Sigmund Freud's office at Bergasse 19, in the Alsergund district of Vienna, 2005. The Sigmund Freud Museum is at this location. Above left, Freud's waiting room, photograph by H. Israel. Photograph on right ©Science Source.

generations. My random tour throughout the city was clear evidence of this. I discovered a massive sculpture in the center of a main square. The 'Memorial Against War and Fascism' is a reminder of Austria's Nazi past and one can see a hypodermic syringe being injected into an emaciated Holocaust victim. Just behind this massive sculpture is a monument of a bearded elderly Jewish man, restrained by barbed wire scrubbing the cobblestone street revealing true events that occurred there (Figure 20). After the Anschluss, this was a common 'entertaining' scene with enthusiastic local Nazi supporters as smiling onlookers.

The last monument that I had passed in 2005 further demonstrated Austria's acknowledgement and desire for atonement, having been active participants in support of the Nazi regime. There was a stone memorial in front of an empty green lawn. The heading of the memorial indicated 'Never Forget' and marked the location of the Gestapo headquarters in Vienna.

Following this random jogging tour of the city of Vienna, I realized that I had seen first-hand so many sites that had great significance which reflected this dark epoch in Austria's history. I was in awe of what I had seen, particularly as it related to the reason why I was in Vienna. Being emotionally drained and totally exhausted, it was time for a 'mental hygiene' session. Thus, I needed to see a 'shrink.' I found ***his*** office, but the waiting room was empty and so it was time to end the jogging tour, leave Vienna and return home (Figure 21).

Notes

1. H. Israel, 'The Nazi Origins of Pernkopf's Atlas of Topographic and Applied Human Anatomy: A Lesson in Biomedical Ethics.' 17th Annual International Conference of Oral & Maxillofacial Surgeons, Vienna, Austria, September 2005.
2. V. Nutton, 'Galen,' *Encyclopedia Britannica*, 11 April 2025. https://www.britannica.com/biography/Galen.

12

The Train Conductors – Dr. William Seidelman and Dr. Sabine Hildebrandt

The five decades immediately following the end of the Nazi regime were characterized by continual denial and obfuscation of the truth of complicity by the medical profession and institutions that had been under the Nazi regime. The cases of Hallervorden, Voss, Stieve, Gross and Hirt are just a few of the many examples where public exposure of their crimes revealed the true role of anatomists, physicians and academic institutions as active participants in horrific medical experiments and executions. Further detailed investigations of Nazi medicine which belatedly began three decades ago have continued, providing significant important lessons for the doctors of today and in the future. Often, the stimulus for an investigation would come from individuals who discovered a history that was ethically unacceptable, and after reporting individually, would be confronted by denials and maintenance of the status quo. However, over these past three decades I have been blessed to know and collaborate with two individuals whose passion for pursuing the truth, academic excellence and influence have encompassed most of the investigations, revelations and initiatives to date, Dr. William Seidelman and Dr. Sabine Hildebrandt.

Dr. Seidelman and Dr. Hildebrandt have each been a driving force, the 'conductors of a train,' that began decades ago. That train was, and continues to be headed for the truth, based on documentary and physical evidence, leading to appropriate investigations, memorialization of victims and changes in medical education to ensure the maintenance of bioethical principles. I feel quite fortunate to have been one of the passengers on that train. There have been many other individuals who have been 'train conductors' in the pursuit of historical truths and relevance of exposing the role of Nazi medicine as perpetrators of unethical experiments and murder. These scholarly 'train conductors' have also emphasized that the transgressions of the medical profession during the Third Reich are not unique in history, with human nature having the capacity to perform both good and evil acts. As leaders in this important field of study, they have provided directions for the future, and their scholarly works are referenced frequently in this writing. However, my personal experience, long-time collaboration and friendship with Drs. Seidelman and Hildebrandt warrant a further detailed reflection on the tremendous impact they have had on the importance of understanding this history and education in medical bioethics.

For over six decades Dr. Seidelman (Bill) has been providing insight into the dark history of Nazi medicine during the reign of the Third Reich and its continued influence on the medical profession. In a presentation he delivered at the Vienna Psychiatric Hospital Baumgartner Hohe in 1998, Bill recalled his family's Austro-Hungarian roots dating back to the 1850s and their eventual migration to North America. His grandfather and namesake, William Seidelman, was born in Budapest, and eventually settled in Vancouver, British Columbia. Bill's great uncle, Edward Joseph Seidelman served in the British army during the First World War and was killed in the October 1917 battle for Ypres, Belgium, and buried somewhere in an unknown grave. Lance Corporal Adolph Hitler also fought in the battle of Ypres as a soldier in the German army.[1]

Bill graduated from medical school at the University of British Columbia (UBC) in 1968 and practiced family medicine at McMaster University, Ontario Canada in the 1980s. He became interested in the history of the German medical profession of the 1930s, based on his review of publications in the *Journal of the American Medical Association* combined with his passion for justice. After meeting with Visiting Professor on the History of Medicine, Michael Kater at McMaster University, Bill became interested in studying the history of Professor Verschuer, head of genetics at the University of Münster in Germany after the Second World War, who had published on genetic research on twins. Dr. Verschuer was also the mentor for Dr. Josef Mengele, the infamous Nazi physician who became known as the 'Angel of Death' for his gruesome medical experiments on twins and other prisoners at the Auschwitz concentration camp. As Bill Seidelman studied the dark history of Nazi medicine, his interest and research increased significantly, with more global questions as to how doctors can ethically place different values on human life based on race, and whether data from Nazi medical experiments should be used. Dr. Seidelman's increasing interest and research in the 1980s included publications on the continued use of anatomical remains from Nazi victims in German medical schools and institutions, including the Universities of Tübingen, Heidelberg, Cologne and the Max Planck Institute of Brain Research.[2,3] Dr. Seidelman called for the commemoration of the victims, appropriate burial of the mortal remains and for the international medical community to confront the legacy of Nazi medicine and the potential for doctors to perform evil acts in the name of science.

Dr. Seidelman has undeniably been a major force in the pursuit of the truth leading to major investigations of the many doctors and institutions that were the perpetrators of Nazi crimes. This past tainted history of medicine under the Nazi regime had remained hidden and denied for many decades following the conclusion of the Second World War. I was so fortunate to have such a colleague and friend with the passion and persistence to collaborate with, in the pursuit of the true origins of the Pernkopf Atlas. Dr. Seidelman has developed many collaborative relationships over the years, which will ensure that the pursuit of the truth and the importance of medical bioethics education will continue in the future.

Dr. Seidelman, upon the occasion of the fiftieth reunion of the University of British Columbia Medical School class of 1968, recalled:[4]

> *Inspired by the UBC medical historian, Dr. Bill Gibson, I pursued medical history with a focus on medicine in Nazi Germany. I sort of fell into this not realizing what I was getting into. In reality I was poking my finger into a seething cauldron of secrets and lies carefully covered up by the universities and the academic and scientific elite. My questions were not well received and the work became increasingly engaging............Fortunately, a new generation of German and Austrian scholars is pursuing this subject to a degree that I could never have imagined.*

In 2006 Dr. Sabine Hildebrandt's article titled 'How the Pernkopf Controversy Facilitated a Historical and Ethical Analysis of the Anatomical Sciences in Austria and Germany: A Recommendation for the Continued Use of the Pernkopf Atlas' was published in the journal

Clinical Anatomy.[5] At that time, Dr. Hildebrandt held an academic position in the Division of Anatomical Sciences at the University of Michigan Medical School. This article was published at a time when a shift in attitudes had gradually occurred in Austrian and German medical schools and anatomy departments, that belatedly started four decades after the fall of the Nazi regime. Of great significance was the background of the author, Sabine Hildebrandt. Born and educated in Germany, she had lived through and experienced the post-Second World War environment that existed. Her early education introduced her to the facts of National Socialism and during her medical school studies at Philipps-Universität Marburg in the 1980s she became increasingly interested in the history of doctors during the Nazi era. Dr. Sabine Hildebrandt continued to absorb more knowledge of this hidden history upon reading the publications in the 1980s on investigations into the role of the medical profession and institutions as perpetrators of crimes based on National Socialist ideology. The conflict between the ethical principles of 'do no harm' that she learned in medical school and the reports of horrific crimes of Nazi doctors must have been overwhelming. Dr. Hildebrandt has written 'I felt drawn to this history, as I needed to know why the people I lived with had become part of a clearly atrocious past.'[6]

Dr. Hildebrandt moved to the US and obtained a faculty appointment at the University of Michigan, teaching anatomy to medical students. Following the investigation of the Anatomical Institute at the University of Vienna, and the significant media attention on Pernkopf and his atlas, a colleague anatomist asked Dr. Hildebrandt her opinions regarding the issues raised. This query by her anatomist colleague sent Dr. Hildebrandt on a 'quest for information.' She soon discovered that there was a detailed history with previously unexplored documents in German and Austrian archives that needed to be uncovered and studied, which held important lessons to be learned for medical professionals of the future. While many were proponents of banning the Pernkopf Atlas, Dr. Hildebrandt's landmark paper on the Pernkopf controversy in 2006 called for continued publication of the atlas as an historical document. She reasoned that continued use of the atlas would honor the victims and provide for education of physicians not only to further their knowledge of anatomy, but also serve as a guide for teaching ethics and history to medical professionals as an essential component of the education of healers of the future. Additionally, as an anatomist, Dr. Hildebrandt confirmed that the anatomical pictures in Pernkopf's Atlas are the very best in detail and accuracy and cannot simply be replaced. Banning the book or ending its publication would be tantamount to the burning of books and the suppression of knowledge and ideas that occurred under the Nazi regime.[5,6]

Following Dr. Hildebrandt's career path, she has become one of the world's most respected authorities on the history of anatomy and medicine in the Third Reich and emphasizes the relevance today, with the need to educate future health professionals. She has published extensively, given presentations throughout the world, and has authored the landmark book first published in 2016, *The Anatomy of Murder - Ethical Transgressions and Anatomical Science During the Third Reich,* a detailed scholarly account of the history of the many ethical transgressions that took place in the anatomical sciences under the Nazi regime.[6-10] She has been a driving force in the creation of *The Lancet* Commission on Medicine, Nazism and the Holocaust, convened by Lancet's Editor-In-Chief, Robert Horton in 2023.[11] Dr. Hildebrandt (Boston Children's Hospital, Harvard Medical School, Boston, Mass.) currently serves as the co-Chair of *The Lancet* Commission, along with Drs. Herwig Czech (University of Vienna, Austria) and Schmuel P. Reis (Hebrew University, Jerusalem, Israel). These leading scholars emphasize learning from the past to reinforce bioethical principals necessary for medical practice.

The importance of the educational component of this history cannot be overemphasized. One may consider that prior to the Nazi era, the academic medical institutions in Germany and Austria were considered the finest in the world. Numerous Nobel Laureates were produced as a result of the academic prowess of these institutions. The University of Vienna's medical faculty included four Nobel prize recipients: Robert Barany (1914), Julius Wagner-Jauregg (1927), Karl Landsteiner (1930) and Otto Loewi (1936).[12] The list of giants in the field of medicine from German and Austrian academic institutions is extensive and among these are Robert Koch, who discovered microbes as the basis for infection, Rudolph Virchow, a pioneer in cellular pathology, and Abraham Flexner, who innovated major changes in medical education. William Osler, a Canadian born physician, enhanced his medical education in Germany and Austria, studying in these great institutions, and ultimately became a pioneer in medical education in the United States, Europe and throughout the world. He established the system of medical training in residency programs with bedside teaching, making rounds on patients with doctors in training and emphasizing the importance in obtaining a detailed medical history from the patient. Osler became one of the founding members of the Johns Hopkins Hospital in Baltimore, establishing the first residency program for physicians in the US.[13]

The impact of the influence of Austrian and German medical institutions prior to the Nazi regime cannot be overstated. However, with the purge of faculty who would not pledge allegiance to Hitler, who were Jewish or non-Aryans, along with adopting the principals of racial hygiene as the scientific rationale for implementing policies of 'eliminating the unfit through sterilization and other means,' these former prestigious academic institutions fell into disgrace. The main point here is that if such a scientifically advanced society could reach the pinnacle of research and education in medicine and other related fields, and then fall into the depths of mass extermination of populations of people, what can prevent such historical events from repeating itself? Therefore, the repetition of genocide throughout world history, with the transgressions of medicine during the Nazi reign being an extreme example, must be investigated, studied, exposed, and taught to future generations to prevent the unthinkable potential for average people and intellectuals to become killers. These are major factors that have driven William Seidelman, Sabine Hildebrandt, and others to become powerful forces for ethical medicine and 'conductors of the train.'

Notes

1. W. Seidelman, 'Memory, Medicine, and Morality: The Meaning of the Exploitation of the Human Body in the Third Reich,' Presentation at Symposium: 'The History of Nazi Euthanasia in Vienna,' Vienna Psychiatric Hospital Baumgartner Hohe, 29-30 (January 1998).
2. W. Seidelman, 'In Memoriam: Medicine's Confrontation with Evil,' *Hastings Center Report*, (November/December 1989), pp5-6.
3. A. Silversides, 'Canadian MD Fights to Put Remains of Nazi Victims to Rest,' *Canadian Medical Association Journal*, 162, 11(2000), p.1648.
4. W. Seidelman, 'University of British Columbia Medicine Alumni, MD Class of 1968 – 50th Reunion,' (2018).

5. S. Hildebrandt, 'How the Pernkopf Controversy Facilitated a Historical and Ethical Analysis of the Anatomical Sciences in Austria and Germany: A Recommendation for the Continued Use of the Pernkopf Atlas,' *Clin. Anat.*, 19, (2006), pp. 91-100.
6. S. Hildebrandt, *The Anatomy of Murder - Ethical Transgressions and Anatomical Science During the Third Reich*, (New York and Oxford: Berghahn Books, 2016), pp: 1-4.
7. S. Hildebrandt, Anatomy in the Third Reich: An Outline. Part 1. National Socialists Politics, Anatomical Institutions and Anatomists. *Clin Anat.* 22, (2009), pp. 883-93.
8. S. Hildebrandt, 'Anatomy in the Third Reich: An Outline. Part 2. Bodies for Anatomy and Related Medical Disciplines,' *Clin Anat.* 22 (2009), pp. 894-905.
9. S. Hildebrandt, 'Anatomy in the Third Reich: An Outline. Part 3. The Science and Ethics of Anatomy in National Socialist Germany and Postwar Consequences,' *Clin Anat.* 22 (2009), pp. 906-15.
10. S. Hildebrandt, Letter in Response to Winkelmann and Schagen, Seidelman and Levi, 'Call for New Era in Research on "Medicine in the Third Reich." ' *Clin Anat*, 23 (2010) p. 124.
11. H. Czech, S. Hildebrandt, S.P. Reiss, et. al., 'The *Lancet* Commission on Medicine, Nazism, and the Holocaust: Historical Evidence, Implications for Today, Teaching for Tomorrow,' *Lancet* online, November 8, 2023.
12. E. Ernst, 'A Leading Medical School Seriously Damaged: Vienna 1938,' *Ann Intern Med*, 122, 10 (1995), pp.789- 92.
13. M. Bliss, *William Osler: A Life in Medicine*, (Oxford: Oxford University Press, 2007).

13

Medical Ethical Dilemmas Arising from the Nazi Atlas

The Development of the 'Vienna Protocol'

The decades following the revelations surrounding the Pernkopf Atlas were filled with many more investigations uncovering Nazi medical atrocities and the use of mortal remains and research data from that dark era. The essential questions of medical ethics which accompanied these revelations remained unanswered. Should medical information from Nazi atrocities be used? How should we deal with Holocaust era human remains? Complex issues surrounding this debate continue to this day and perhaps will never be adequately resolved for many. However, the pursuit for answers to these difficult questions remained and two decades following the University of Vienna's investigation of anatomical sciences during the Pernkopf era, The 'Vienna Protocol' was developed, providing guidance when dealing with these complex issues.

In 1982, a plastic surgeon who was in the midst of advanced fellowship training in neurosurgical research, peripheral nerve and hand surgery, discovered Pernkopf's Atlas as an anatomical resource that provided unparalleled details of the complexity and variability in the anatomy of peripheral nerves. During her fellowship training in hand surgery, she used the atlas as her 'dissection partner' in the anatomy laboratory of Johns Hopkins Hospital and the atlas has followed her throughout her professional career. The knowledge gained from her study of this unique anatomy atlas, helped her perform complex surgeries on patients with nerve injuries suffering from severe pain, paralysis, and disability. That surgeon, Dr. Susan Mackinnon performed the world's first successful nerve allotransplantation (donor graft is from the same species and not genetically identical to the recipient) in 1988 and she became a leading expert in peripheral nerve surgery. As a pioneer in the field of nerve surgery, Dr. MacKinnon was awarded the prestigious Gold Medal Award in Surgery by the Royal College of Physicians and Surgeons in Canada in 1988. Her contributions leading to major advances in nerve transplantation, medical education and to the field of plastic and reconstructive surgery have changed the practice of surgery, enhancing quality of life for so many patients. Clearly, Dr. Mackinnon's accomplishments are due to her intellectual abilities and talents as a surgeon, which did not come from a book. However, the fact that this innovative and brilliant researcher and surgeon was aided by her use of the Pernkopf Atlas is important to note.[1,2]

In 2018 I became aware of Dr. Susan Mackinnon, Chief, Division of Plastic and Reconstructive Surgery at Washington University School of Medicine and Shoenberg Professor of Plastic and Reconstructive Surgery. As a medical educator, Dr. Mackinnon and Andrew Yee, a surgical education specialist at the medical school who soon was to be awarded his PhD, were developing a library of educational videos that had been greatly influenced by the Pernkopf Atlas. Aware of the tainted history of the atlas created by Nazis who performed dissections on executed victims, they acknowledged that the ethical dilemma thus created was significant and raised many questions.[1] Susan Mackinnon and Andrew Yee sought answers from those who were experts in dealing with the atlas, Sabine Hildebrandt and Bill Seidelman, and following this, they were introduced to me. I do recall having conversations with Dr. Mackinnon regarding the ethical dilemma which we both had faced on a daily basis: should we use the atlas during surgery and/or as a tool for the education of our residents in training? I informed Susan that I had never fully resolved this ethical dilemma to my satisfaction. In general, I avoided using the book, but when I was confronted with a complex case, I would prepare for surgery using the Nazi anatomy atlas to help me navigate through complex surgery. I found that it was interesting that Susan had a similar response initially, indicating that she always felt the need to keep the atlas near the operating room, 'in my OR locker,' and would use it when needed, 'always with respect, gratitude, solemnity and disclosure, and also with some discomfort.'[1] I also discovered that Susan and Andrew were working on a research project involving a survey of nerve surgeons' assessment of the Pernkopf Atlas, which greatly piqued my interest.

Although I was included in many of the communications between Sabine, Bill, Susan, and Andrew regarding the development of guidelines on the issue of ethics surrounding the use of this atlas, and analogous scenarios, this was essentially to keep me up to date on these developments. I learned that Dr. Michael Grodin, Professor of Health Law, Ethics and Human Rights at Boston University and Rabbi Joseph Polak, Chief Justice Rabbinical Court of Massachusetts and New England, and also a child-survivor of the Westerbork Bergen-Belsen concentration camps, were going to study these issues and provide a response from the perspective of Jewish Law (Halacha). A Rabbinic Responsum is a written treatise provided by a rabbi to a question, based on a study of Jewish law. Rabbi Polak was put to the task, with invaluable perspectives on human rights, health law, medical ethics provided by Dr. Michael Grodin.

On 14 May 2017 a special symposium was held at Yad Vashem in Jerusalem, Israel titled 'How to Deal with Holocaust Era Human Remains.' Dr. William Seidelman served as the Symposium Chair, and presentations were provided by world renowned experts on this topic, including Dr. Gotz Aly, a German historian and author, Dr. Margit Berner, from the Vienna Museum of Natural History, Dr. Yoram Haimi, an archeologist from the Israel Antiquities Authority, Dr. Miriam Offer, Senior Lecturer in Holocaust Studies at Western Galilee College, Professor Heinz Wassle, Emeritus Director of the Max Planck Institute for Brain Research and Professor Paul Wiendling, Professor in the History of Medicine at Oxford-Brookes University. Drs. Seidelman and Hildebrandt also gave presentations. Perhaps the most important and relevant outcome of this symposium was the presentation ' "Vienna Protocol" for when Jewish or Possibly-Jewish Human Remains are Discovered' delivered by Rabbi Joseph Polak.[3]

Rabbi Polak reviewed the Jewish laws regarding the handling of mortal remains, which are very strict and specific, requiring burial without delay. A dignified burial is for the benefit of the deceased, to be done before the process of decay, and is also part of the process of redemption for the sins of the deceased. Burial without delay benefits the mourners permitting them to begin the grieving process. Deriving any benefit from Jewish human remains, photographing the dead and cremation are not permitted under Jewish law. However, the 'Vienna Protocol' also indicates that Jewish law puts the highest priority on saving or preserving a life (in Hebrew 'pikuach nefesh'). If the use of the images of anatomical depictions in the Pernkopf Atlas can save a life or preserve quality of life, then this would be permitted as an overriding factor. The use of the atlas for medical education as a method of training doctors to save and/or preserve a life would also be included under the 'Vienna Protocol.' However, the 'Vienna Protocol' also indicates that the use of these images must also be accompanied by the obligation of the user to provide full disclosure of the origin of the human remains, with commemoration of the victims for their sacrifice and preserving their dignity.[3]

Although the 'Vienna Protocol' is based on Jewish law, the strict and specific guidelines on how to deal with human remains can potentially serve as a guideline for those who must decide whether or not to use the book, irrespective of one's religious beliefs. The 'Vienna Protocol' does not provide the treating doctor with the answer to the question, 'should I or shouldn't I use this book?' The answer is a personal decision that must be based on the individual's full knowledge of the background of the origin of the book. It is neither right nor wrong to use the book, as that depends on the doctor's individual beliefs and freedom to make decisions. Most importantly, the use of the book is accompanied by the obligation to honor the victims with full acknowledgment and disclosure. Therefore, students and doctors in training who are shown pictures from the Pernkopf Atlas during their education, must be informed of the horrific history. I have delivered presentations regarding the Nazi origins of the atlas, so there is full disclosure of the history. However, when I have given lectures on the administration of local anesthesia and surgical techniques, where I previously avoided showing anatomical pictures from the Pernkopf Atlas, I now use them for teaching purposes with full disclosure to the audience regarding the origins of the book and the sacrifice of Nazi victims. The reactions of students upon this disclosure can usually be described as 'shock,' that the anatomical picture that is being projected on a power point slide shows the corpse of a person who was likely murdered by the Nazis. Doctors who want to use the atlas in preparation for a surgical procedure are obligated to obtain permission from their patients, disclosing the history of its origins along with honoring the victims.

And now another coincidence. A *New York Times* article from 12 May 2020 highlights a Palestinian surgeon in Israel who uses the Pernkopf Atlas in preparing for surgery.[4] The surgeon, Dr. Madi El-Haj at the Hadassah Medical Center in Jerusalem had a Jewish patient who required complex nerve surgery. When the patient was a 13-year-old boy he stepped on a mine laid by Palestinian militants resulting in a severely wounded foot that had caused significant chronic pain, despite multiple surgeries over eighteen years which failed to provide relief. The patient, who was now a 31-year-old adult, had indicated that his mother had relatives that perished in the Holocaust. Dr. El-Haj informed the patient that he would prefer to use an anatomy atlas in the operating room which would help him navigate this complex surgery, but also indicated the illustrations in this book created by Nazis were likely based on executed victims. Dr. El-Haj also informed the patient that he could operate without using the atlas, but that would make the surgery more difficult. The patient was given the choice and decided that his surgeon use the book. The surgery was a success, significantly reducing the pain and suffering that had greatly affected his quality of life. The patient indicated 'It sounds like a good joke…the Muslim surgeon with the Nazi atlas operating on a Jew.' Dr. El-Haj, who indicated that he used the Pernkopf Atlas in approximately 90% of his operations, received his training as a peripheral nerve surgeon under Dr. Susan Mackinnon.

An interesting coincidence related to this true story found its way to me when my close friend Shelley Sherman, who was an officer in the Hadassah organization, returned to the US from her trip to Hadassah Medical Center. Shelley informed me that she met a Palestinian surgeon, Dr. Madi El-Haj, who knew of me. Yes, this was true, as Bill Seidelman had invited Dr. El-Haj to have dinner at his home in Jerusalem, and through our routine e-mail correspondence Bill had informed me of the Mackinnon-trained Palestinian peripheral nerve surgeon, Dr. El-Haj, who was treating Jews and Muslims at Hadassah Medical Center and routinely used the Pernkopf Atlas adhering to the 'Vienna Protocol.'

Following the creation of the 'Vienna Protocol,' the bioethical issues for doctors, students and patients still persist. In a 2021 article Rabbi Polak reflected on the moral dilemma faced by doctors who choose to use the book to enhance their abilities to heal and relieve human suffering:[5]

> *I know that while Pernkopf's collection is obscene, untouchable by any measure – the surgeon needing to consult its secrets is holy …. her patient is holy, and the skills and processes of healing are holy …. the surgeon, students and the patient are partners with the*

Almighty, Who is surely present in the operating theater. The atlas must be used if it can heal the patient……. but every living person involved with such a case; patient, family, students, staff – must be told from whence these illustrations come, and why it was necessary to use them……. immortalizing his victims.

Notes

1. S. Mackinnon, 'When Medical Information Comes from Nazi Atrocities,' *BMJ*, 368, (2020), p.17075.
2. The University of Toronto Division of Plastic Reconstructive & Aesthetic Surgery Website, Hall of Fame featuring Susan E. Mackinnon, MD, FRCSC, FACS, 2024. https://www.uoftplasticsurgery.ca/about/division/hall-of-fame/
susan-mackinnon/
3. J. Polak, ' "Vienna Protocol" for when Jewish or Possibly-Jewish Human Remains are Discovered,' Symposium titled 'How to Deal with Holocaust Era Human Remains,' Yad Vashem, The World Holocaust Remembrance Center, Jerusalem, Israel, (14 May 2017).
4. I. Kershner, 'In Israel, Modern Medicine Grapples With Ghosts of the Third Reich,' *The New York Times*, 12 May 2020.
5. J. Polak, 'The "Vienna Protocol" and Reflections on Nazi Medicine: Murder a la Carte,' *Journal of Biocommunication*, 45, 1(2021), pp. 95-97.

14

Assessment of Pernkopf's Atlas by Neurological Surgeons and Oral & Maxillofacial Surgeons 2017-21

The years 2017-21 were quite tumultuous for me both professionally and personally. My professional activities as an academician and oral and maxillofacial surgeon were associated with the creation of a new dental school, Touro College of Dental Medicine in Hawthorne, New York. I had numerous responsibilities in education, research, clinical care, and administration at the new school. As a Professor of Clinical Dental Medicine, I directed courses in temporomandibular disorders (TMJ), pain and anxiety control, and chronic oral-facial pain. Additional responsibilities included mentoring students in scholarly projects with clinical research and I also served as Vice Dean for Academic Affairs for an abbreviated period of time. Additionally, the COVID pandemic was raging during this period creating havoc in dental education programs and there were months when the dental school had to close its doors to patient care due to concerns for transmission and spread of infection. Living in Queens, New York City, my wife and I were sequestered in a high-rise apartment, avoiding entry into a tiny elevator with the risk of being sneezed upon by persons who didn't believe in masking or airborne spread of infections. Still, I was able to maintain most of my professional activities by delivering lectures and conducting courses and examinations remotely. Administratively, meetings were held remotely, and this was quite a challenge as the school was preparing for a site visit for accreditation by the Commission on Dental Accreditation of the American Dental Association.

Nerve Surgeons' Assessment of the Role of Pernkopf 's Atlas in Surgical Practice

Still, amongst all of these complex factors, my support and participation with the efforts of Susan Mackinnon, Andrew Yee, Sabine Hildebrandt and William Seidelman were extremely important. As I had indicated previously, I initially was a relatively passive participant in these discussions as the efforts leading to the 'Vienna Protocol' proceeded. However, when Susan and Andrew informed me of their survey of Nerve Surgeons of the role of Pernkopf's Atlas, we realized that these efforts could be supplemented by a survey of those within my specialty of oral and maxillofacial surgery. The survey of surgeons was focused on determining if attitudes and use of the Pernkopf Atlas would change if they followed ethical guidelines, largely based on the 'Vienna Protocol.'

In a February 2019 issue of *Neurosurgery* Andrew Yee, Susan Mackinnon, et al. reported on the results of their survey of nerve surgeons in their assessment of Pernkopf's Atlas and proposed guidelines for an ethical approach for the use of the book in surgical planning and education.[1] The results indicated 182 nerve surgeons participated in the survey and 69% of respondents aware of the atlas' Nazi background were still comfortable using the book, while 15% were uncomfortable and 17% undecided about using the atlas. However, when provided with the ethical guidelines that were proposed by the authors, 76% of those who were either uncomfortable, or undecided became comfortable with the use of the atlas to enhance patient care. Additionally, the respondents rated Pernkopf's Atlas superior to another excellent and very popular atlas (Netter's), with respect to anatomical detail and usefulness for surgeons. The guidelines proposed for the ethical use of the Pernkopf Atlas included the following conditions:

1. A formal and educational disclosure displayed prior to viewing the atlas discussing its historical origin and a discussion of the ethical issues.
2. A consensus from bioethicists validating its specific use for benefiting the lives of patients.
3. A consensus validating its use according to Jewish law according to the principle that the preservation of human life overrides virtually any other religious consideration.

4. An official memorial existed dedicated to the victims in the creation of the atlas.

The aforementioned ethical guidelines were developed as a result of and were consistent with the 'Vienna Protocol.'

Oral and Maxillofacial Surgeons' Assessment of the Role of Pernkopf's Atlas in Surgical Practice: Unexpectedly a 'Bumpy Road'

As I observed my colleagues at Washington University School of Medicine working diligently to complete their research survey of nerve surgeons, I began to pursue research on a similar survey of oral and maxillofacial surgeons' (OMSs) responses to the Pernkopf Atlas in 2017. For numerous reasons, a survey of oral and maxillofacial surgeons was most appropriate, as it was my advanced surgical specialty training that was greatly enhanced by my study of the Pernkopf Atlas, as had been the case with Susan Mackinnon as a peripheral nerve surgeon. Similarly, as I progressed in my career as an academician, I had used the knowledge gained from the anatomical depictions in the atlas, to treat patients and educate my students and oral and maxillofacial surgeons in residency training.

The success of this project depended mostly on my collaboration with Andrew Yee, as a surgical education expert. We worked diligently to adapt the survey that had previously been given to nerve surgeons to be made relevant to specialists in OMS. This required numerous changes, and in particular, deciding on those anatomical pictures of the head and neck which were most indicative of the Pernkopf Atlas, for comparison to other anatomy atlases. The next challenge was getting as many OMSs as possible to participate in the survey. Initially this was a relatively easy task, since I was a member of numerous OMS professional organizations and through my publications and research, I was well known in my field of expertise, management of chronic oral-facial pain and arthroscopic surgery of the temporomandibular joint. The two best known professional OMS organizations in the US are the American Association of Oral and Maxillofacial Surgeons (AAOMS) and the American College of Oral and Maxillofacial Surgeons (ACOMS). Both of these organizations require members to pledge their commitment to ethical principles as health care professionals. These organizations conduct numerous educational programs for OMSs throughout the year and both organizations have a major annual scientific meeting, with presentations on the latest advances in the field. The vast majority of presentations at these meetings are related to clinical surgery, with research related to ethics, although extremely relevant to patient care, being extremely uncommon. However, I had no difficulty getting permission from these major organizations and responses to the survey that was created by Andrew Yee and myself, titled 'Surgical Assessment of Pernkopf's Anatomical Atlas' from ACOMS and AAOMS.[2] However, cooperation from another professional organization, of which I was an active member, was not forthcoming to my great dismay.

To further boost the number of participants, the survey was sent to members of several smaller organizations, such as the New York State Society of Oral and Maxillofacial Surgeons, and those attending the New York Institute of Clinical Oral Pathology conferences, with successful participation. However, an important, but small organization consisting of one hundred plus members provided some interesting feedback as well as pushback. I shall refer to this organization as X.org, to maintain anonymity. Prior to administering the survey, I contacted the appropriate committee of the organization to obtain permission for its distribution amongst membership. I was directed to the two appropriate members of X.org, both of whom were quite influential within the organization and amongst OMSs in general. The first individual responded positively indicating 'I was not aware of any of this until taking the survey, and now would like to know more. It certainly raises important and relevant ethical questions that are worthy of broad discussion and consideration.' Needless to say, the survey was approved for distribution to the membership by this individual and the link to the survey was sent to the membership. The second individual (Dr Y) did not respond to the request for permission to conduct the survey. Once the survey went to the membership, the responses that I received were both disappointing and shocking. Most members did not take the survey on the grounds that it was inappropriate for our membership, indicating that X.org was not a forum for having a political, religious, and philosophical discussion. Although some were supportive and saw the relevance of the biomedical ethical issues that were important to OMSs, those who did not take the survey did not have the opportunity to realize the relevance of the issues being raised. Instead, many public and private reactions to a simple request for survey participation, assumed that there was a political or religious agenda that was being promoted, without knowing the history or understanding the relevance of the issues raised by the atlas survey. What was most distressing to me was the public response provided by Dr Y, who never responded to my initial request for permission but only responded to the entire membership after the survey was distributed. The following summarizes Dr Y's public response to the membership:

- *Professor Z (anonymous and quite famous in OMS, not Pernkopf) fought for the Nazis and was forced to follow Nazi doctrine. Should his work and name be expunged and honorary membership in OMS organizations be removed? No.*
- *None of the fellow members of X.org know of the horrific situation that Pernkopf had been placed in, nor do we know what his beliefs actually were.*
- *Did Pernkopf oppose exterminations, but was worried about saving the lives of members of his family?*
- *Famous Professor Z, who fought for the Nazis would have been imprisoned or executed if he refused. Pernkopf may have been faced with the same dilemma.*
- *I am not supporting what Pernkopf did in his professional life and anatomical research, but did he have a choice; follow the evil doctrine and live, or be executed?*
- *There are other excellent anatomy books that OMSs should feel free to use.*

Dr Y provided a public defense of Pernkopf to our membership, without having any idea of the true origins of the atlas, the suffering of the victims, Pernkopf's political agenda on the role of medicine, nor the intent of this research survey. For unknown reasons, Dr Y assumed that behind this survey was an agenda to expunge Pernkopf's Atlas from our use, which was a totally false assumption. To put it succinctly, I was outraged by this public response to the membership of X.org. Although we had very few responses to the survey, I was not done with the X.org and the issues which arose from the members of this organization. Upon reflection, I wondered why there was an assumption that there was a

Comparison of Oral & Maxillofacial Surgeons and Nerve Surgeons Responses to Survey Assessing the Role of Pernkopf's Atlas in Surgical Practice

	OMSs[3]	Nerve Surgeons[1]
Number of Respondents	181	182
Aware of Background and **comfortable** using the atlas	42%	69%
Aware of Background and 'uncomfortable' using the atlas	33%	15%
Aware of Background and 'undecided' using the atlas	25%	17%
Following provision of ethical guidelines for using the atlas: change from uncomfortable to comfortable	53%	59%
Following provision of ethical guidelines for using the atlas: change from undecided to comfortable	98%	93%
Ethical guidelines changing the attitudes of those previously uncomfortable or undecided to comfortable	75%	76%
Pernkopf v Netters Atlas Anatomical detail	Pernkopf>Netter (4 Anatomical Plates) 76-91%	Pernkopf>Netter (6 Anatomical Plates) 79-91%
Surgical utility	76-81%	66-82%

Table II. Survey findings demonstrated that OMSs and Nerve Surgeons had remarkably similar responses regarding the use of the Pernkopf Atlas. Those who were resistant to using the atlas in preparation for surgery, when provided with ethical guidelines for the use of the book, changed to being comfortable. OMSs and Nerve surgeons found Pernkopf's Atlas had superior anatomical detail and surgical utility comparing 4-6 anatomical plates with Netter's Atlas.[1,3,4]

religious and political agenda to expunge the book, especially for those who did not take the survey. The essential historical information was included in the survey.

After having received the responses of 181 OMSs, it was time to analyze the data, which involved a coordinated effort amongst Andrew Yee, me and two more brilliant individuals. As an educator and mentor, I seized upon the opportunity of recruiting two of our brightest and most talented students at Touro College of Dental Medicine, Jessica Li and Joshua Lilly, both of whom had decided to apply for postgraduate training in oral and maxillofacial surgery in the future. Educating students, residents, and all future health professionals on the role of doctors as willing perpetrators of genocide and unethical medical experiments is a critical component of creating ethical practitioners and researchers of the future.

After much diligence and hard work, the four of us were able to analyze the survey data and provide the results, which were strikingly similar to the responses of the nerve surgeons

Following analysis of the data, we decided to submit an abstract for presentation at the annual meeting of X.org. Within this small organization it is relatively rare for an abstract to be rejected. Our abstract was one of four that were rejected, with twenty-one abstracts being accepted for the 2019 X.org meeting. I sent e-mails to the three reviewers, requested a reason for the rejection of the abstract, and specifically whether the material in the abstract was deficient scientifically. I only received a response from one of the reviewers who indicated that the rejection was based on the material being inappropriate for X.org because it was not relevant to the treatment of patients. My reaction was to withdraw my membership in this organization and have the material submitted and published elsewhere.

The abstract was then submitted to the American College of Oral and Maxillofacial Surgeons (ACOMS) and accepted for presentation at their 2019 annual meeting in Albuquerque, New Mexico. My brilliant dental students, Jessica Li and Joshua Lilly, who were one year away from graduation and applying to OMS postgraduate training programs, did an excellent job presenting the purpose of the survey and the results to the ACOMS membership, highlighting the issues raised by the use of scientific information created by unethical methods.

The air was filled with significant tension in the large room where the multitude of poster presentations were to be viewed and evaluated. As students, Jessica and Josh were nervous because giving a presentation before a group of oral and maxillofacial surgeons was intimidating, especially because these same people could be the ones who would interview them as applicants for a residency program. Of course I was slightly worried for them, but I knew that they were well prepared after they had practiced so many times. However, I was quite tense with respect to the reactions they would be getting, with the potential for a repeat of what I had experienced with X.org. Was this audience going to view this abstract as having a political or religious agenda, rather than a true understanding that the real theme was medical ethics?

The presentation was extremely well received, allaying all of our concerns, and there also was an interesting side note to this story. One of the members of X.org, who refused to participate in the Pernkopf survey with his opinion being it was 'not appropriate with a religious and political agenda' attended the ACOMS abstract presentation. This OMS listened intently to the content of the information that Jessica and Josh were presenting on the Pernkopf Atlas and the survey results. Following the presentation this OMS did apologize to me as his initial reaction at X.org was based on assumptions that were made prior to really understanding the purpose of the research. It was a happy time, and I was so immensely proud of Jessica and Josh, who I knew would become excellent oral and maxillofacial surgeons.

Following the presentation of this material at the ACOMS meeting, the entire team, especially Andrew Yee, worked diligently to have a full manuscript of the oral and maxillofacial surgeons' assessment of the Pernkopf Atlas published. We were successful with acceptance of the manuscript in the scholarly journal, *Annals of Anatomy*.[3] I felt enormously proud to be a member of this team of individuals who were passionate about the importance of ethical medicine principles in the education of current and future healthcare professionals.

Triumph and Tragedy

In September 2020 I received an invitation from Andrew Yee to remotely attend the defense of his PhD thesis titled 'Implementation of Innovation and Ethics Using Video-Based Learning in Nerve Surgery.' Andrew's PhD studies were through Utrecht University in the Netherlands largely based on his video education modules and research on medical ethics. I felt honored to attend Andrew's thesis defense remotely as he answered many tough questions regarding his research which included the assessment of the role of the atlas on surgical practices of nerve and oral and maxillofacial surgeons. Although this subject was just one of many that were included in his thesis defense, I was able to see the depth and breadth of Andrew's knowledge. I was elated, along with Susan Mackinnon, Sabine Hildebrandt and Bill Seidelman when we found out that Andrew was successful and earned his PhD in Healthcare Professions Education.

My brilliant students, Jessica Li and Joshua Lilly were accepted into the oral and maxillofacial surgery postgraduate training program at Nassau County Medical Center, in New York. Jessica has stayed in communication with me on a regular basis throughout her training and I was ecstatic when she discussed some of the more difficult and challenging cases that she had encountered. I specifically recall two patients with severe, intractable chronic oral and facial pain, which had not been successfully controlled, despite the attempts at treatment by prior surgeons. Jessica, although at a very early stage in her development as an OMS persisted, reviewed the literature, spoke to colleagues, and did everything possible to come up with creative ideas to relieve the suffering of these patients. Jessica's commitment to her ethical obligations as a healer did not allow her to give up, and I was extremely gratified to find out that she, along with a team of other surgeons, was able to provide significant relief of pain and improved quality of life for both patients. I know that Dr. Jessica Li will continue as a healer with the highest degree of medical ethics in caring for each individual patient.

Dr. Joshua Lilly was heading along the same path as a brilliant, young, talented oral and maxillofacial surgeon. A terrible tragedy occurred when his life was taken in a motor vehicle accident in 2022. I am truly heart broken by this loss, as are all who knew this fine young man. May his memory be a blessing in our hearts and minds.

Notes

1. A. Yee, D. Coombs, S. Hildebrandt, W. Seidelman, J.H. Coer, S. Mackinnon, 'Nerve Surgeons' Assessment of the Role of Eduard Pernkopf's Atlas of Topographic and Applied Human Anatomy in Surgical Practice,' *Neurosurgery*, 84, 2 (2019), pp. 491-8.
2. 'Surgical Assessment of Pernkopf's Anatomical Atlas (OMS),' (2018). https://www.surveygizmo.com/s3/4604660/Surgical-Assessment-of-Pernkopf-s-Anatomical-Atlas-AAOMS, (2018). (link to survey no longer active).
3. A. Yee, J. Li, J. Lilly, S. Hildebrandt, W. Seidelman, D. Browne, P. Kopar, J.H. Coert, S. MacKinnon, H.A. Israel, 'Oral and maxillofacial surgeons'

assessment of the role of Pernkopf's Atlas in surgical practice,' *Annals of Anatomy*, 234, 151614 (2021), pp. 1-10. https://doi.org/10.1016/j.aanat.2020.151614.

4. F. H. Netter, *Atlas of Human Anatomy, Sixth edition*, (Philadelphia: W. B. Saunders, 2014).

15

Dentists During the Third Reich and Nazi Gold

This educational journey does not end. Being an oral and maxillofacial surgeon, I wondered how the dental profession as well as my specific specialty fared under the rule of the Third Reich. I was soon to be shocked again as luck intervened, compelling me to explore this complex history which influenced the dental profession in the US.

Academic Dentists from the University of Vienna and Their Confrontation with Evil

In the fall, 2018 I had contacted Dr. Bruce Sanders, a colleague, friend, academic oral and maxillofacial surgeon and an Adjunct Professor at University of California Los Angeles (UCLA) School of Dentistry in California. Amongst several topics, I had asked him if he had received the survey on the assessment of the Pernkopf Atlas, which he indicated that he had completed. While we were on the topic, he informed me that he had lectured to dental students at UCLA on the impact of academic dentists originally from the University of Vienna who fled Austria and had a profound influence on dentistry and dental education in the US. Bruce sent me a copy of his presentation including a fascinating article which focused on five dentists at the University of Vienna who emigrated to America and had a significant impact on dental education and research.[1,2]

The dental profession in the US prior to the 1930s was viewed as having technical expertise, but significantly deficient in the basic biomedical sciences (anatomy, physiology, cell biology, biochemistry, pathology, microbiology) and research. US dental schools were technique-oriented, but few had emphasized education on the biological basis for disease, unlike their professional school counterparts in Europe, and in particular Austria. At the University of Vienna, dentistry had evolved as a specialty of medicine, thus requiring an education which emphasized the biomedical sciences and research. The University of Vienna's Medical faculty were world-renowned and included Julius Tandler. As Chair of Anatomy Tandler had pioneered education in oral anatomy with the publication of the book *Anatomy for Dentists* by Tandler and Sicher in 1928. By the turn of the century and even prior to 1900 the University of Vienna's faculty were known for publications and advances in dentistry, oral biology and pathology, and included the prominent names Heider, Wedl, and Scheff.[1-5]

The most prominent faculty members who emigrated to the US from the faculty of the University of Vienna were Bernhard Gottlieb, Balint Orban, Harry Sicher, Joseph Weinmann and Rudolf Kronfeld. When I became aware of these famous names, I realized that many of the textbooks that I had used in my courses at Columbia University School of Dental and Oral Surgery were authored by these individuals. I had been a student studying from their books to enhance my education from 1973 and beyond. The textbook *Orban's Oral histology and embryology* was one I had used on a regular basis as the required text reference for the study of oral histology at Columbia University. Sicher's *Oral Anatomy* was not a required textbook, but it had been in the medical center library and was commonly used as a reference. Since my go to anatomy book was Pernkopf's Atlas, I had used Sicher's book only occasionally.[1,2]

Bernhard Gottlieb and Harry Sicher completed their medical school studies at the University of Vienna and were greatly influenced by the Chair of Anatomy, Julius Tandler. From the 1920s through the 1930s the Dental Research Institute at the University of Vienna, under Gottlieb, became well known in Europe for its prominence among oral scientists. Gottlieb was a brilliant oral pathologist who became internationally known following the International Dental Congress meeting in 1926, helping him establish relationships with the more prominent dental schools in the US such as Chicago College of Dental Surgery at Loyola.[1,2]

Balint Orban, following his medical school training at the University of Budapest in 1922, became a faculty member at the Dental Research Institute at the University of Vienna, under Gottlieb's leadership. Orban was a prolific researcher, publishing numerous papers and by 1927 he moved to the US obtaining a faculty position at Loyola. Faculty from other dental schools came to Chicago to hear the dynamic researcher

Dr. Balint Orban lecture and present his research findings explaining the biologic processes involved in the oral sciences. Orban's textbook titled *Dental histology and embryology* was first published in 1928. Following a very influential two years at Loyola, which had a profound impact on dental education in the US, Orban returned to the University of Vienna in 1929 to continue his research.[1,2,6]

Dr. Rudolf Kronfield completed medical school training at the University of Vienna in 1926 and proceeded to work under Gottlieb as a brilliant and prolific researcher. When Orban left Loyola in 1929, Kronfeld became his replacement, leaving the University of Vienna for the Chicago College of Dental Surgery at Loyola, with the full support and influence of Gottlieb. Kronfeld established himself as a very prominent researcher and became very active in the International Association for Dental Research (IADR). During Kronfeld's eleven years at Loyola, he was very productive making contributions to the scientific literature on the development of the human jaws and surrounding structures and histopathology. He obtained private funding for the establishment of the Foundation for Dental Research, a state-of-the-art dental research laboratory at Loyola's School of Dentistry in 1935. The philanthropic donor, President and Chairman of the Board of Pepsodent Corporation, was swayed by the strength of the research work of Kronfeld and Orban. Kronfeld became Director of Loyola's Foundation Dental Research laboratory. Tragically, Kronfeld committed suicide in 1940 just prior to becoming President of the International Association of Dental Research.[1,2,7]

Harry Sicher continued his academic career as Professor of Anatomy and Oral Surgery at the University of Vienna until 1939, when he fled to the US following Pernkopf's purge of the University of Vienna Medical Faculty. He obtained a position at Chicago Medical School as an Associate Professor of Neuroanatomy. In 1942 he became an Associate Professor of Anatomy and Histology at the College of Dental Surgery, Loyola University in Chicago. Throughout his academic career he authored at least 80 publications on topics related to oral anatomy, histology, applied anatomy relating to local anesthesia and temporomandibular joint disorders.[1,2,8]

Joseph Weinmann became a research associate under Gottlieb following his graduation from the University of Vienna School of Medicine in 1923. He was an eminent researcher in the field of oral pathology but his academic career in Austria ended in 1938. Weinmann fled to the US to escape the Nazis and spent the next few years on the faculty of the College of Dentistry at the University of Illinois, followed by Columbia University, and then Loyola University School of Dentistry. By 1949 Weinmann became Professor and Head of the Division of Oral Pathology at the University of Illinois. His academic research career was extremely productive, obtaining significant grant support from the National Institutes of Health.[1,2]

Bernard Gottlieb, who had trained so many of these brilliant scientists, eventually fled the Nazis escaping to Palestine and joined the University at Tel Aviv. However, due to war, he had to leave Palestine and eventually was able to obtain a position at Baylor College of Dentistry in Dallas, Texas. Due to limitations in financial resources and faculty with limited research experience, Gottlieb did not have great success in establishing a research program at Baylor and passed away in 1950.[1,2]

The forced migration of dentists from Germany and Austria was not accompanied by a welcoming dental profession in the US. The American Association of Dental Schools held a meeting in 1939 on the issue of refugee dentists' applications for successful completion of their studies, since dental school graduation in the US was a requirement by local state dental boards for licensure. State dental boards would not accept graduation from a German or Austrian dental school, with 90% of states requiring graduation from an American dental school. Many dental schools viewed the refugee professors as competitors, who would absorb all available faculty positions, while some dental schools realized that the European dentists were much stronger in the basic sciences and research who potentially could greatly enhance the dental profession as researchers and physicians of the oral cavity. However, the dental profession in the US considered the refugee dentists as technically less proficient than their American counterparts and remained resistant to accepting them.

Although the academic dental community in the US demonstrated mixed opinions regarding accepting refugee dentists, there were two powerful organizations that were clearly resistant toward facilitating licensure for these dentists. The National Association of Dental Examiners was an organization which would administer examinations to dentists who had graduated from dental schools. Passing this mostly clinical examination was a requirement for licensure by most state dental boards. Some members of the National Association of Dental Examiners strategized to protect the interests of the American-born graduating dentists as well as those dentists who were already in practice. Although some members of the National Association of Dental Examiners organization had legitimate concerns about maintaining the standards of clinical practice to ensure quality dentistry for the patients, most state board members were mostly concerned about the influx of foreign dentists on competition with their constituent practicing American dentists. Therefore, dentists emigrating from Europe had difficulty in obtaining dental school acceptance and state licensure in many instances. The most exceptional dentist scientists, such as those from the University of Vienna, were ultimately able to secure faculty positions in pursuit of continuing their careers in education and research.[1,2]

Although I was completely familiar with the purge of faculty at the University of Vienna when Pernkopf became the Medical School Dean in 1938, I had no knowledge that these events would have a direct influence on my education. Due to the purge of faculty who were either Jewish or who would not pledge their allegiance to Hitler and the National Socialist agenda, these brilliant dentist-scientists were forced to flee from Vienna, with their ultimate destination being the US, where they made great contributions to the advancement of dental research and dental education. Until I had spoken to Dr. Bruce Sanders, I did not realize that the eminent faculty from the University of Vienna who fled the Nazis and came to the America, were giants in the field of dental research and education. I studied and gained knowledge from their publications. How ironic is this? Eduard Pernkopf, the Nazi creator of my most used anatomical atlas reference, led the purge of Viennese academic dentists. Gottlieb, Orban, Sicher and Weinmann were all Jewish who were forced to flee Austria due to National Socialism. Kronfeld, also of Jewish ancestry, left Vienna for the US in 1929 driven in part by antisemitism. These five dentist-scientists whose research and emigration to the USA greatly influenced the dental profession had also authored books that I studied as part of my education.[1,2,6,8]

When confronted with the purge of faculty and antisemitism, the dentist-scientists from the University of Vienna were faced with threats to their survival. Aside from the loss of their careers, these scientists and their families were in grave danger of losing their lives. Many residents of Vienna committed suicide, while others were deported to concentration camps. In retrospect it is incredible that Orban, Sicher, Gottlieb and Weinmann were able to flee to America and also continue to make enormous contributions to science. Their struggle to survive and then continue to contribute to our understanding of the biological basis of oral diseases is a testament to how truly great these individuals were. I find it incredible that only now, fifty years since my graduation, I was a beneficiary of their knowledge and teachings, along with so many of my professional colleagues. Their courage and response to evil has had a positive impact on so many doctors and their patients, leaving a legacy that very few are aware of.

Nazi Dentists – More Monstrous Deeds

In 2015 my education on the dissection of evil continued and reached new heights. I was asked to be a reviewer for an article submitted to *Vesalius, the Journal of the International Society for the History of Medicine.* Prior to publication in a peer reviewed article, the editors of that journal send unpublished copies of the manuscript to experts who are to provide a critique of the article to determine if it provides information that adds to our historical and scientific knowledge. The title of the manuscript to be reviewed by me was 'Nazi Dental Gold: from Dead Bodies to Swiss Banks,' authored by Xavier Riaud, DDS, PhD, an eminent scientist and historian from France. I learned that Riaud completed his PhD studies on the History of Sciences and Technics and was an Associate member of the National Academy of Dental Surgery in France. The content of the manuscript was both fascinating and horrifying and this article was accepted for publication.[9] I had known that the Nazis used the gold from the teeth of those who were exterminated in concentration camps, but beyond that my knowledge was minimal. The information that follows summarizes what I learned from this article, and being further stimulated to discover more, I researched additional material to get a full picture of Nazi dentists, Nazi gold, prisoner dentists and the fate of the gold plundered by the Nazis following the Second World War.

With the rise of National Socialism in Germany, Hitler became Chancellor in 1933. It was a time when the German economy was suffering significantly from the effects of the worldwide depression, inflation and from punishing reparations from the Treaty of Versailles upon its surrender ending the First World War. Nazi currency, the Reichsmark, was not accepted by many countries as Germany began its military buildup under Hitler. In 1934 an agreement was reached between Germany and Switzerland by which gold would be converted into Swiss Francs, a currency that would be accepted by many countries that were considered 'neutral.' Therefore, this agreement enabled Germany to trade and make purchases with neutral countries such as Sweden, Switzerland, Portugal, Spain, Turkey and Argentina, to supply natural resources required for the Nazi industry to manufacture military weapons and other industrial products necessary for a wartime economy. This funding of the Nazi war machine through the conversion of gold to Swiss Francs allowed Germany to become powerful militarily, in addition to greatly improving economic conditions. Thus, the accumulation of gold became the necessary driving force to fuel the German economy, military buildup and enable the Third Reich to expand beyond its borders.

The Nazi invasion of surrounding countries not only provided more territory for Germany but was also accompanied by the plundering of the gold bullion from the central banks of these countries. The tremendous wealth accumulated by the Nazis through stealing gold bullion from the vaults of the central banks provided the funds for the Third Reich to create enormous military power that ultimately led to the Nazi empire in Europe, with expansion to Poland, Czechoslovakia, Hungary, Belgium, the Netherlands, Denmark, France, and Norway. However, gold bullion from the central banks of Europe was not the only source of Nazi gold. Non-monetary gold from the citizens of those countries which had been invaded by Germany was an important and necessary source of gold required to fund the Nazi war machine.[9]

In 1940, Dr. Victor Scholtz from the Medical University Stomatology Institute in Breslau, Germany, successfully defended his doctoral dissertation. The focus of his thesis was dental gold from the mouths of the dead being vital for the economy of the Third Reich. Pertaining to dental gold Scholtz wrote 'this is not an end in itself, rather a beginning.' In September 1940, Heinrich Himmler, head of the SS and Gestapo, ordered SS doctors to collect gold teeth from the mouths of both the living and the dead. Sondercommando teams consisting of

Figure 22. Auschwitz, Poland 1944. Surviving prisoners outside of the gas chambers and burning bodies. Removing items from corpses, of value to the Nazi state and extraction of gold teeth was standard procedure. Permission courtesy of The Archive of The State Museum Auschwitz-Birkenau in Oświęcim and Yad Vashem Photo Archive5318/200.

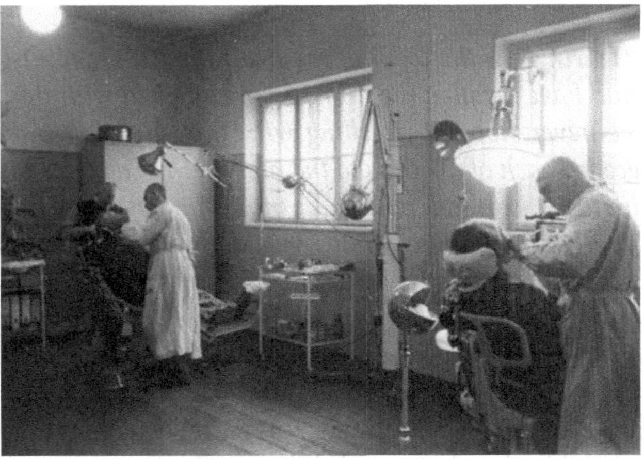

Figure 23. Auschwitz, Poland 1941, Dentists at the Auschwitz concentration camp working on prisoners in the dental clinic. Extraction of gold teeth on live patients as well as the remains of the executed was standard procedure and a source of gold for the Nazi war machine. Permission courtesy of The Archive of The State Museum Auschwitz-Birkenau in Oświęcim and Yad Vashem Photo Archive FA157/28.

concentration camp prisoners, extracted dental gold from the dead immediately following the removal of the corpses from the gas chambers at Auschwitz and other concentration camps. Nazi dentists in the German army also extracted gold teeth from prisoners while they were alive (Figures 22 and 23).[9]

The Agony of Dentist Prisoners

Prisoner dentists were forced to assist the Nazis in obtaining gold. Franz Feldmann and Paul Katz were French Jewish dentist prisoners at Birkenau, who were forced to remove gold teeth following the extermination of concentration camp victims who had been cremated. Cases of gold teeth were also accumulated from those who had been exterminated in the gas chambers. The gold was melted into cylinders or bars and this gold of dental origin was then sent to Berlin.[9]

The incredible suffering and torment experienced by dentist prisoners is documented in the book *The Dentist of Auschwitz – a Memoir* by Benjamin Jacobs.[10] As a prisoner at the Auschwitz Fursengrube Subcamp, Jacobs was forced to remove teeth of those who had been executed. His reflections in this emotionally challenging memoir include:

> *.... tearing out the teeth of the dead moved me to disgust...what would have befallen me if I had not complied with this order?......I have never stopped wrestling with that question.....Repugnance preceded each of my trips to the morgue.....The tools I used for this grim task I kept in a red box.... most inmates who saw me walking to the morgue...knew what I was doing....my father and brother also knew, though I never told them.*

It is impossible to imagine the enormity of human suffering and mental anguish experienced by Jacobs and other prisoner dentists when given the orders received by their Nazi captors. Picture being placed in the scene depicted in the photograph (Figure 22). There are no words that can adequately convey this horror.

With the Allied troops rapidly approaching, Nazis captors attempted to hide the enormity of the genocide they had committed and attempted to evacuate remaining living prisoners from the concentration camps.

Many died on this march to nowhere of starvation, disease or execution. Miraculously, Benjamin Jacobs was able to survive a death march. He also survived a disaster on the Baltic Sea when a ship that he and other prisoners were on was torpedoed. By 1949 he was able to emigrate to the US, settling in Boston. He applied for admission to dental school only to be denied admission for many years. After having survived the horrors of being a prisoner dentist in a concentration camp, this was the greeting that he and other 'foreign dentists' faced from the dental profession in the US. Jacobs was told by the school's administration that due to the GI Bill passed by Congress, there was preferential admission for soldiers returning from the war. It is difficult to imagine the plight of Benjamin Jacobs, somehow surviving the physical and mental torture of being a prisoner dentist in Auschwitz, only to be rejected by the dental profession in the US.

In 1953, eight years after the end of the war, a dental school had encouraged Dr. Jacobs to reapply for admission. He declined. Benjamin Jacobs had become a successful businessman.[10]

The Fate of Nazi Dentists

Most of the dental gold specimens from concentration camps were collected by SS officers on a regular basis and sent to the Reichsbank of Berlin, but some of the gold was routed elsewhere. Officers of the SS, upon request, sometimes received gold for their dental treatment which originated from the teeth of concentration camp victims. Gold theft by SS soldiers also occurred as well as trafficking of dental gold with living prisoners exchanging their extracted gold teeth for food.[9] A 2009 article in the United Kingdom's newspaper, *The Telegraph,* claimed that Hitler may have had dental restorations that originated from the gold teeth of concentration camp victims. This sensational headline must have sold many newspapers, but the evidence was very circumstantial, without proof, and most likely bogus.[11]

When one thinks of Nazi doctors who committed horrible atrocities, such as Mengele and Rascher, the role of dentists is not generally considered. However, Nazi dentists included many who performed monstrous deeds and were convicted of war crimes. Amongst these notorious dentists included Hugo Blaschke, who was the personal dentist of Hitler, Himmler, Goering and Eva Braun. Blatschke was in charge of all dental services for the SS and organized the collection of dental gold from those exterminated in concentration camps. After the war he was sentenced to ten years in prison for war crimes and crimes against humanity. Herman Pook was an SS dentist who was responsible for the centralization of the gold from the concentration camps and organized the dispatch of the victim gold to the Reichsbank in Berlin. Pook was sentenced to ten years for war crimes but served time in prison for less than six years.[9,12]

Willy Frank was the Director of the Dental Clinic at Auschwitz and participated in concentration camp selections of prisoners to be murdered in the gas chambers. The second dental officer under him, Willi Schatz, also participated in selections.[13] Both Frank and Schatz were able to continue their dental careers after the war. However, two decades later they were arrested and tried for war crimes and crimes against humanity. Interestingly Frank was found guilty and sentenced to seven years in prison,[13] while Schatz was acquitted for lack of evidence at the 1965 Frankfurt Auschwitz Trials and was able to continue practicing dentistry. However, years later, there was conclusive photographic evidence that proved Schatz's participation in prisoner selections, but he never served prison time for his crimes.[14]

Dr. Wilhelm Henkel, a dentist at the Mauthausen concentration camp, was sentenced to death for the murders of camp prisoners. Henkel was hanged by the Allies in 1947.[15] Dr. Walter Sonntag was a dentist and a member of the Waffen-SS who actively participated in the atrocities at the Ravensbrück concentration camp. Sonntag, who was married and had one child, was witnessed brutally mistreating the critically ill, beating up prisoners, abusing females and allegedly sending approximately 2,000 women for transport to their deaths at a sanatorium in Berlin. He participated in the selection process at Ravensbrück sending prisoners to be exterminated. Sonntag was sentenced to death for war crimes and murder by a British court and hanged in September 1948.[12,16]

Nazi Oral and Maxillofacial Surgeons

It is abundantly clear that the potential for human beings to become perpetrators of unimaginable monstrous acts exists. For those in the healing professions, the performance of acts of torture, medical experimentation and murder, were not isolated to the medical profession and included members of the dental profession as well. Research has demonstrated that the medical profession had the highest proportion of members in the Nazi party (NSDAP, National Socialist German Workers Party, *Nationalsozialistische Deutsche Arbeiterpartei)* estimated to be 45 percent. The legal and teaching professions had an estimated Nazi party membership of 25 percent. As an oral and maxillofacial surgeon, I was very curious about the statistics on the participation of my specialty during the Third Reich. I was astounded to discover that within the healthcare professions, the specialty of maxillofacial surgeons had the greatest participation in Nazi party membership, comprising 62% of German and Austrian specialists in maxillofacial surgery (German 64.5%, Austrian 54.3%).[17]

The disproportionately high numbers of NSDAP members amongst maxillofacial surgeons may possibly be explained by their direct involvement in dealing with wartime facial and jaw injuries. In addition, maxillofacial surgeons are experts in people born with facial deformities, such as cleft lip and palate, considered to be unhealthy to the Aryan gene pool by the Nazis. The expertise of maxillofacial surgeons was often needed when decisions on forced sterilization were required under National Socialist ideology and law.[17] When I discovered the name of a world renowned oral and maxillofacial surgeon amongst those who were members of the NSDAP, I was shocked and dismayed. Yes, Professor Z, who in 2005 I had met in Vienna and was mentioned in an embarrassingly uninformed e-mail to the members of X.org that provided pushback to participation in the Pernkopf Atlas survey to OMSs, was a member of the Nazi party. Why did he join the NSDAP? Joining the Nazi party was not a requirement, as 117/187 maxillofacial surgeons in Germany and Austria participated as party members.[17] Since party membership was voluntary (37% of maxillofacial surgeons did not join the party) one can only speculate if Professor Z was forced to join the Nazi party. There is no suggestion that Professor Z did anything other than treat all of his patients to the best of his abilities. Furthermore, his contributions to the advancement of the specialty of oral and maxillofacial surgery had an enormous impact on increasing surgeons' skills and enhancing the lives of so many patients. How and why Professor Z joined the Nazi party remains a question that most likely will never be answered.

What Happened to all that Nazi Gold?

Following the end of the Second World War there was a huge accumulation of gold that had been stolen by the Nazis. This consisted of gold which had been plundered from the banks of the countries that had been invaded by the Nazis and victim gold. Some victim gold came from the theft of the possessions of individuals and institutions in countries overtaken by the Nazis. However, there was much gold that came from Holocaust victims, whether from extracted teeth or from their possessions. A German SS officer, Bruno Melmer was in charge of delivery of gold from the concentration camps to the central bank in Berlin, the Reichsbank. This 'Melmer Gold' was converted into bullion and stored in the vaults of the Reichsbank and then transferred to Switzerland banks in exchange for Swiss Francs, the currency that permitted German industry to obtain resources from other countries, building its war machine and stimulating the economy.[9,12]

In late March 1945 US General George Patton's army crossed the Rhine River and entered Germany. The US army advanced on the German village Merkers, which had potassium mines. Military intelligence operatives who had interviewed miners and other villagers obtained information that led them to believe the mine may contain gold and stolen art. On 8 April 1945 the 90th Infantry Division of the US army blasted a hole in a vault wall revealing the storage of a huge amount of gold bars, coins, bullion, jewelry and precious works of art which had been stolen by the Nazis (Figure 24).[18] The value of the Nazi gold recovered from Merkers mine was estimated to be $256 million in1945 dollars,[19] equivalent to approximately 4.5 billion dollars in 2024. Some percentage of this gold came from the mouths of Holocaust victims. It has been estimated that the value of the gold recovered from Merkers mine was less than half of the estimated total amount of $625 million plundered by the Nazis.[20] This staggering amount represents approximately 11 billion 2024 dollars. But what happened to the gold that was missing at the time of the discovery of Merkers mine? Since Switzerland was the largest gold distributor in Europe and had established financial arrangements with Nazi Germany, it was assumed that the rest of the missing gold was in vaults of Swiss Banks.[20]

In 1946 the Tripartite Gold Commission (TGC) was established by the US, Great Britain and France, to permit European countries to receive restitution for the stolen gold that had been recovered. Five

Figure 24. Merkers mine in Germany discovered by the US army in April 1945 stored an estimated $256 million dollars (4.5 billion in 2024 dollars) of gold, jewelry and art treasures stolen by the Nazis. This discovery represented less than half of the total amount of plundered valuables (estimated at 11 billion in 2024 dollars). The missing gold was assumed to be in the vaults of Swiss banks. © Everett Collection/Shutterstock with permission.

decades later, US President Bill Clinton commissioned Stuart E. Eizenstat, the Under Secretary of Commerce for International Trade, to prepare a report on the status of unrecovered assets, including gold, that had been stolen or hidden by Germany under the Nazi regime. Eizenstat was especially qualified to coordinate the participation of the appropriate agencies as he also held the position of Special Envoy of the Department of State on Property Restitution in Central and Eastern Europe.[18,21,22]

Eizenstat and William Z. Slany, Department of State Historian, completed the preliminary study which was the basis of a congressional hearing before the Committee on Banking and Financial Services in

June 1997.[21,22] The report indicated that there had been an estimated $185 - $289 million dollars in looted gold in the Swiss National Bank at the end of the Second World War. The Swiss banks only paid $58 million in monetary gold to the Tripartite Gold Commission (TGC) to be redistributed to claimant countries in 1946. This was far short of the total amount of monetary gold which accumulated in Swiss banks at the end of the war. The $58 million that had been recovered by the TGC was only used for claimant countries that had massive destruction of buildings, bridges, roads, factories, and other vital components of infrastructure. The rationale for providing restitution to these countries was for rebuilding infrastructure as a result of the devastating effects war had on Europe. The Western Allied countries were preoccupied with the Cold War with the Soviet Bloc of nations and prioritized the rebuilding of the economies of free European countries. Restitution for individual Nazi victims, both Jewish and non-Jewish was not a priority of the TGC. Therefore, there was no mechanism for restitution of Holocaust victims or their heirs, although victim gold was certainly a component of the gold that had been recovered. Non-monetary gold from victims, such as gold coins, jewelry, personal items and dental gold was smelted into bars and mixed with monetary gold as part of the entire gold pool that had either been recovered by the TGC or remained in Swiss bank vaults.[21,22]

The US State Department had estimated that between 1946 and 1996, $4 billion in 1996 dollars from the TGC was received by claimant countries including Albania, Austria, Belgium, Czechoslovakia, France, Greece, Italy, Luxembourg, The Netherlands, Poland and Yugoslavia. Claimant countries had received 65% of their original claims. But what about the victims and their heirs who had suffered so much? Where was the justice in leaving billions of dollars of Nazi monetary gold in Swiss bank vaults while the victims and their families, who had suffered so much physical pain, torture, medical experimentation, death as well as theft of their assets and gold from their teeth, were not compensated?[21,22]

As a result of the findings of the Eizenstat report, along with pressure from Bill and Hilary Clinton, Edgar Bronfman, President of the World Jewish Congress and Senator Alphonse D'Amato (New York), Chair of the US Senate Banking Committee, significant negative publicity on the Swiss banking industry was reported in newspapers, including The New York Times.[23,24] This negative publicity was not well received in

Switzerland. The State Department of the US was not in a position to force the Swiss Banks to pay reparations, however, the economic power of the financial district in New York City was able to provide the impetus for some restitution for Nazi victims. Alan Hevesi, Comptroller of New York City, pressured the Swiss Bank with sanctions. A class action lawsuit was filed in Brooklyn Federal Court by Holocaust survivors (with the support of the World Jewish Congress) and their heirs against the Swiss Banks, seeking $20 billion dollars in compensation.[25] The continued negative publicity that the Swiss banks received, along with pressure from the financial community particularly in New York City, created strain in the relations between Switzerland and the US. Eizenstat, who served as a mediator in the negotiations with the Swiss banks, refused a settlement offer of $300,000 million indicating that it was only a 'fraction of the $2.8 billion dollars in Nazi gold that the Swiss received on behalf of Nazi Germany by the Swiss central bank.'[26]

Ultimately, the Swiss banks settled the litigation on 12 August 1998, in Brooklyn Federal Court for the sum of $1.25 billion dollars. Although considered a large settlement by some, this was a small amount compared to the original class action seeking $20 billion dollars in compensation, and the $2.8 billion dollars of Nazi gold sitting in Swiss bank vaults. Among the eligible claimants were Jewish victims and their heirs, homosexuals, the physically and mentally handicapped, Romani (Gypsies) and Jehovah's Witnesses all of whom had suffered as victims of the Nazis. The settlement between Holocaust victims and the Swiss Banks resulted in the payment of approximately $1.288 billion dollars to over 458,400 Holocaust victims and their heirs, located in every state of the US and more than 80 nations. A significant amount of the distribution of $720 million dollars went to those who owned bank accounts and other assets that had been deposited in the Swiss banks.[27] In the end, amongst all classes of the 458,400 Holocaust victim claimants, the average settlement amount was $2,810 per Holocaust victim claimant.

Further details on the issue of assets which had been deposited in Swiss banks is necessary to understand the reaction of those individuals and families who were not able to escape from Germany's army as they swept across Europe. Realizing that the Nazis were going to steal and plunder anything of value, which was a requirement to fund their industrial military war machine, many of those who knew that they were

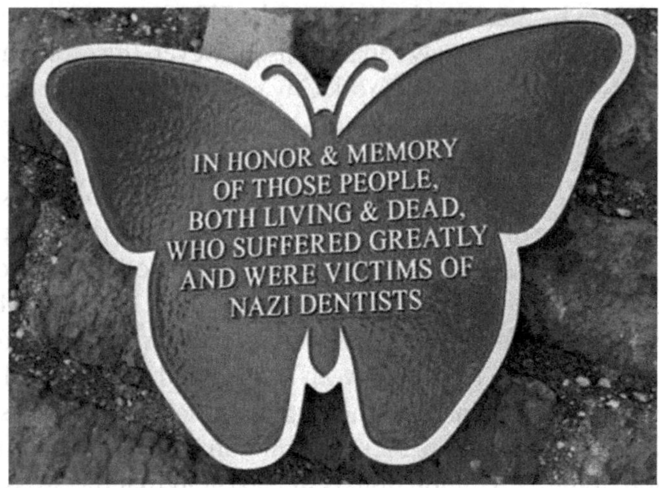

Figure 25. Memorial plaque honoring the victims of Nazi dentists, from the Holocaust Museum and Tolerance Center, Nassau County, New York, USA. Photograph by H. Israel.

going to be likely victims sought to safely shield their assets by depositing money and valuables in the banks of neutral Switzerland. However, with the extermination of millions of people by the Nazis these accounts remained dormant. Survivors and their heirs could not reclaim these assets because they were unable to produce a death certificate. The unclaimed assets remained in the Swiss banks. Auditors determined that the total estimated value of the assets in these dormant accounts was approximately $1 billion dollars.[28] Therefore, the allocation of up to $720 million dollars for Holocaust victim claimants and their heirs was close to, but still less than the amount that had originally been deposited.

When one reflects on the average settlement amount amongst all classes of claimants being $2,810 per Holocaust victim resulting from this litigation, the words 'very unsettling' come to mind. How does one put a price on the inhumane suffering and losses that were incurred by Holocaust victims and their families? Where are the memorials for the victims of Nazi dentists? I have delivered presentations on this topic at several professional meetings, medical and dental schools, and at local community groups. To commemorate those who were victims and suffered in a manner beyond human comprehension, a limited amount of money was donated. A small memorial plaque to honor the memory of the victims of Nazi dentists was placed in 2016 and can now be seen at the Holocaust Museum and Tolerance Center, Nassau County, New York (Figure 25).

Influence of the Nazi Purge of Jewish Dentists in the US After the Second World War: Antisemitism at a US Dental School

The impact of the purge of physicians and dentists from Europe under the Nazi regime had a lingering influence on discrimination in medical and dental schools following the Second World War.[29]

Recently, I attended an International Holocaust Remembrance Day program, with members of the Rocky Mountain Jewish Historical Society from the Center for Judaic Studies at Denver University in Colorado. Sitting just behind me was a relative of Dr. Perry Brickman, an oral and maxillofacial surgeon who authored the book, *Extracted – Unmasking Rampant Antisemitism in America's Higher Education.*[30] Dr. Brickman's memoir recounts the shame he had experienced in 1952 after he was unceremoniously dismissed from Emory University Dental School despite his excellent grades. There was no explanation, and he lived with the haunting memory of this demoralizing experience throughout his life, as he proceeded to successfully complete his dental education at the University of Tennessee, followed by successful completion of oral and maxillofacial surgery training. Dr. Brickman progressed with his brilliant career and become a leader in his community for decades, although he continued to harbor a deep and personally painful secret. In 2006 he stumbled upon an exhibit that demonstrated gross antisemitism in Emory University's dental school between 1948-61. There were many other Jewish dental students who were either dismissed or never accepted solely due to antisemitism. Similar to Dr. Brickman, these dental professionals harbored this hidden painful shame.

Following his retirement, Dr. Brickman courageously spent years researching archival documentary evidence, digging up the past, and contacting those students who had been unknowing victims of antisemitism. Ultimately, Dr. Brickman was able to influence Emory University officials to announce a public apology for their previous antisemitic policies. In 2012 a special ceremony was held at Emory, with

University President James Wagner, delivering a public apology. Many of those dentists who had been targets of this antisemitism attended, coming from all parts of the country with their families.

Confrontations with unethical initiatives, discrimination based on race/religion and purges of faculty, students and employees in the workforce are not limited to totalitarian regimes or the past.

Notes

1. B. Sanders, 'The History of the Dental Profession in the US: The Stranger Dentists Within Our Gates, The Vienna Dental Scientists Who "Saved' American Dentistry." ' Presentation delivered by Dr. Sanders to dental students at UCLA School of Dentistry, (2018).
2. N.W. Kremenak, C.A. Squier, 'Pioneers in Oral Biology: The Migrations of Gottlieb, Kronfeld, Orban, Weinmann, and Sicher from Vienna to America,' *Crit Rev Oral Biology Med*, 8 , 2 (1997), pp. 108-128.
3. C. Wedl, *Pathology of the Teeth: Anatomy and Physiology*, (Philadelphia: Lindsay & Blakiston, 1872).
4. M. Heider, C. Wedl, *Atlas to the Pathology of Teeth*, (Leipzig: Verlag Von Arthur Felix, 1869).
5. J. Scheff, *Handbook of Dentistry*, (Vienna: Holder, 1891).
6. C. Bergmann, D. Gross, 'A fairytale career in spite of political disenfranchisement: The Jewish oral pathologist Bálint Orbán (1899-1960),' *Pathology-Research and Practice*, 216, (2020), pp. 1-7. https://doi.org/10.1016/j.prp.2020.152862.
7. K. Reinecke, J. Westemeier, D. Gross, 'In the shadow of National Socialism: Early emigration and suicide of the oral pathologist Rudolf Kronfeld (1901–1940),' *Pathology-Research and Practice*, 215, 12, (2019), p. 152682.
8. T. Schunck, D. Gross 'From Nazi victim to honored scientist: The two lives of Jewish anatomist Harry Sicher (1889–1974),' *Annals of Anatomy*, 235 (2021), p.1-10.
9. X. Riaud, 'Nazi Dental Gold: From Dead Bodies to Swiss Banks,' *Vesalius, Journal of the International Society for the History of Medicine*, 21, 1 (2015), pp. 33-55.
10. B. Jacobs, 'The Dentist of Auschwitz – a Memoir,' (Lexington: The University Press of Kentucky (1995).
11. D. Wroe, 'Hitler had fillings made from gold torn from the mouths of Jews,' *The Telegraph*, 8 October 2009.

12. X. Riaud, 'Medical Ethics under a Totalitarian Regime: German Dentists and the Third Reich,' *Dental Historian: Lindsay Club Newsletter*, 7, 45 (2007), pp.76-86.
13. M. Krischel, 'Dentists in National Socialist Germany: A Fragmented Profession,' in S, Hildebrandt, M. Offer, M.A. Grodin (eds). *Recognizing the Past in the Present: New Studies on Medicine Before, During and After the Holocaust.* (New York and Oxford: Berghahn Books Publisher, 2020), pp. 190-203.
14. E. Schwanke, D. Gross, 'Progressive Entanglements? Activity Profiles, Responsibilities and Interactions of Dentists at Auschwitz. The Example of 2nd SS Dentist Willi Schatz,' *Med. Hist*, 643, 3 (2020), pp.374-400.
15. R.D. Speers, W.G. Brands, E. Nuzzolese, et al, 'Preventing dentists' involvement in torture – The developmental history of a new international declaration,' *JADA*, 139 (2008), pp. 1667-73.
16. L.A. Bitterich, C. Rinnen, D. Gross, 'Nazi dentists before British courts: aspects on the role of the German dental profession in the Third Reich,' *British Dental Journal*, 123, 10 (2021), pp. 647-53.
17. L.A. Bitterich, D. Gross, 'Maxillofacial surgeons in the Third Reich and their connection to National Socialism,' *Journal of Cranio-Maxillo-Facial Surgery*, 49 (2021), pp. 329-35.
18. G. Bradsher, 'Nazi Gold: The Merkers Mine Treasure' Prologue: *Quarterly of the National Archives and Records Administration, US*, 31, 1 (Spring 1999).
19. G.M. Taber, *Chasing Gold – The Incredible Story of How the Nazis Stole Europe's Bullion*, (New York and London: Pegasus Books, 2014).
20. A. Smith, *Hitler's Gold: The Story of the Nazi War Loot*, (Oxford England, Providence Rhode Island, USA: Berg Publishers, 1989).
21. S.E. Eizenstat, W.Z. Slany, 'The U.S. and Allied Efforts to Restore Gold and Other Assets by Nazis During Second World War. Preliminary Study,' US Congressional hearing before the Committee on Banking and Financial Services, May 1997.
22. S.E. Eizenstat, W.Z. Slany, 'The Eizenstat Report and Related Issues Concerning US and Allied Efforts to Restore Gold and Other Assets by Nazis During Second World War. Hearing before the Committee on Banking and Financial Services House of Representatives, 105th Congress, First Session, 25 June 1997.
23. A. Cowell. 'The Swiss and Holocaust Money,' *The New York Times, Week in Review*, 27 October 1996.

24. A. Cowell, Swiss 'Central Bank to Fight Holocaust Claims,' *The New York Times, Week in Review*, 4 April 1998.
25. G. Bradsher, 'Turning History into Justice: Holocaust-Era Assets Records, Research and Restitution March 1996 – March 2001,' Lecture, University of North Carolina, presented by Dr. Greg Bradsher, Director Holocaust-Era Assets Records Projection, National Archives and Records Administration, 19 April 2001.
26. D.E. Sanger, 'How a Swiss Bank Gold Deal Eluded a U.S. Mediator,' *The New York Times*, 12 July 1998.
27. J. Gribetz, S.C. Reig, 'Special Masters' Final Report on the Swiss Banks Holocaust Settlement Distribution Process,' Case 1:96-cv-04849-ERK-JO Document 5040 Filed with the US District Court Eastern District of New York, 28 March 2019.
28. Official Website of the Swiss Banks Settlement: In Holocaust Victim Assets Litigation, U.S. District Court for the Eastern District of New York, Judge Edward R. Korman Presiding. CV-96-4849, updated 14 April 2020. https://www.swissbankclaims.com/New%20docs/Final%20Report.pdf
29. E. Halperin. 'The Jewish Problem in U.S. Medical Education, 1920-1955,' *Journal of the History of Medicine and Allied Sciences*, 56, 2 (2001), pp. 140-167.
30. P. Brickman, *Extracted - Unmasking Rampant Antisemitism in America's Higher Education*, (New York, London, Nashville Tn, Melbourne Australia, Vancouver Canada: Morgan James Publishing, (2020).

16

Impact of the Investigation of the Pernkopf Atlas

The issues surrounding the Pernkopf Atlas are not unique and represent just one example of the numerous ethical transgressions in medicine that took place during the Third Reich. Reasons for recounting these horrific deeds are many. First, my personal involvement and questions regarding Pernkopf and the creation of his atlas was my introduction into a world of horror. I had minimal knowledge of the enormity of crimes perpetuated by the medical profession and academicians prior to my discovery of the Nazi origins of this anatomy atlas. Having been introduced to this world of doctors performing monstrous deeds by many scholars, and especially Dr. Seidelman, one realizes the necessity for healthcare providers to become educated on this history and the power they wield with the potential to cause unimaginable suffering. Secondly, there was a period of at least fifty years following the end of the Second World War, where individuals and institutions in Europe remained silent. This was accompanied by denial, rationalization, blaming others or actively denying the demise of morality, particularly in the medical profession, during the Nazi regime. This denial and delay in uncovering the truth by itself, was unethical, with the continued use of data and specimen material from executed individuals. Thirdly, one learns that as horrific as the truth is, the stories of these ethical transgressions by the medical profession must be retold, especially with acknowledgment of the sacrifices of the victims, whose suffering must be memorialized. This knowledge and education must be passed on to future generations, to be vigilant in preventing such events from ever happening again.

The journey which brought this unknowing oral and maxillofacial surgeon into the history of Nazi medicine and its relevance continues to this day. This education leads one to reflect on the cry for '*never again*' and the famous quotes:

The only thing necessary for the triumph of evil is for good men to do nothing.
Those who don't know history are doomed to repeat it.

The question remains, why do human beings continue to participate in mass murder and genocide? What does one do when confronted with such transgressions of moral values? Is there any way for humanity to prevent history from repeating itself?

I have continued to communicate with Bill Seidelman on a regular basis since the University of Vienna released its 1998 report on the Anatomical Sciences during the Nazi era. We frequently reflect on the progress that has been made over the past three decades with the Pernkopf Atlas controversy playing a key role in stimulating studies into the past and ethical debates regarding how to handle useful scientific information that was created through unethical means. Exploring these issues has led to more research and education of the past, with the goal of preventing reoccurrences of the moral degradation of humanity and distortion of science. However, we also lament at the many failings that are so evident in today's world. The recurring wars in the Middle East, significant increases in hate crimes against Asians, Blacks, Muslims and Latinos, antisemitism, authoritarian countries seeking more land and power, refugee crises from those who are dispossessed, are just some examples of humankind's inability to learn from the past. How is it possible that deportations, purges and discrimination of minorities have become commonplace in nations that are supposed to be looked upon as the stalwarts of democracy?

A *New York Times* article from 12 August 2024, titled 'A Nazi Villa So Tainted Berlin Can't Give it Away' reveals the dilemma surrounding the Nazi mansion of Joseph Goebbels, Hitler's propaganda minister.[1] This huge estate, which is in disrepair, is owned by the State of Berlin and the cost of maintenance upkeep has become a significant financial burden. The government has given up trying to sell or develop this property and is willing to give it away for free. However, the Berlin government cannot get rid of the property out of fear that Nazi sympathizers will use it as a center and symbol for the re-emergence of the past. There now are extreme right-wing groups that deny the legitimacy of the current German government with some members on trial for plotting to overthrow the government. The author reports:[1]

> *the far right has re-emerged in German politics, there has been a shift in sentiment toward remembering the past, in order to never forget it.*

This trend with re-emergence of far right political groups throughout the world is quite alarming and reinforces the necessity of educating current and future generations on the history of the emergence of Nazi ideology and the potential for 'average' people to be swayed to eventually perform acts of violence and evil, that seem unfathomable. We must do everything possible to prevent the professions and the public to be influenced by groups that potentially will lead to a violent repeat of history with the scapegoating of those who are labelled as being 'less worthy of life.' Today, the danger is upon us.

Prior to the University of Vienna Senatorial investigation (1997-98), there were publications revealing the active role of academic institutions and the medical profession in mass exterminations. There had also been the 1989 University of Tübingen investigation, driven by the protests of medical students, revealing the use of anatomical specimens from the Nazi era, and the University of Marburg's Professor of Anatomy Gerhard Aumüller leading efforts for the medical profession to take responsibility for its dark past. It is logical to assume that the silence and denial in Germany and Austria for decades after the war was largely due to the generation of people who were either 'de-Nazified' or just lived through that period and were not able to confront or reconcile the horrors of the past, attempting to live a 'normal' family life. It is interesting that in the 1980s through the 1990s the next generation, medical students, academicians, and others were driving forces within Germany and Austria to acknowledge the medical profession's complicity in the past. It was this generation of individuals who became leaders in Germany and Austria to memorialize Nazi victims, promote education on the Holocaust, acknowledge the plundering of gold, art and other treasures, and restore their countries toward a civilized society with ethical values. Although the Pernkopf investigation amongst other revelations did have an impact, it occurred at a time when Austria and Germany were ready to acknowledge the past and do what was necessary to move forward. Therefore, it is difficult to quantify the impact of the Pernkopf Atlas issue. Were the revelations exposed by the University of Vienna in 1997-98 on the origins of the atlas the trigger for future investigations? Or perhaps the revelations that followed were a part of the trend toward revealing the truth by the next generation of Germans and Austrians. It is likely that both were important factors in creating the change in attitudes in Europe with acknowledgment of their role in this dark period of history.

When one searches the OVID medical literature database for articles using the search terms 'Pernkopf, Nazi, Anatomy, Atlas' there are a total of eighty-eight publications. It is interesting to note the significant increase in scholarly articles on the atlas since the University of Vienna's investigational report, with seventy publications since 1998. There has been a more recent increase in interest in the Pernkopf Atlas since Rabbi Polak's responsum, the 'Vienna Protocol' in 2017 (Figure 26). These figures do not take into account the use of different search terms that can be used for an OVID literature search, other medical literature databases, or the myriads of articles and media coverage appearing in newspapers, magazines, and broadcasts.

It is apparent that the University of Vienna investigation in 1998 had struck a chord within the medical profession and in the media. The

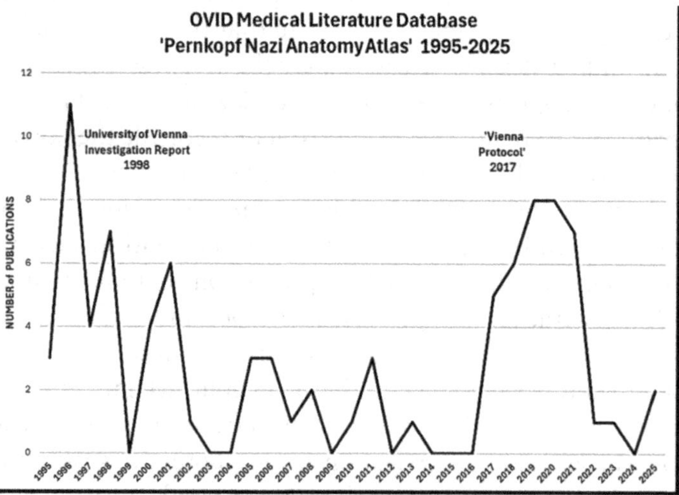

Figure 26. Search terms 'Pernkopf, Nazi, Anatomy, Atlas' in the peer reviewed medical literature reveals a total of 88 publications. Since 1998 following the University of Vienna investigation into the Pernkopf Atlas controversy there have been 70 publications. Of note are the increased numbers of publications following the introduction of the 'Vienna Protocol' providing ethical guidelines for those considering using the atlas for patient care and medical education.

ethical debate as to whether one should use valuable scientific information that could save lives, but was created by the perpetrators of exterminations, torture and medical experiments continues. When Sabine Hildebrandt, a faculty member in the Department of Anatomy at Michigan University, and a German born physician learned about the controversy surrounding the Pernkopf Atlas, she felt compelled to do further research. The result was the 2006 publication on the historical and ethical analysis of the Pernkopf controversy and its influence on the sciences in Austria and Germany.[2] From that starting point, Dr. Hildebrandt has become a leading world expert, publishing, lecturing and exerting influence to continue to make positive changes today with an emphasis on education on bioethics for healthcare professionals today and in the future. Dr. Hildebrandt is currently the Co-Chair of *The Lancet* Commission on Medicine, Nazism, and the Holocaust, launched on 8 November 2023. When I recall the rejections Bill Seidelman and I received upon submission of our manuscript titled 'The Swastika and the Cadaver: Eduard Pernkopf and Anatomy in the Third Reich,' from the *New England Journal of Medicine* and *The Lancet* in 1996, one could say that great progress has been made on the importance of this area of study. More recently *The Lancet* has taken a leading role in recognizing previous and current ethical shortcomings in the health professions, with emphases on incorporating this history into medical education.

The Lancet Commission

An email communication I received from Bill Seidelman on 6 November 2020, included 'Major Development' on the subject heading.[3] From the tone of his writing, I could tell that Bill was extremely excited about a breakthrough. He informed me of the efforts to have the prestigious medical journal, *The Lancet*, form a commission dedicated to the education of healthcare professionals on the importance of the history of the Holocaust and the medical profession's active role in exterminations, medical experimentation and torture. Although there was much documentation on the role of medicine during the Third Reich, there remained a major void in the establishment of a sustained permanent central program for research, documentation and education. A major goal of this proposed commission was to establish an international central network to educate the doctors of today and in the future on the layers of complex factors that led to genocide. Through education the focus would be to prevent reoccurrences of these unimaginable transgressions that have been repeated throughout history, as exemplified by the medical profession during the Nazi regime.

The events leading to the formation of *The Lancet* Commission were numerous, but a commentary by Richard Horton, the Editor-in-Chief of *The Lancet*, titled 'Offline: Medicine and the Holocaust – it's time to teach,' had a significant impact.[4] Horton's powerful 2019 commentary indicated that the medical profession is a hierarchical profession with 'inherent risks for abuse' and has 'enormous power over the lives of individuals and communities.' Horton concluded:

> *teaching medical students about the Holocaust would instill lessons about the equal worth of human beings, the limits of human experimentation, the importance of ethical regulation of research and practice and the balance between notions of public health and the duty of health professionals to the welfare of individuals.*

With this published commentary by the Editor-in-Chief of *The Lancet* demonstrating his strong advocacy for including the Holocaust in the curriculum of health professionals, a group of international experts developed a proposal for this project. An outline of the proposal titled 'Teaching Medicine and the Holocaust' was created by Professor William E. Seidelman, MD, University of Toronto (Emeritus), Professor Volker Roelcke, MD, University of Giessen, Germany, Professor Sabine Hildebrandt, MD, Harvard Medical School and Professor Shmuel P. Reis, MD, Hebrew University of Jerusalem, and was submitted to *The Lancet* on 21 October 2020.[5] With acceptance of this proposal *The Lancet* was to establish a special commission of international experts and to publish a special edition dedicated to the relevance of the Holocaust to the medical profession. This newly created *Lancet* Commission was to promote webinars, seminars, teaching and scholarships to further the education of health care professionals on the relevance of these issues in the present and prevent a repeat of the history that led to the atrocities that had been committed by the medical profession.[5]

The Lancet Commission on Medicine, Nazism and the Holocaust consists of international scholars in the field of medical education, the

Holocaust and the history of medicine, many of whom are academic physicians and bioethicists. The commission also receives significant input from a student advisory council with fifteen members from ten countries. The co-chairs of the commission are Professor Herwig Czech, PhD, Department of Ethics, Collections and History of Medicine at the Medical University of Vienna, Austria, Professor Sabine Hildebrandt, MD, Harvard Medical School, Boston, Massachusetts, and Professor Shmuel P. Reis, MD, Hebrew University of Jerusalem, Israel. The other members of the commission are listed on the initial report, which was published in *The Lancet* online on 8 November 2023.[6] These members of *The Lancet* Commission are the international leaders and driving forces for renewed emphasis on learning from history in medical education.

The launch event and symposium for '*The Lancet* Commission on Medicine, Nazism, and the Holocaust: historical evidence, implications for today, teaching for tomorrow,' took place at the Medical University of Vienna on 9 November 2023, and was attended by individuals throughout the world, either remotely or in person. This landmark symposium and the report of the commission summarized their central messages as follows:

> *1) to provide the skills required to detect and prevent crimes against humanity and genocide.*
>
> *2) to care for the victims of atrocities.*
>
> *3) to uphold the healing ethos central to the practice of medicine.*
>
> *4) to foster history informed morally courageous health professionals who will speak up when necessary.*[7]

The location of the symposium for the launch event for *The Lancet* Commission in the historic building, the Josephinum, at the Medical University of Vienna, was very significant and most appropriate for this landmark event (Figure 27). The Josephinum is a late-eighteenth-century palace which is now a museum dedicated to the study of the history of medicine, in the Department of Ethics, Collections and History of Medicine, under the leadership of Professor Herwig Czech.

Figure 27. The Josephinum at the Medical University of Vienna, Department of Ethics, Collections and History of Medicine was an appropriate venue for the launch of *The Lancet* Commission on Medicine, Nazism and the Holocaust on November 9, 2023. The original paintings from the Pernkopf Atlas are kept there preserving the historical significance of these meticulous anatomical representations. Photograph courtesy of © Josephinum / Reiner Riedler with permission.

As a leading scholar on the history of Pernkopf's Atlas, Czech[8] described the fate of the artists' anatomical paintings following the University of Vienna's investigations and report in 1998, concluding that these paintings depicted executed victims of the Nazi judicial system. Ultimately, the original publisher, Urban and Schwarzenberg ceased publication of the Pernkopf Atlas in 1994 but continued to own the original drawings and publishing rights, until 2003 when these were sold to the company Elsevier, a leading publisher in medicine and science. Therefore, Pernkopf's artists' original paintings were owned by Elsevier, and there was great concern raised on the fate of these paintings as the ethical debate regarding the Pernkopf specimens raged on. Although there were those who urged that the atlas, and thus the paintings be banned, there were many individuals, including myself, who felt that banning the book would be equivalent to the burning of books performed by the Nazis. One cannot erase the history behind the creation of the atlas and the immense suffering of the victims. Memorializing the victims and using the creation of the atlas as an historical lesson for future medical professionals to prevent the path taken when healers became killers, was the approach that many scholars had recommended. Therefore, the fate of the original paintings took on great significance. Ultimately, given the historical significance of the meticulous anatomical representations created by Pernkopf and his artists, Elsevier agreed to donate the original paintings to the Medical University of Vienna which are now in their historical collections in the Josephinum.[8] Yes, the University of Vienna was definitely the appropriate venue for the launch of *The Lancet* Commission on Medicine, Nazism and the Holocaust.

The Center for Bioethics and Humanities

When my wife and I moved to Colorado in 2023, we knew that we were moving to a less tumultuous environment than the overcrowded New York metropolitan area, where we had always lived. It also helped to be living four minutes from our son's family. When I told Bill Seidelman and Sabine Hildebrandt, they immediately indicated that the University of Colorado Anschutz Campus had a very active Center for Bioethics and Humanities under the Directorship of Dr. Matthew Wynia. I quickly learned that the Center for Bioethics and Humanities was fully involved with *The Lancet* Commission with Dr. Wynia being a member of *The Lancet* commission. The center includes a special steering committee on Holocaust Genocide & Contemporary Bioethics (HGCB) to promote educational programs. I attended the International Holocaust Remembrance Day program, where Dr. Wynia delivered an incredible presentation titled 'How Healers Became Killers: Nazi Doctors and Modern Medical Ethics.'[9] Was this simply good luck, fate or was it just meant to be? Regardless, within a very short time I had the opportunity to meet and work with Matt Wynia, the director, Lisa Culhane, program coordinator, and Dr William Silvers, a moving force who was instrumental in the creation of the Holocaust Genocide & Contemporary Bioethics program. After Dr. Wynia delivered his presentation on 29 January 2024, I knew I was in a special place that prioritized the education of health professionals to be aware of the power of the medical profession and its potential to do great harm if bioethics is not emphasized. When I was invited to serve as member of the Holocaust Genocide Contemporary Bioethics Steering Committee, I felt honored and privileged to accept this assignment.

Just by chance I learned that Sabine Hildebrandt was an invited speaker for the Holocaust Memorial Day (Yom HaShoah) Programs in May 2024 at the Center for Bioethics and Humanities. Dr. Hildebrandt delivered a fabulous Grand Rounds Presentation titled 'From Routine to Murder: Anatomy in Nazi Germany and its Legacies for Today.'[10] This lecture focused on the complicity of anatomists and the medical profession leading to the horrific events that became the Holocaust. I was so fortunate to be able to meet up with Sabine, my friend and colleague. A major highlight for me personally was to participate in a panel discussion with Sabine and Matt titled 'Unraveling the Past, Confronting the Present, and Charting an Ethical Future in Medicine: The History and Legacy of the Pernkopf Atlas.' This stimulating discussion recounted the events leading to the Pernkopf investigation and the implications for today and lessons for the future.[11] The aforementioned presentations at the University of Colorado Center for Bioethics and Humanities, as well as many of the Center's programs, can be viewed on You Tube.[9,10,11]

The great news is that the University of Colorado Center for Bioethics and Humanities is just one example of the many programs at institutions throughout the world that are focused on the education of future health professionals. With the creation of *The Lancet* Commission on Medicine, Nazism and the Holocaust, medical schools are beginning to incorporate this history into the curriculum. This provides great hope for the future, so that healthcare professionals become acutely aware of the power they possess on the fate of individual lives, and the necessity of maintaining the highest ethical principles which must always be an essential component in their interactions with each individual patient. For me, it was 'bashert' (coincidence? luck?) that after living in the New York Metropolitan area my entire life, I had moved to a location that was an important academic center for *The Lancet* Commission. The Holocaust Genocide Contemporary Bioethics program at the Center for Bioethics and Humanities is at the forefront of educational initiatives that embraced concepts which have become an essential part of my being due to lessons that I had learned from a Nazi anatomist.

Can it happen again?

Central questions in the aftermath of the genocide committed during the Nazi era are:

1. Can mass murder with physicians as perpetrators occur again?
2. How can we prevent a reoccurrence of such mass murder?

Many hold the belief that the physicians and scientists who participated in mass murder were evil sadistic monsters who simply abused their power towards the end of creating a "master race." From the vantage point of a physician, or medical student in today's world, one may conclude that since 'I am not evil or sadistic' this horrendous history is unlikely to be repeated. However, we must be extremely cautious if one takes the stance that it is impossible for mass genocide on the scale of the Nazi era cannot happen again. History has revealed that such gross ethical transgressions can and do occur, with the susceptibility of human beings to perform both unthinkable acts of cruelty, as well as performing deeds that result in tremendous good. Based on human nature and a review of history, one can surmise that the answer to the first question is yes, mass murder by human beings can and does occur, and doctors are no exception to becoming willing perpetrators.

My education on the answers to these questions continues to grow. With the initiatives of the Holocaust, Genocide, Contemporary Bioethics Steering Committee, we were quite fortunate to have Dr. Volker Roelcke, a founding Co-Chair of *The Lancet* Commission on Medicine, Nazism and the Holocaust and a world-renowned scholar on the medical profession during the Nazi era, come to Colorado to educate us during Holocaust Memorial week activities. I attended a special Holocaust Memorial Presentation on 23 April 2025, where Dr. Volker Roelcke delivered a medical grand rounds presentation at the University of Colorado Anschutz Medical Campus, Center for Bioethics and Humanities. Volker Roelcke, MD, PhD, Professor and Chair of the Institute for the History of Medicine, Giessen University, Germany, provided an audience filled with medical residents, students and faculty a lecture on 'Nazi Medical Crimes and Their Aftermath: Facts, Ethics and Lessons.' Dr. Roelcke debunked several myths regarding the Nazi physicians and their role as perpetrators of sterilization, mass murder and unethical medical experimentation. He emphasized several key points:[12]

- *Nazi doctors were not forced by political pressure to perform their active role as perpetrators of sterilization, euthanasia and medical experimentation.*
- *Physicians provided the initiative and rationale for their acts based on their belief in racial hygiene theory and eugenics.*
- *Racial hygiene and eugenics were considered accepted scientific disciplines at that time, based on research which took place throughout the academic world in the US, Great Britain and other countries.*
- *In Nazi Germany, there was a reversal of public health policy, in which the 'collective good' health of the overall population (the Volk), took priority over the 'individual good.'*
- *The political ideology which focused on the health of the Aryan population, combined with the initiatives and willingness of physicians to promote racial hygiene goals, resulted in a collusion between the Nazi state and the medical profession.*
- *Under these extreme conditions, sterilization, euthanasia, mass murder and unchecked medical experimentation occurred.*

The answers to the second question, 'how can we prevent such history from repeating itself,' are not known. However several principles have arisen, which ultimately have become the focus of this writing.

- *Education on the importance of understanding the history of the origins of genocide is essential, and needs to be reinforced in medical schools, dental schools, and all institutions of learning.*
- *Individuals must speak out when unethical transgressions do occur.*
- *The longer one waits to speak out, there is greater potential for that voice to be ineffective in promoting change.*

Notes

1. S. Maslin Nir, 'A Nazi Villa So Tainted Berlin Can't Give it Away,' *The New York Times*, 12 August 2024.
2. S. Hildebrandt, 'How the Pernkopf Controversy Facilitated a Historical and Ethical Analysis of the Anatomical Sciences in Austria and Germany: A

Recommendation for the Continued Use of the Pernkopf Atlas,' *Clin. Anat.*19 (2006), pp. 91-100.

3. W. Seidelman, Personal correspondence with Dr. Howard Israel, 6 November 2020.
4. R. Horton, 'Offline: Medicine and the Holocaust – it's time to teach,' *Lancet*, 394 (2019), p. 105.
5. W. Seidelman, V. Roelcke, S. Hildebrandt, S.P. Reis, 'Project: Teaching Medicine and the Holocaust – Outline,' Proposal submitted to *The Lancet*, 21 October 2020.
6. H. Czech, S. Hildebrandt, S.P. Reis, et al, '*The Lancet* Commission on Medicine, Nazism, and the Holocaust: historical evidence, implications for today, teaching for tomorrow,' *Lancet*, 402, 10415 (8 November 2023), pp. 1867-1940.
7. T. Chelouche, H. Czech, M.A. Fox, et al, 'Statement on *The Lancet* Commission on Medicine, Nazism and the Holocaust,' *Lancet*, 402, 10415 (8 November 2023), pp. 1816-17.
8. H. Czech, C. Druml, M. Muller, et al, 'The Medical University of Vienna and the legacy of Pernkopf's anatomical atlas: Elsevier's donation of the original drawings to the Josephinum,' *Annals of Anatomy*, 237 (2021), pp. 1-8.
9. M. Wynia, 'How Nazi Doctors became Killers,' International Holocaust Remembrance Day program at University of Colorado Anschutz Medical Campus, Center for Bioethics and Humanities, 29 January 2024. https://youtu.be/czaFD9EEfqE?si=POhVl04jbciU6cwz
10. S. Hildebrandt, 'From Routine to Murder: Anatomy in Nazi Germany and its Legacies for Today,' Medical Grand Rounds, University of Colorado Anschutz Medical Campus, Center for Bioethics and Humanities, 8 May 2024. https://youtu.be/_urEgmwgnyo?si=st2xQKUX0sNBHMqw
11. S. Hildebrandt, H. Israel, M. Wynia, 'Unraveling the Past, Confronting the Present, and Charting an Ethical Future in Medicine: The History and Legacy of the Pernkopf Atlas,' Panel Discussion University of Colorado Anschutz Medical Campus, Center for Bioethics and Humanities, 7 May 2024. https://youtu.be/RJez1AvgHU0?si=UyQ7dGKs6dpJEol8
12. V. Roelcke, 'Nazi Medical Crimes and Their Aftermath: Facts, Ethics and Lessons.' Medical Grand Rounds, University of Colorado Anschutz Medical Campus, Center for Bioethics and Humanities, 23 April 2025.

Epilogue

A former professor of mine at Columbia University and director of the oral pathology diagnosis course said something that I have never forgotten. He delivered a lecture on rare disease entities and said, 'although some individual diseases are quite rare, if you add up all of the uncommon diseases that you will encounter in clinical practice, the overall category of rare diseases is actually quite common.' At that time, I was a student, and his point did not seem very remarkable to me. However, over the years of clinical practice as an oral and maxillofacial surgeon, I have recalled how true his statement really was. I have learned and taught my students and residents of the importance of establishing a diagnosis as an essential component prior to performing treatment on a patient. Although the diagnosis is often straightforward, there are many times when something appears a bit unusual, and one is uncertain of the diagnosis. When this occurs a series of tests or procedures are performed to ultimately arrive at the most likely condition that requires treatment. If the patient does not respond to the treatment, one must go back to the drawing board, often doing a literature search or contacting an 'expert' colleague, to discover that rare condition.

Through the years, I have found my oral pathology professor's statement to be quite true, rare diseases as an overall group of conditions appear commonly, but you must be persistent in searching for the answers. Discovering the correct answer or the right path rarely happens just by chance but occurs with diligence, hard work and commitment to fulfill the obligation of doing the best for each individual patient. Failure or giving up should never be an option, although invariably we cannot succeed one hundred percent of the time. Successful outcomes didn't happen by chance or random events. One had to be proactive and persistent. The terms luck, destiny or 'bashert' never seemed relevant to me, especially when it was related to my education, development as a surgeon, educator and provider of care for my patients.

The Yiddish term 'bashert' has been used throughout the chapters in this book. I have avoided attempting to define a concept that I really do not understand and for me remains vague and mysterious. Yet, as I recall the events of the past fifty years, the only word that I can think of that comes close to describing the many improbable events, meetings, coincidences, luck, chance encounters, is the word 'bashert.' When one Googles 'bashert' there are a variety of interpretations of the English translation of this Yiddish word. The following are some of the descriptions of its meaning: 'destiny, preordained, inevitable, it was meant to be.' It is often used when referring to a marriage of two people or finding one's soulmate. Another interpretation is that it describes an event that seems to be divinely ordained. None of these various definitions seem to hit on the essence of my use of the term 'bashert' in this writing. Suffice it to say that when I have used the term 'bashert' I am referring to a series of chance events that defy any explanation and led to some positive outcome. Perhaps there have been a series of many rare events and coincidences that just occurred randomly within the past fifty years that has led me to this moment in time.

In retrospect, the following events include some of the many inexplicable random occurrences, chances of luck, and coincidences that have occurred along this journey, which I will call 'bashert.' In a routine conversation with my bride to be, Mindy, I mention that I wasn't learning anatomy to my satisfaction with the book that was required for the course at Columbia University in 1973. My professor indicated that an atlas by Pernkopf was the most detailed available, used by surgeons and anatomists, but was prohibitively expensive for a student. Mindy takes note of this brief conversation and amazingly finds Pernkopf's Atlas in a lower Manhattan bookstore near her work, and surprises me with this gift. I was shocked and couldn't believe that she spent $50 on this gift in 1973, which would be equivalent to $371 today! How did she find the book? How did she remember the name Pernkopf or even know how to spell the name? Where did Mindy find the money to pay for this 'masterpiece' medical book? How did I become so dependent on this one book, which was clearly the most influential and used reference throughout the years of my development as an oral and maxillofacial surgeon? Little did we know then the impact this book was going to have throughout the next fifty years of our lives. Should one call this bashert?'

I depend on Pernkopf's Atlas for a period of over twenty years as I develop my knowledge of anatomy and surgical skills. I write down each step required for every major surgery I perform on a yellow pad, the day prior to surgery, with Pernkopf's Atlas by my side reviewing the anatomical relationships that were going to be encountered the following day. When I enter the operating room with my yellow pad, the students and residents sometimes laugh inside giving me strange looks, trying to figure out why the 'expert' needs a yellow lined 'cheat sheet.' I tell them, 'today, in this operating room, I will be doing the surgery for a second time, the first time having been written on my yellow lined pad the night before the procedure.' My pal Pernkopf always came through and I was never going to allow a complication during surgery because I didn't review the detailed anatomy.

A chance remark by a colleague who stops by my office just to say hello and chat, changes my world. With my copy of the Pernkopf Atlas open preparing for the next day's surgery, he closely observes what I had been doing and says, 'I heard that Pernkopf was a Nazi.' He didn't have to say anything more than a friendly greeting. How could I be so unaware of the source of material I had been reviewing for over twenty years? Were the lessons that I learned coming from a Nazi? Who were the people whose anatomy had been depicted in this atlas? This brief random encounter with my colleague could not have been inevitable, or was it? Was it 'bashert?'

I intensively investigate everything I could find regarding Pernkopf and his atlas. What I find is horrifying. Swastikas and other Nazi icons in 1937 and 1943 German language editions of the book. An essay by Weissman titled 'Springtime for Pernkopf' describing his rise to academic power as the Dean of the University of Vienna's Medical School in 1938, who tells his faculty that medicine must heal the *Volk*, the body of the Aryan people' by eliminating the unfit through 'sterilization and other means.' Rave reviews in the *New England Journal of Medicine* and the *Journal of the American Medical Association* describe Pernkopf's Atlas as a 'masterpiece'. An article on the history of Pernkopf's Atlas and his artists suggests that the corpses he used were from victims executed by the Nazis. Why were the swastikas erased from my $50 dollar English language version of the book, but the anatomical pictures were the same as those in the older German language editions? What a horror, a nightmare.......was it possible that I had benefited from the execution of Nazi victims for over twenty years? What do I do with this?

My Rabbi recommends that I read Dr. Robert Lifton's book, *Nazi Doctors*. I read the book with both fascination, horror and disgust, learning how physicians who took an oath to be healers, became the executioners for the Third Reich. Was it 'bashert' when I see a posting at Columbia Presbyterian Medical Center, that Dr. Robert Lifton was going to be giving a presentation at the 1994 Holocaust Memorial program? How lucky was I to be able to contact him and drive him from his home to the medical center and get a chance to meet with him and discuss my dilemma? Was it 'bashert' that he would connect me with Michael Kater, who then connected me to perhaps the world's leading expert investigating anatomical specimens at academic medical centers in Germany still in use from the Nazi era? That expert and colleague became my first 'email friend', Bill Seidelman, whose wisdom, research, knowledge and passion to find the truth, memorialize the victims, learn from medicine's dark history under the Nazi regime and educate future healthcare professionals continue to amaze me every day. Certainly, I feel so fortunate to have Bill Seidelman as one of my dearest friends. Was this friendship and collaboration 'bashert?'

Other coincidences continue to amaze me. My friend and fellow congregant, Kurt Kellman, helped me with German to English translations during those early years of investigation. Was it 'bashert' to find out that he became a Bar Mitzvah in the Seitenstettengasse Temple in Vienna, the only synagogue that was able to survive the Nazis and avoid destruction. I was so fortunate to be able to visit that synagogue in 2005, when I delivered a presentation on the legacy of the Nazi anatomy atlas at the International Association of Oral and Maxillofacial Surgeons Annual Meeting, which miraculously was held in Vienna. The numerous chance events that followed me during that trip to Vienna still mystify me.

How fortunate was it to have chance encounters with two individuals, Drs. George Hindels and Gertrude Schneider, who lived through experiences in Vienna under the Nazis and who had direct knowledge of Pernkopf's agenda for the role of medicine in the Third Reich? Hindels attended the University of Vienna Medical School and Julius Tandler's anatomy course, where Jews learned about the mysteries of the human body, while National Socialists took Pernkopf's course, where they were taught the anatomy of the superior Aryan human race and the concept of racial hygiene to preserve the Aryan *Volk*. Hindels somehow survived Dachau, emigrated to America and became a member of the faculty at Columbia University School of Dental and Oral Surgery, located on the Health Sciences Campus of Columbia University where, by chance, I was to make courtesy rounds on his ailing wife, providing me with the opportunity to learn of his eyewitness experiences in Vienna under the Third Reich. My visit with Gertrude Schneider, who had authored a book on the Jews of Vienna provided tremendous insight into the source of corpses for Penkopf's work. Dr. Schneider's research ultimately led me to the names of Jewish men, along with biographical information, who had been imprisoned at the *Wiener Landesgericht*, and no record of leaving. Their punishments, along with the many non-Jewish Communists, resistance fighters, or those with anti-Nazi sentiments, were death, providing a ready source of corpses for the Institute of Anatomy under Pernkopf's direction. Meeting with both of these individuals provided a direct window into the horrors these victims faced. What fate provided me with the opportunity to meet face to face with these first-hand witnesses?

Why did I receive an e-mail in 2018 from a woman whose grandfather had been a medical student at the University of Vienna School of Medicine. The granddaughter's e-mail suggested that I read the journalist G.E.R. Gedye's *Fallen Bastions*, chronicling his eyewitness account of the events in Vienna after the Nazis annexed Austria in 1938? Gedye's account of a Jewish family that had committed suicide and been taken in a cart labelled for the Anatomy Institute haunts me still, as I envision the building, the corpses and the 'dumpster' taken directly to the basement of Pernkopf's Anatomy Institute.

A patient with a chipped tooth mistakenly makes an appointment with me. This encounter leads to the article in the 26 November 1996, *The New York Times Science Section*, which brings the issues associated with the Pernkopf Atlas to the general public. One day later, the publication in the *Journal of the American Medical Association* authored by me and Bill Seidelman stimulates much attention and debate in the medical profession. Both of these publications provide additional pressure on the University of Vienna to conduct a thorough investigation of the anatomical sciences during the Pernkopf era, 1938-45. Through Bill's miraculous contacts and reputation, he is able to meet with the leaders of Yad Vashem in Jerusalem, Israel and convinces them to provide leadership as the world organization to officially request an investigation into the origin of the Pernkopf anatomical specimens. Original confidential letters are drafted by Bill and I which needed to be hand delivered to Yad Vashem in Jerusalem. Was it just a coincidence that Bill's daughter, Rhona, then a student at Hebrew University in Jerusalem, was visiting a friend across the street from the Columbia University campus, allowing me to provide Rhona with these confidential letters to directly hand deliver to the Vice Chair of Yad Vashem?

How lucky was it that Professor Alfred Ebenbauer, the Rector of the University of Vienna could see through the deception and denial of his faculty members when questioned about the Pernkopf specimens? Ebenbauer's moral compass resulted in a reversal of the denial of a dark history that had pervaded Austria and the University of Vienna for fifty years, resulting in the investigation confirming that executed Nazi victims were the source of Pernkopf's corpses.

Perhaps one of the most haunting and memorable experiences in this entire saga revolved around my five days in Vienna, when I delivered a presentation on the legacy of the Pernkopf Atlas. It was not the presentation or the meeting that mystifies me. My random jogging through the streets of Vienna in 2005 and the numerous significant coincidences in such a short period of time brought my sense of the inexplicable to a new level. Were these events 'bashert' on steroids? Without having any specific plan my first random jog to nowhere in particular, brought me to the entrance of the Medical School of the University of Vienna, where I discovered a newly constructed memorial to Jewish Nazi victims. The monument, identified as a synagogue on the campus map, was immediately adjacent to the building for 'Oral Surgery.' A few blocks away was a huge fortress-like building, the *Wiener Landesgericht*, the local district court of Vienna which had been notorious for execution of Nazi victims. Within walking distance was Pernkopf's Anatomy Institute, and across the street was the Urban and Schwarzenberg medical bookstore. My jogging legs took me to the scene of horrendous crimes against innocent victims from 1938-45. The Urban and Schwarzenberg medical bookstore had an antique book collection with the 1943 original volumes of Pernkopf's Atlas on the shelf, each book with a cost of well over 100 Euros. The exception was one volume, which was only fifty Euros, and I felt compelled to purchase this volume, since my original gift from Mindy cost $50 US dollars. At the 2005 International Conference of Oral and Maxillofacial Surgeons I meet the world famous oral and maxillofacial surgeon, 'Professor Z.' At that time I had no knowledge that he had been a member of the National Socialist Party during the war years, as over 60% of the oral and maxillofacial surgeons in Germany and Austria had become. Another day's jog took me to the only synagogue that survived the Nazis, Seitenstettengasse Temple. Since my friend, Kurt Kellman had become a Bar Mitzvah there, I was compelled to enter and attended a fascinating presentation on the history of the Jews of Vienna. The entire sanctuary was surrounded by hundreds of memorial plaques of those who had passed away, where my eyes felt compelled to view the names, but I didn't get past the first memorial plaque that I saw for 'Chaim Ben Israel,' my name in Hebrew.

I struggle to define 'bashert' as it relates to the many inexplicable events that have occurred throughout this journey on the legacy of an anatomy book. For one to label these improbable coincidences as 'bashert,' these random events must lead to some positive outcome. A series of inexplicable coincidences that are interesting, fascinating, but have no impact or significance, is not 'bashert.' The series of events that led to the mass extermination and torture of millions of people by the medical profession cannot be reconciled as anything other than acts of evil. Perhaps it is incomprehensible to explain how human beings who pledged an oath to heal the sick and relieve suffering, from prestigious institutions in Germany and Austria, could turn into murderers. The institutions many of these doctors came from were world-renowned for their breakthroughs in medicine and had produced many Nobel Laureates. By what mechanism can a human being rationalize such a reversal from good to evil and call it a science, namely racial hygiene? Although unfathomable, inexplicable, these events did occur, and it is terrifying to know that history continues to repeat itself. Do we have any control over such events, and can we prevent mass genocides, torture, evil and suffering?

Irrespective of whether this journey was fueled by chance, luck, childhood memories of the scene with Grandpa Max, or disgust with my ignorance of a very dark period in the history of medicine, the year 1994 began the transformation of the person I had been. From that day when my colleague suggested that I was studying anatomical pictures created by Nazis, I slowly discovered that there were greater lessons to be learned from Pernkopf's Atlas other than preparation for surgery. The changes that took place in me as a person, although gradual, were quite dramatic. I learned the true importance of studying history and passing this history from generation to generation.

When I look back at the beginning of this journey it seems unreal that a brief comment by my colleague would have such a significant impact. Clearly there was much luck with mystifying coincidences, as well as many setbacks on this journey, but ultimately that small incident, along with the passion of many others, helped to launch a chain reaction of events that continue to have an impact today. I was a changed person. I learned that one infinitesimally small voice is important and has the potential to make a difference. But to truly make an impact and create change, requires many voices together with persistence and empathy replacing complacency.

Picture a scene just outside of the entrance to Temple Isaiah of Great Neck, New York on a spring day with a clear blue sky amidst blossoming flowers in 2007. Many people congregated in front of the entrance of this very small Temple which had a membership that barely reached 100 families. As President of the congregation, I was committed to ensuring that the buried history of each person's story had a place where it can be preserved. Congregants and many other members of the community gathered to dedicate the Holocaust Memorial and Archive of Temple Isaiah with a plaque dedicated to Sonia Hochman. A chance meeting with a local resident named Sonia, living in our community, revealed that she and her family had survived the Nazis by living in underground caves for 494 days. Her story of survival as a child was chronicled by her Grandmother, Esther Stermer in the book *We Fight to Survive.*[1] This became the first story in this Holocaust Archive of our tiny congregation. There remained an open invitation for anyone in the community, regardless of one's affiliation or religious faith, to provide a memory of a history that was significant so that we never forget. What followed were dozens of stories that were preserved in the Temple Isaiah computer archive, filled with photographs, memoirs, artifacts and video interviews to ensure that these stories were preserved and passed on to future generations. As we gathered items for entry into the archive database, my education of this history grew significantly and continued to reinforce the importance of retelling the stories of the past so that one can live with the hope of a brighter future.

As a clinician and educator, I strived to relay these stories to my students as well as others in the community. For current and future doctors the most important lesson is that bioethics must take the highest priority in their education, influencing decisions made on each individual patient by healthcare professionals. There is no choice here. One must be diligent about the importance of maintaining high ethical standards in our powerful role as healers who are constantly making complex decisions that affect the lives of each individual patient. Through education, religion, and independent thinking, one cannot remain silent when ethical boundaries are breached. There is great hope for the future with the creation of many programs throughout the world as exemplified by the symposium launch of '*The Lancet* Commission on Medicine, Nazism, and the Holocaust: historical evidence, implications for today, teaching for tomorrow.' With the wisdom, knowledge and dynamism of physicians and historians such as Bill Seidelman, Sabine Hildebrandt, Herwig Czech, Shmuel Reis, Matthew Wynia, William Silvers, Volker Roelcke and others, along with fellowships, curricular change and emphasis for medical students and other healthcare professionals, the essential components of medical bioethics, compassion and care for each individual can prevail in the future.

On 8 March 2005, a sculpture memorializing the victims of the Nazi 'Angel of Death' was unveiled in the German Bavarian town, Gunzburg, where Josef Mengele was born. The broadcast 'Mengele Hometown Opens Victim memorial,' revealed the inscription on this sculpture as follows:

> *No one can divorce himself from the history of his people. One should not and must not let history rest because otherwise it can rise again and become part of the present*

The sculpture was erected on the grounds of the town's elementary school, a most appropriate location for teaching future generations.[2]

In this universe which stretches to infinity how improbable is it that we exist here on Earth, where there is life? Shouldn't it be a moral obligation and a requirement for all who have been given this gift as living, breathing human beings to do everything possible to preserve life, protect life and reduce suffering? Through education, empathy and diligence we must prevent a repeat of history and fully pursue our obligation to preserve this rare gift that for some inexplicable reason has been given to us.

Notes

1. E. Stermer, *We Fight to Survive*, (Igi Press, 2008).
2. DW News. 'Mengele Hometown Opens Victim Memorial,' 8 March 2005. https://www.dw.com/en/mengele-hometown-opens-victim-memorial/a-1512050

Bibliography

Angetter DC, 'Anatomical science at University of Vienna 1938-45,' *Lancet*, 355 (2000), pp. 1454-57.

Anonymous. Letter sent to Dr. Howard A. Israel, in response to Nicholas Wade's 1996 article 'Doctors Question Use of Nazi's Medical Atlas, *Science Times, The New York Times*, Personal letter dated 29 November 1996.

Associated Press, 'France Honors Jewish Victims of Nazi Anatomy Professor,' *The Jerusalem Post*, 11 December 2005.

Aumüller G, 'Anatomy in the Nazi Era,' in Medical Student Council of Philipps University of Marburg (ed), *Responsibility of Medicine Under National Socialism*, (Marburg: Schuren Press, 1991), pp 87-111.

Berger RL, 'Nazi Science - The Dachau Hypothermia Experiments' *N Engl J Med*, 322, 20 (1990), pp.1435-40.

Bergmann C, Gross D, 'A fairytale career in spite of political disenfranchisement: The Jewish oral pathologist Bálint Orbán (1899-1960),' *Pathology-Research and Practice*, 216, (2020), pp. 1-7. https://doi.org/10.1016/j.prp.2020.152862.

Bitterich LA, Gross D, 'Maxillofacial surgeons in the Third Reich and their connection to National Socialism,' *Journal of Cranio-Maxillo-Facial Surgery*, 49 (2021), pp. 329-35.

Bitterich LA, Rinnen C, Gross D, 'Nazi dentists before British courts: aspects on the role of the German dental profession in the Third Reich,' *British Dental Journal*, 123, 10 (2021), pp. 647-53.

Bliss M. *William Osler: A Life in Medicine*. (Oxford: Oxford University Press, 2007).

Bradsher G, 'Nazi Gold: The Merkers Mine Treasure' Prologue: *Quarterly of the National Archives and Records Administration, US*, 31, 1 (Spring 1999).

Bradsher G, 'Turning History into Justice: Holocaust-Era Assets Records, Research and Restitution March 1996 – March 2001,' Lecture, University of North Carolina, presented by Dr. Greg Bradsher, Director Holocaust-Era Assets Records Projection, National Archives and Records Administration, 19 April 2001.

Breedem A, 'A French University Confronts Medical Crimes and its Nazi Past,' *The New York Times*, 27 July 2022.

Brickman P, *Extracted - Unmasking Rampant Antisemitism in America's Higher Education*, (New York, London, Nashville TN, Melbourne Australia, Vancouver Canada: Morgan James Publishing, 2020).

Broder J, 'The Corpses That Won't Die,' *The Jerusalem Report*, 22 February 1996.

Charatan F, 'Investigation of the Nazi Anatomy Textbook to Start,' *BMJ*, 70, (February 1997), pp. 335-6. https://www.bmj.com/archive/7080n.htm

Chelouche T, Czech H, Fox MA, et al, 'Statement on *The Lancet* Commission on Medicine, Nazism and the Holocaust,' *Lancet*, 402, 10415 (8 November 2023), pp. 1816-17.

Cowell A, Swiss 'Central Bank to Fight Holocaust Claims,' *The New York Times, Week in Review*, 4 April 1998.

Cowell A. 'The Swiss and Holocaust Money,' *The New York Times, Week in Review*, 27 October 1996.

Czech H, Druml C, Muller M, et al, 'The Medical University of Vienna and the legacy of Pernkopf's anatomical atlas: Elsevier's donation of the original drawings to the Josephinum,' *Annals of Anatomy*, 237 (2021), pp. 1-8.

Czech H, Hildebrandt S, Reis SP, et al, '*The Lancet* Commission on Medicine, Nazism, and the Holocaust: historical evidence, implications for today, teaching for tomorrow,' *Lancet*, 402, 10415 (8 November 2023), pp. 1867-1940.

Dafni R, Letters from Yad Vashem to Presidents of Universities of Vienna, Innsbruck, Urban and Schwarzenberg, cc. H. Israel, 23 March 1995.

Dickman S, 'Scandal over Nazi Victims' Corpses Rocks Universities,' *Nature* 337, (1989), p. 195.

DW News. 'Mengele Hometown Opens Victim Memorial,' 8 March 2005. https://www.dw.com/en/mengele-hometown-opens-victim-memorial/a-1512050

Ebenbauer A, Letter to Ambassador Johanan Bein, Vice Chairman Yad Vashem, 17 December 1996.

Ebenbauer A, Letter to Professor H. Israel, Columbia University with attached documents, letters, reports from faculty of the University of Vienna and additional experts, 18 March 1996.

Ebenbauer A, Letter to Professor Howard Israel, Columbia University with attached documents from August 1997 entitled 'Information for the Users of the Pernkopf-Atlas.' 24 September 24 1997.

Ebenbauer A, Schutz W. 'Origins of the Pernkopf Anatomy Atlas - In Reply,' *JAMA*, 277, 14, (1997). p.1122.

Ebenbauer A, 1945-2007 o. Univ.-Prof. Dr. phil, University of Vienna. https://geschichte.univie.ac.at/en/persons/alfred-ebenbauer

Eizenstat SE, Slany WZ, 'The Eizenstat Report and Related Issues Concerning US and Allied Efforts to Restore Gold and Other Assets by Nazis During Second World War. Hearing before the Committee on Banking and Financial Services House of Representatives, 105th Congress, First Session, 25 June 1997.

Eizenstat SE, Slany WZ, 'The U.S. and Allied Efforts to Restore Gold and Other Assets by Nazis During Second World War. Preliminary Study,' US Congressional hearing before the Committee on Banking and Financial Services, May 1997.

Ernst E, 'A Leading Medical School Seriously Damaged: Vienna 1938,' *Ann Intern Med*, 122, 10 (1995), pp.789- 92.

Ferner H (ed), *Eduard Pernkopf Atlas of Topographical and Applied Human Anatomy, Volume I, Head and Neck*, (Philadelphia Pa and London, W.B. Saunders Company, 1963), pp. 1-345.

Firbas W, Letter to Rector of the University Professor Alfred Ebenbauer, 30 March 1995.

Forster WR, *Farewell Berlin*, (Thornton, CO: Farewell Berlin, LLC, 2018), pp.27-8.

Franzblau M, 'Throw Away Evil Atlas,' letter to the editor, *The New York Times, Editorials/Letters Section*, 3 December 1996.

Fritsch E, Letter to Ambassador Johanan Bein, Vice Chairman Yad Vashem, 29 September 1995.

Fritsch E, Letter to Ambassador Johanan Bein, Vice Chairman Yad Vashem, 26 February 1996.

Fullerton Z, 'The Protection of Individual Inviolability: Nazi Doctors and their Mark on Biomedical Research,' *Senior Capstone Projects*, 402, (Vassar College Digital Library, Thesis, Open Access, 2015), pp1-70.

Gedye GER, *Fallen Bastions, The Central European Tragedy*, (London: Victor Gollancz LTD Publisher,1939).

Gisel A, Letter to Rector of the University of Vienna Professor Alfred Ebenbauer, 26 April 1995.

Grant JCB (ed.), *Grant's Atlas of Anatomy*, Sixth Edition, (Baltimore: The Williams & Wilkins Company 1972).

Gribetz J, Reig SC, 'Special Masters' Final Report on the Swiss Banks Holocaust Settlement Distribution Process,' Case 1:96-cv-04849-ERK-JO Document

5040 Filed with the US District Court Eastern District of New York, 28 March 2019.

Gruber H. Letter (unpublished) sent to the Editor *Ann Intern Med*, 12 July 1995.

Halperin E. 'The Jewish Problem in U.S. Medical Education, 1920-1955,' *Journal of the History of Medicine and Allied Sciences*, 56, 2 (2001), pp. 140-167.

Hast HM, 'Pernkopf Anatomy: Atlas of Topographic and Applied Human Anatomy, vol1, Head and Neck, 3rd ed, Platzer W (ed), *Journal of the American Medical Association*, 263, 15 (1990), p. 2115.

Heider M, Wedl C, *Atlas to the Pathology of Teeth*, (Leipzig: Verlag Von Arthur Felix, 1869).

Hildebrandt S, 'From Routine to Murder: Anatomy in Nazi Germany and its Legacies for Today,' Medical Grand Rounds, University of Colorado Anschutz Medical Campus, Center for Bioethics and Humanities, 8 May 2024. https://youtu.be/_urEgmwgnyo?si=st2xQKUX0sNBHMqw

Hildebrandt S, 'How the Pernkopf Controversy Facilitated a Historical and Ethical Analysis of the Anatomical Sciences in Austria and Germany: A Recommendation for the Continued Use of the Pernkopf Atlas,' *Clin. Anat.*19 (2006), pp. 91-100.

Hildebrandt S, Israel H, Wynia M, 'Unraveling the Past, Confronting the Present, and Charting an Ethical Future in Medicine: The History and Legacy of the Pernkopf Atlas,' Panel Discussion University of Colorado Anschutz Medical Campus, Center for Bioethics and Humanities, 7 May 2024. https://youtu.be/RJez1AvgHU0?si=UyQ7dGKs6dpJEol8

Hildebrandt S, Krebs C, 'From body image – Pernkopf's anatomical gaze and eyewitness accounts on the process of creating images from Nazi victims'bodies,' *Anat Sci Educ*, 18, 3 (2025), pp.277-288. https://doi.org/10.1002/ase.70001

Hildebrandt S, *The Anatomy of Murder – Ethical Transgressions and Anatomical Science During the Third Reich*, (New York and Oxford: Berghahn Books 2016).

Hildebrandt S, 'Anatomy in the Third Reich: An Outline. Part 1. National Socialists Politics, Anatomical Institutions and Anatomists,' *Clin Anat.* 22 (2009), pp. 883-93.

Hildebrandt S, 'Anatomy in the Third Reich: An Outline. Part 2. Bodies for Anatomy and Related Medical Disciplines,' *Clin Anat.* 22 (2009), pp. 894-905.

Hildebrandt S, 'Anatomy in the Third Reich: An Outline. Part 3. The Science and Ethics of Anatomy in National Socialist Germany and Postwar Consequences,' *Clin Anat.* 22 (2009), pp. 906-15.

Hildebrandt S, Letter in Response to Winkelmann and Schagen, Seidelman and Levi, 'Call for New Era in Research on "Medicine in the Third Reich." ' *Clin Anat*, 23 (2010) p. 124.

Hindels G, Personal interview, 23 August 1996.

Historical Museum of the City of Vienna Special Exhibition, '*Wien 1938*,' (Vienna: Documentation Archives of the Austrian Resistance, 11 March – 30 June 1988). pp. 196-222.

Hollinshead WH (ed.), *Anatomy for Surgeons, Volume 1, Second Edition, The Head and Neck*, (Hagerstown, Maryland, New York, San Francisco and London: Harper & Row Publishers, Inc., 1968), pp. 306-29.

Horton R, 'Offline: Medicine and the Holocaust – it's time to teach,' *Lancet*, 394 (2019), p. 105.

Hubenstorf M, 'Anatomical science in Vienna, 1938-45 (Commentary),' *Lancet*, 355 (2000), pp. 1385-6.

Hutton EB, 'In Reply Pernkopf Anatomy,' *JAMA*, 276, 20 (1996), p. 1634.

Hutton EB, President and CEO Waverly, Inc. Letter to H. Israel, Columbia University School of Dental & Oral Surgery, 29 August 1996.

Israel H, 'The Nazi Origins of Pernkopf's Atlas of Topographic and Applied Human Anatomy: A Lesson in Biomedical Ethics.' 17th Annual International Conference of Oral & Maxillofacial Surgeons, Vienna, Austria, September 2005.

Israel H, Seidelman W, Letter to the editor. 'Nazi origins of an anatomy text: The Pernkopf Atlas,' *JAMA*, 276, 20 (1996), p. 1633.

Jacobs B, 'The Dentist of Auschwitz – a Memoir,' (Lexington: The University Press of Kentucky, 1995).

Jacobson B, Letters from the Anti-Defamation League to the Presidents of the Universities of Vienna and Innsbruck, cc H. Israel, 7 March 1995.

Kasten FH, 'Unethical Nazi Medicine in Annexed Alsace-Lorraine: The Strange Case of Nazi Anatomist Professor Dr. August Hirt,' in G. Kent, G. Mason (eds.), *Historians and Archivists: Essays in Modern German History and Archival Policy*, (Fairfax, Virginia: University Press, 1991), pp. 173-208.

Kasten FH. Personal correspondence, 29 November 1994.

Kater, MH, 'Unresolved Questions of German Medicine and Medical History in the Past and Present,' *Central European History*, 25, 4 (1993), pp. 407-423.

Kater MH, *Doctors Under Hitler*, (Chapel Hill NC and London: The University of North Carolina Press,1989).

Kater MH, Letter to R. Lifton and H. Israel, 21 July 1994.

Kershner I, 'In Israel, Modern Medicine Grapples With Ghosts of the Third Reich,' *The New York Times*, 12 May 2020.

Krause H. Letter (unpublished) sent to the Editor *Ann Intern Med*, 9 November 1995.

Krause W. Letter to Rector of the University of Vienna Professor Alfred Ebenbauer, 13 April 1995.

Kremenak NW, Squier CA, 'Pioneers in Oral Biology: The Migrations of Gottlieb, Kronfeld, Orban, Weinmann, and Sicher from Vienna to America,' *Crit Rev Oral Biology Med*, 8 , 2 (1997), pp. 108-128.

Krischel M, 'Dentists in National Socialist Germany: A Fragmented Profession,' in S, Hildebrandt, M. Offer, M.A. Grodin (eds). *Recognizing the Past in the Present: New Studies on Medicine Before, During and After the Holocaust.* (New York and Oxford: Berghahn Books Publisher, 2020), pp. 190-203.

Lang H, 'August Hirt and "extraordinary opportunities for cadaver delivery" to anatomical institutes in National Socialism: A murderous change in paradigm,' *Ann Anatomy*, 2195 (2013), pp.373-380.

Lehner M. 'The Medical Faculty of the University of Vienna 1938 – 1945 (Dissertation),' University of Vienna, May 1990.

Lerner BH, Rothman DJ, 'Medicine and the Holocaust: Learning More of the Lessons,' (Editorial), *Ann Intern Med*, 122, 10 (1995), pp. 793-4.

Lifton R, *The Nazi Doctors: Medical Killing and the Psychology of Genocide*, (New York: Basic Books, 1986).

Macintyre B, *The Spy and the Traitor: The Greatest Espionage Story of the Cold War*, (New York: Broadway Books, 2019).

Mackinnon S, 'When Medical Information Comes from Nazi Atrocities,' *BMJ*, 368, (2020), p.17075.

Malina P, 'Eduard Pernkopf's atlas of anatomy or: The fiction of pure science,' *Wien Kinische Wochenschrift*, 109, (1997), pp. 935-201.

Maslin Nir S, 'A Nazi Villa So Tainted Berlin Can't Give it Away,' *The New York Times*, 12 August 2024.

Massry SG, Smogorzewski, M, 'The Hunger Disease of the Warsaw Ghetto," *Am J Nephrol*, 22 (2002), pp. 197-201.

Moe K, 'Should the Nazi research data be cited?' *Hastings Center Report*, 14, 6 (1984), pp.5-7.

Muhlberger K, Letter to Rector of the University of Vienna Professor Alfred Ebenbauer, 3 April 1995.

Netter FH, *Atlas of Human Anatomy, Sixth edition*, (Philadelphia: W. B. Saunders, 2014).

Neufeld N, 'Wernher Von Braun and the Nazis,' *American Experience: Chasing the Moon.* Public Broadcasting Service, 20 May 2019. https://www.youtube.com/watch?v=9e4Hy-Qcs1s

Nutton V, 'Galen,' *Encyclopedia Britannica*, 11 April 2025. https://www.britannica.com/biography/Galen.

Official Website of the Swiss Banks Settlement: In Holocaust Victim Assets Litigation, U.S. District Court for the Eastern District of New York, Judge Edward R. Korman Presiding. CV-96-4849, updated 14 April 2020. https://www.swissbankclaims.com/New%20docs/Final%20Report.pdf

Panush R, Letter to the editor. *JAMA*, 276, 20 (1996), p. 1633.

Paroli EM, 'The Atlas Portrays the Horrors of the Reich,' *Tempo Medico*, 6 March 1996.

Peiffer J, 'Neuropathology in the Third Reich: Memorial to those Victims of National-Socialist Atrocities in Germany who were used by medical science,' Brain *Pathol*, 1 (1991), p. 125-31.

Pernkopf E, '*Originalabhandlungen Nationalsozialismus und Wissenschaft' Wien Klinische Wochenscrift,* 51 (1938), p. 545.

Personal communication, 1994.

Piotrowski VC, An Anatomic Classic with Swastikas,' *Science and Technology, Frankfurter Rundschau*, 53, 113/20 (January 1997), p 8.

Platzer W, Letter to Rector of the University of Innsbruck Professor Hans Moser, 3 April 1995.

Polak J, ' "Vienna Protocol" for when Jewish or Possibly-Jewish Human Remains are Discovered,' Symposium entitled 'How to Deal with Holocaust Era Human Remains,' Yad Vashem, The World Holocaust Remembrance Center, Jerusalem, Israel, (14 May 2017).

Polak J, 'The "Vienna Protocol" and Reflections on Nazi Medicine: Murder a la Carte,' Journal *of Biocommunication*, 45, 1(2021), pp. 95-97.

Reinecke K, Westemeier J, Gross D, 'In the shadow of National Socialism: Early emigration and suicide of the oral pathologist Rudolf Kronfeld (1901–1940),' *Pathology-Research and Practice*, 215, 12, (2019), p. 152682.

Riaud X, 'Medical Ethics under a Totalitarian Regime: German Dentists and the Third Reich,' *Dental Historian: Lindsay Club Newsletter*, 7, 45 (2007), pp.76-86.

Riaud X, 'Nazi Dental Gold: From Dead Bodies to Swiss Banks,' *Vesalius, Journal of the International Society for the History of Medicine*, 21, 1 (2015), pp. 33-55.

Roelcke V, 'Nazi Medical Crimes and Their Aftermath: Facts, Ethics and Lessons.' Medical Grand Rounds, University of Colorado Anschutz Medical Campus, Center for Bioethics and Humanities, 23 April 2025.

Sanders B, 'The History of the Dental Profession in the US: The Stranger Dentists Within Our Gates, The Vienna Dental Scientists Who "Saved' American Dentistry." ' Presentation delivered by Dr. Sanders to dental students at UCLA School of Dentistry, (2018).

Sanger DE, 'How a Swiss Bank Gold Deal Eluded a U.S. Mediator,' The *New York Times*, 12 July 1998.

Scheff J, *Handbook of Dentistry*, (Vienna: Holder, 1891).

Schneider G, *Exile and Destruction The Fate of Austrian Jews 1938-1945*. (Westport Connecticut and London: Bloomsbury Publishing, 1995).

Schneider G. Personal interview, 6 December 1996.

Schoettler C, 'Do Surgeons Use Images of Nazis' Victims?' *The Toronto Star and Baltimore Sun,* August 1997.

Schunck T, Gross D. 'From Nazi victim to honored scientist: The two lives of Jewish anatomist Harry Sicher (1889–1974),' *Annals of Anatomy*, 235 (2021), p.1-10.

Schuster H, Harris A, 'Nazi Medicine,' IMPACT CNN and Time's weekly broadcast newsmagazine, 19 October 1997. https://youtu.be/B4-FrCrio0w

Schwanke E, Gross D, 'Progressive Entanglements? Activity Profiles, Responsibilities and Interactions of Dentists at Auschwitz. The Example of 2nd SS Dentist Willi Schatz,' *Med. Hist,* 643, 3 (2020), pp.374-400.

Seidelman W, 'Dissecting the History of Anatomy in the Third Reich – 1989-2010: A Personal Account,' *Annals of Anatomy*, 194 (212), pp.228-36.

Seidelman S,'Nuremberg Lamentation: For the Forgotten Victims of Medical Science.' *BMJ* 313, 7070 (1996), pp.1463–67. https://doi.org/10.1136/bmj.313.7070.1463.

Seidelman W, 'Academia Under Scrutiny: An Agenda for the Next Century' presented at Symposium 'Doctors Under Scrutiny,' The University of Vienna, 7-8 October 1999.

Seidelman W, 'Complicity, Complacency and Conspiracy: The Enduring Legacy of Medicine in the Third Reich,' Presented at the Conference 'Hippocrates Betrayed: Medicine in the Third Reich,' The U.S. Holocaust Memorial Museum, Washington, D.C. 24 January 1996.

Seidelman W, 'From the Danube to the Spree: Deception, Truth and Morality in Medicine,' Documentation Archive of the Austrian Resistance (ed.), Vienna. *Yearbook* (1999), pp.15-32.

Seidelman W, 'In Memoriam: Medicine's Confrontation with Evil,' *Hastings Center Report*. (November/December 1989), pp. 5-6.

Seidelman W, 'Medspeak: for Murder: The Nazi Experience and Culture of Medicine,' in A. Caplan (ed), *When Medicine Went Mad: Bioethics and the Holocaust,* (Totowa, New Jersey: Humana Press 1992), pp271-9.

Seidelman W, 'Memory, Medicine, and Morality: The Meaning of the Exploitation of the Human Body in the Third Reich,' Presentation at Symposium: 'The History of Nazi Euthanasia in Vienna,' Vienna Psychiatric Hospital Baumgartner Hohe, 29-30 (January 1998).

Seidelman W, 'University of British Columbia Medicine Alumni, MD Class of 1968 – 50th Reunion,' (2018).

Seidelman W, Israel H, 'Anatomy in Vienna,' *Lancet,* 356, 2000, p.343.

Seidelman W, Letter to H. Israel upon return from meeting with Yad Vashem, 10 January 1995.

Seidelman W, Personal communication with H. Israel, 8 August 1994.

Seidelman W, Personal correspondence with Dr. Howard Israel, 6 November 2020.

Seidelman W, Roelcke V, Hildebrandt S, Reis SP, 'Project: Teaching Medicine and the Holocaust – Outline,' Proposal submitted to *The Lancet*, 21 October 2020.

Silversides A, 'Canadian MD Fights to Put Remains of Nazi Victims to Rest,' *Canadian Medical Association Journal*, 162, 11(2000), p.1648.

Smith A, *Hitler's Gold: The Story of the Nazi War Loot,* (Oxford England, Providence Rhode Island, USA: Berg Publishers, 1989).

Snell RS, Pernkopf Anatomy: Atlas of Topographic and Applied Human Anatomy, vol. 2 Thorax, Abdomen and Extremities, 3rd ed. Platzer W (ed), Monsen H (Transl).' *The New England Journal of Medicine,* 323, 3 (1990), p. 205.

Spann G, et al, 'Investigations of Anatomical Science in Vienna - Results of the Senate Project of the University of Vienna,' B. Matouschek Editor (November 1998), pp 1-12.

Speers RD, Brands WG, Nuzzolese E, et al, 'Preventing dentists' involvement in torture – The developmental history of a new international declaration,' *JADA*, 139 (2008), pp. 1667-73.

Stermer E, *We Fight to Survive*, (Igi Press, 2008).

Surgical Assessment of Pernkopf's Anatomical Atlas (OMS),' (2018). https://www.surveygizmo.com/s3/4604660/Surgical-Assessment-of-Pernkopf-s-Anatomical-Atlas-AAOMS, (2018). (link to survey no longer active).

Symposium Program. 'Doctors Under Scrutiny,' The University of Vienna, 7-8 October 1999.

Symposium Program. 'A Period of Darkness: The University of Vienna's Medical School and the Nazi Regime,' World Congresses of Gastroenterology, Society of Physicians, Vienna, Austria, 6 September 1998.

Taber GM, *Chasing Gold – The Incredible Story of How the Nazis Stole Europe's Bullion*, (New York and London: Pegasus Books, 2014).

Thaler M, Franzblau M, Personal correspondence, 1994.

The University of Toronto Division of Plastic Reconstructive & Aesthetic Surgery Website, Hall of Fame featuring Susan E. Mackinnon, MD, FRCSC, FACS, 2024. https://www.uoftplasticsurgery.ca/about/division/hall-of-fame/susan-mackinnon/

Toledano R, 'Anatomy in the Third Reich – The Anatomical Institute of Reich Universität Strassburg and the Deliveries of Dead Bodies' Ann *Anatomy*, 205 (2016), pp.128-44.

University of Vienna Press Conference regarding the origins of 'Topographic Human Anatomy' by Eduard Pernkopf' announcing the research project initiated for this purpose 'Investigations into the Anatomical Science at the University of Vienna 1938-1945.' 12 February 1997.

University of Vienna. Document entitled 'Information for Users of the Pernkopf Atlas.' August 1997.

Vendantam S, 'Anatomy of Horror,' The *Philadelphia Inquirer Health & Science section*, pD1, 18 August 1997.

Wade N, 'Doctors Question Use Of Nazi's Medical Atlas,' Science *Times, The New York Times*, 26 November 1996.

Wahlberg D, 'Medical Book Stirs Controversy, Nazi Ties to Anatomical Illustrations Create Ethical Dilemma,' *Michigan Live: Ann Arbor Edition*, 14 April 1997. https://www.mlive.com/ann-arbor/medbook

Wedl C, *Pathology of the Teeth: Anatomy and Physiology*, (Philadelphia: Lindsay & Blakiston, 1872).

Weisel E, Letter sent to Dr. Howard A. Israel, in response to Nicholas Wade's 1996 article 'Doctors Question Use of Nazi's Medical Atlas, *Science Times, The New York Times*, Personal letter dated 26 November 1996.

Weissman G, 'Springtime for Pernkopf,' *Hospital Practice*, (15 October 1985), pp.142-68.

Weissman G, 'Springtime for Pernkopf', in *They All Laughed at Christopher Columbus: Tales of Medicine and the Art of Discovery*, (New York: Times Books, 1987), pp. 48-69.

Williams D, The history of Eduard Pernkopf's *Topographische Anatomie des Menschen*,' *J of Biocommunication*, 15, (1988), pp. 2-12.

Winau R, Experimentation on Humans and Informed Consent: How We Arrived Where We Are.' in W. Lafleur, G. Bohme, & S. Shimazono (Eds.), *Dark Medicine: Rationalizing Unethical Medical Research*. Indianapolis, (Indianapolis: Indiana University Press, 2007), pp 46-56.

Winick M (ed). *Hunger Disease*, (New York: Wiley,1979).

Wroe D, 'Hitler had fillings made from gold torn from the mouths of Jews,' *The Telegraph*, 8 October 2009.

Wynia M, 'How Nazi Doctors became Killers,' International Holocaust Remembrance Day program at Colorado University Anschutz, Center for Bioethics and Humanities, 29 January 2024. https://youtu.be/czaFD9EEfqE?si=POhVl04jbciU6cwz

Yad Vashem Documents from their Central Archives entitled 'Secret State Police Vienna State Police Control Office' Records of ten males arrested by the Gestapo and sent for hearings at the *Wiener Landesgericht* 1940-1943, Obtained by Dr. Gertrude Schneider with copies sent to Dr Howard Israel in 1997 July.

Yaros KA, 'Don't Censor Atlas, However Odious Its Origin,' letter to the editor. *The New York Times, Editorials/Letters Section,* 3 December 1996.

Yee A, Coombs D, Hildebrandt S, Seidelman W, Coer JH, Mackinnon S, 'Nerve Surgeons' Assessment of the Role of Eduard Pernkopf's Atlas of Topographic and Applied Human Anatomy in Surgical Practice,' *Neurosurgery*, 84, 2 (2019), pp. 491-8.

Yee A, Li J, Lilly J, Hildebrandt S, Seidelman W, Browne D, Kopar P, Coert JH, MacKinnon S, Israel HA, 'Oral and maxillofacial surgeons' assessment of the role of Pernkopf's Atlas in surgical practice,' *Annals of Anatomy*, 234, 151614 (2021), pp. 1-10. https://doi.org/10.1016/j.aanat.2020.151614.

Yudkin J, 'Hunger Disease: Studies by the Jewish Physicians in the Warsaw Ghetto.' Book review, M. Winick M (ed), Hunger *Disease,* (New York: Wiley, 1979). *J R Soc Med.*, 72, 10 (1979), p. 790

Zwerdling W, 'Interview of Dr. Howard Israel regarding the Nazi Origins of the Pernkopf Atlas controversy,' *All Things Considered*, National Public Radio Broadcast, February 1996.

Appendix

RECEIVED

BY

APR 1 ! 1995

YAD VASHEM יד ושם

The Holocaust Martyrs' and Heroes' Remembrance Authority רשות הזכרון לשואה ולגבורה

DIVISION OF ORAL AND MAXILLOFACIAL SURGERY

Jerusalem, March 23, 1995

Dr. Alfred Ebenauer
President
University of Vienna
Dr. Karl Lueger Ring 1
A-1010 Vienna
Austria

Honorable President Ebenauer,

It has recently come to our attention that some of the work of the Austrian anatomist, Professor Eduard Pernkopf, may have included human subjects who were victims of the Nazis. We are therefore requesting a formal investigation into this matter.

The facts are that Professor Pernkopf was the author of a major atlas of human anatomy entitled Topographische Anatomie des Menschen which was first published in 1937. Pernkopf's atlas of human anatomy consists of paintings of dissections performed at the Istitute of Anatomy of the University of Vienna. The 1943 and 1952 German language editions include illustrations in which the artists incorporated Nazi icons (swastika and "SS" symbols) into their signatures. Relevant examples are:

1. LEPIER SIGNATURE WITH SWASTIKA
Anatomic Dissection of a Pregnant Woman
Edition 1943, Volume 2, Page 586, Figure 168.

2. ENTRESSER SIGNATURE WITH "SS" SYMBOL IN HIS NAME
Anatomic Dissection of the Thigh of a Circumcised Male
Edition 1943, Volume 2, Figure 188, Tafel 102, (opposite page 672)

3. BATKE SIGNATURE WITH "SS" SYMBOL FOR THE YEAR '44
Anatomic Dissection of the Neck
Edition 1952, Volume 3, Figure 14, Tafel 9, (opposite page 48).

The painting signed by Entresser with the "SS" symbol continues to be published in the 1989 English-language edition of the work (Edition 3, Volume 2, Figure 336, Page 338). Given the fact that most circumcised males at that time were Jews, the origins of the subject and the manner of his death are suspet.

1

P.O.B. 3477, JERUSALEM 91034, TEL. 751611, FAX. 433511 .ת.ד. 3477, ירושלים 91034, טל. 751611, פקס

YAD VASHEM יד ושם

The Holocaust Martyrs' and Heroes' Remembrance Authority רשות הזיכרון לשואה ולגבורה

Another illustration from the 1952 edition (Volume 3, Figure 50, Tafel 43, opposite page 97) and signed by Lepier and included in the 1989 English-language edition (Edition 3 Volume 1, Figure 325, Page 325) is that of the head and neck of a cachectic appearing younger man with a haircut resembling that of a concentation camp prisoner. Thus the origins of the subject in this illustration and the cause of his death are also suspet.

While the original dissections were performed during Pernkopf's tenure at the University of Vienna preserved specimens from the Pernkopf collection are reported to be in the Institute of anatomy of the University of Innsbruck.

A similar request is also being made of the President of the University of Innsbruk.

The original publisher of the Pernkopf atlas is Urban and Schwarzenberg Ltd. They continue to publish the work. The original paintings of the Pernkopf dissections are believed to be the property of the publisher. We are also informing Urban and Schwarzenberg of our concerns.

You may be aware that similar questions were raised concerning the origins of human specimens in the patho-anatomical collections of a number of institutions in Germany. This matter engendered considerable publicity at that time and public burials of suspect specimens were conducted in Munich, Frankfurt and Tubingen in March, July and December of 1990.

Rather than cause difficult publicity, it is our wish that a proper investigation be conducted by outside experts with proper documentation. The model for such an investigation is that conducted by the Karl-Eberhardt University of Tubingen and headed by Professor Albin Eser of the University of Freiburg and Director of the Max Planck Institute of International Criminal Law. A copy of the official report of that investigation may be obtained from the office of the President of the university of Tubingen.

Our expectations for such an investigation are:

1. There be proper documentaiton copies of which should be deposited in the archives of Yad Vashem.

2. Upon the completion of the investigation there should be an official published report in the public domain.

2

P.O.B. 3477, JERUSALEM 91034, TEL. 751611, FAX. 433511 .ת.ד. 3477, ירושלים 91034, טל. 751611, פקס

YAD VASHEM יד ושם

The Holocaust Martyrs' and Heroes' Remembrance Authority רשות הזיכרון לשואה ולגבורה

3. If it is established that some of the subjects had, if fact, (or could possibly have) been victims of the Nazis, there should be a public acknowledgement and commemoration to the victims by the institutions and organizations concerned.

4. Specimens shown to have been derived from Jews, which are larger than glass slides, must receive a proper burial in a Jewish cemetery.

The University of Vienna and the University of Innsbruck may wish to consider a joint investigation.

Given the public and political sensitivities involved we are informing the Chancellor of Austria of this matter and copying this letter to him.

We trust that the collections and the documentations will not be in any way disturbed until such time as the examinations can be properly completed.

We would request also that all correspondence on this matter be copied to all those whose names and adresses are attached.

Yours sincerely,

Ambassador Reuven Dafni
Vice Chairman

3

P.O.B. 3477, JERUSALEM 91034, TEL. 751611, FAX. 433511 ת.ד. 3477, ירושלים 91034, טל. 751611, פקס. 433511

YAD VASHEM יד ושם

The Holocaust Martyrs' and Heroes' Remembrance Authority רשות הזיכרון לשואה ולגבורה

cc: Honorable Dr. Franz Vranitzky,
Chancellor of the Federal Republic of Austria
Ballhausplatz 2
1014 Vien

Dr. Josef Govrin
Amb. of Israel
20 Anton Frankgass
1180 Vienna

Professor Dr. Moser
President
University of Innsbruk

Professor, Dr. Howard Israel
Division of Oral and Maxillofacial Surgery
School of Dental and Oral Surgery
Columbia University
116 Str. & Broadway
New York, New York 10 027, U.S.A.

Professor, Dr. William Seidelman
Department of Family and Community Medicine
Faculty of Medicine
University of Toronto
27 Kings College Circule
Toronto, Ontarion M5S 1A1

4

P.O.B. 3477, JERUSALEM 91034, TEL. 751611, FAX. 433511 .ת.ד. 3477, ירושלים 91034, טל. 751611, פקס

Appendix I. Letter from Yad Vashem's Ambassador Dafni to the Universities of Vienna, Innsbruck, and the publisher requesting investigation of the origins of the anatomical illustrations depicted in the Pernkopf atlas. Permission from Yad Vashem Archives AM.2.2/276, pp. 143-146.

Index

Note: Page numbers in italics are illustrations and tables.

9781803710853